AGGREGATE DEMAND AND SUPPLY

Also by B. Bhaskara Rao

COINTEGRATION FOR THE APPLIED ECONOMIST (*editor*)

THE ECONOMETRICS OF DISEQUILIBRIUM MODELS (*co-author*)

Aggregate Demand and Supply

A Critique of Orthodox Macroeconomic Modelling

Edited by

B. Bhaskara Rao
Associate Professor and Director of Postgraduate Studies
School of Economics
University of New South Wales

First published in Great Britain 1998 by
MACMILLAN PRESS LTD
Houndmills, Basingstoke, Hampshire RG21 6XS and London
Companies and representatives throughout the world

A catalogue record for this book is available from the British Library.

ISBN 0–333–69147–4

First published in the United States of America 1998 by
ST. MARTIN'S PRESS, INC.,
Scholarly and Reference Division,
175 Fifth Avenue, New York, N.Y. 10010

ISBN 0–312–21075–2

Library of Congress Cataloging-in-Publication Data
Aggregate demand and supply : a critique of orthodox macroeconomic modelling / edited by B. Bhaskara Rao.
p. cm.
Includes bibliographical references and index.
ISBN 0–312–21075–2
1. Demand (Economic theory) 2. Supply and demand. I. Bhaskara Rao, B., 1939– .
HB842.E85 1998
338.5'21—DC21 97–18334
CIP

This book is printed on paper suitable for recycling and made from fully managed and sustained forest sources.

10 9 8 7 6 5 4 3 2 1
07 06 05 04 03 02 01 00 99 98

Printed and bound in Great Britain by
Antony Rowe Ltd, Chippenham, Wiltshire

Contents

	Preface	xi
	Notes on the Contributors	xiii
1.	**Introduction** **B. Bhaskara Rao**	1
2.	**Aggregate Demand in Principles Textbooks** **Ken McCormick and Janet M. Rives**	
2.1	Introduction	11
2.2	Current Textbook Presentations	11
2.3	Other Effects of Price Changes	17
2.4	Additional Considerations	19
2.5	The Need for Alternatives	21
3.	**Aggregate Demand Curves: A Guide to Use and Abuse Revisited** **Peter H. Hall and Malcolm L. Treadgold**	
3.1	Introduction	25
3.2	The Conventional Curve	26
3.3	Problems with the Conventional Approach	28
	3.3.1 The Volume of Real Aggregate Demand	28
	3.3.2 The Measurement of Excess Demand/Supply	30
	3.3.3 Interdependence of Aggregate Demand and Supply	31

3.4 Two Alternatives 33
3.4.1 Rowan's Curve 33
3.4.2 Corden's Constant-MV Curve 39
3.5 Conclusion 42

4. What is the Matter with Aggregate Demand and Supply?
B. Bhaskara Rao

4.1 Introduction 45
4.2 Aggregate Demand, Supply and the ISLM Model 46
4.3 The Neo Classical Version 56
4.4 The Keynesian Approach 60
4.5 Conclusions 65

5. Walrasian, Non-Walrasian and Post-Walrasian Perspectives on the ADAS Model: Theoretical and Pedagogical Implications
Ralph C. Allen and Jack H. Stone

5.1 Introduction 67
5.2 Institutional Environment 68
5.3 Institutional Environment Behind ISLM 70
5.4 Inconsistencies in ADAS and Proposed Alternatives 72
5.5 Post-Walrasian Coordination in ADAS 76
5.6 Conclusion 80

6. The ADAS Model: Two into One Won't Go
Roy H. Grieve

6.1 Introduction 83
6.2 The Textbook Model 84
6.3 Two Theories, One Model: No Go 88
6.4 The Root of the Problem 90
6.5 Conclusion 93
6.6 Postscript 94

7. Defending ADAS: A Perspective on the ADAS Controversy
Peter Kennedy

7.1 Introduction 95
7.2 The Rise of ADAS 95
7.3 No Internal Inconsistency 97
7.4 ADAS Can be Confusing 99
7.5 Dynamics 102
7.6 Conclusion 104
Appendix to Chapter 7: Survey Instrument 105

8. Theoretical Inconsistencies in the ADAS Model: Can the Model be Rehabilitated?
T. Windsor Fields and William R. Hart

8.1 Introduction 107
8.2 The Textbook ADAS Model 110
8.3 The Aggregate Demand Curve 112
8.4 A Theoretically Consistent ADAS Model 116
8.5 Short Run Aggregate Demand 126

8.6 Price Level and Interest Rate Determination in ADAS Model 128
8.7 Conclusion 135

9. Acceptable and Unacceptable Dirty Pedagogy: The Case of ADAS
David Colander and Peter Sephton

9.1 Introduction 137
9.2 What the ADAS Model is Supposed to Accomplish 138
9.3 Problems with ADAS Analysis 138
9.4 Macro Policy Model 142
9.4.1 The Renaming of the AED Curve 143
9.4.2 Using an Aggregate Supply Path Rather than a Supply Curve 144
9.5 The Aggregate Supply Path Alternative 151
9.6 The More Limited Applicability of the Macro Policy Model 152
9.7 Summary 153

10 Aggregate Demand and Supply Analysis: A Story in the Wrong Language
John W. Nevile

10.1 Introduction 155
10.2 Language of General Equilibrium Comparative Statics 157
10.3 Marshallian Analysis versus General Equilibrium 162
10.4 Not only the Wrong Language but an Unfamiliar Dialect 166
10.5 A Possible Alternative 168
10.6 Conclusion 174

11 A Simple Analysis of Price and Output Determination: A Model with Imperfect Competition

Corrado Benassi, Alessandra Chirco and Caterina Colombo

11.1 Introduction 177
11.2 Aggregate Demand and Supply Under Imperfect Competition 180
11.3 The Role of Wage Rigidities 182
11.4 A Macromodel of Imperfect Competition 185
11.4.1 Firm's Behaviour 185
11.4.2 Union's Behaviour 187
11.5 Aggregate Behaviour of Firms and Unions 189
11.6 Equilibrium Under Full Nominal Flexibility 191
11.6.1 Determination and Properties of Equilibrium 191
11.6.2 Aggregate Demand and Aggregate Supply Under Full Flexibility 195
11.7 Equilibrium Under Nominal Rigidities 195
11.7.1 Equilibrium Under Nominal Wage Rigidity 297
11.7.2 Aggregate Demand and Supply Under Nominal Wage Rigidity 198
11.7.3 Equilibrium Under Nominal Price Rigidity 200
11.8 Concluding Remarks 202
Appendix to Chapter 11 205

Bibliography 209
Index 223

Preface

The aggregate demand and supply model is extensively used in the current macroeconomics textbooks to explain the working of the economy, to evaluate rival macroeconomic paradigms and to illustrate the effects and policy implications of changes in the exogenous variables. However, many teachers are becoming uncomfortable with its logical foundations and the claim that it is general and encompasses alternative macroeconomic paradigms. Although there have been severe criticisms of this model, textbook writers were reluctant to develop more convincing alternative expository models.

That the textbook aggregate demand and supply model has logical pitfalls was pointed out by Rowan (1975), Hall and Treadgold (1982), Hansen, McCormick and Rives (1985) and Rao (1991). Subsequently several important papers have been published in various issues of the *Australian Economic Papers* and the *Southern Economic Journal.* None of this had any significant effect on the textbook model and the way we teach macroeconomics. However, more recently three important papers by Colander (1995), Nevile and Rao (1996) and Grieve (1996) have once again raised doubts about the logical soundness of the derivation of the aggregate demand and supply model. These recent publications have encouraged me to bring out this collection of essays by requesting others, with similar concerns about the logical foundations of the basic macro model, to explore for some logically consistent alternative models for use in the textbooks and classrooms. It is hoped that this collection of essays will encourage many other teachers to extend our efforts.

I am grateful to all the contributors to this volume for readily accepting my request to elaborate their earlier criticisms and suggest alternative models that may eventually replace the current unsatisfactory textbook macro model. I thank Tim Farmiloe, Publishing Director of the Macmillan Press, for his appreciation and timely approval of this project; Sunder Katwala, Commissioning Editor, and Karen Brazier, Editorial Services Controller of the Macmillan Press for their help in preparing the final version of this book and Laser Campus, Madras, and Teresa Attfield, Audio Visual Unit, University of New South Wales, for help with the diagrams and my son, Pankaj, for proof reading parts of the book. My final thanks go to John Nevile and John Lodewijks for helpful discussions on some methodological issues; to Roy Grieve and Malcolm Treadgold for valuable suggestions and corrections; to Kevin Fox for his timely help at a crucial stage in the production of this book; to my graduate students, Debarshi Nandy and Tania Dutta, for help with the preparation of the final version of this book and the index, and to the editors and publishers of the *Australian Economic Papers* for permission to use previously published material in Chapters 3 and 4.

B.B.Rao
Sydney

Notes on the Contributors

Ralph C. Allen is Professor of Economics and currently Head of the Department of Economics and Marketing at Valdosta State University, Valdosta, Georgia, USA. He has published papers on firm location theory, the foundations of macroeconomic models and the economics of crime.

Corrado Benassi is Associate Professor of Economics at the University of Bologna, Italy. His main publications are in the field of the theory of financial intermediation, the micro foundations of macroeconomics and the economics of uncertainty and information.

Alessandra Chirco is Lecturer in Macroeconomics at the University of Bologna, Italy. Her recent publications are on Keynesian economic theories and coordination issues in macroeconomics.

David Colander is the Christian A. Johnson Distinguished Professor of Economics at Middlebury College, Middlebury, Vermont, USA. He has published well over 30 books and 80 research papers on a wide range of topics. He has been on the board and editorial boards of numerous economic societies and journals and has been the President of the Eastern Economic Association and Vice-President of the History of Economic Thought Society.

Caterina Colombo is Lecturer in Economics at the University of Ferrara, Italy. Her main contributions are in the field of New Keynesian economics and its applications to international economics.

Windsor Fields is Professor of Economics at James Madison University, Harrisonburg, Virginia, USA. He has published research papers in journals like *Journal of Monetary Economics, Review of Economics and Statistics, Economic Inquiry, Southern Economic Journal, Economics Letters* and the *Journal of Economic Education.* He has a long-standing interest in economic education.

Roy H. Grieve teaches at the University of Strathclyde, Glasgow, Scotland. His research interests and publications are in the areas of history of economic thought, macroeconomics and development economics. He is the co-editor of a volume of essays on *Bangladesh–Strategies for Development* (1995).

Peter Hall is Associate Professor of Economics in the School of Economics and Management, Australian Defence Force Academy campus of the University of New South Wales, Canberra, Australia. He has worked in macroeconomics and published papers on the economics of innovation, industry and growth, and issues in defence economics. He is the author of *Innovation Economics and Evolution* (1994).

William Hart is Professor of Economics at Miami University in Oxford, Ohio, USA. His research interests include disequilibrium analysis, macroeconomic theory, stabilisation policy, and economic education. He has published papers in the *American Economic Review, Economic Inquiry, Journal of Economic Education, Journal of Macroeconomics, Oxford Economic Papers,* and the *Southern Economic Journal.*

Peter Kennedy is Professor of Economics at Simon Fraser University, Burnaby, British Columbia, Canada. He held visiting positions at Cornell University, London School of Economics, National University of Singapore, Dekin University, University of Cape Town and University of Canterbury (NZ). He is a recipient of four awards for excellence in teaching and the Villard award for research in economic education. He is well known for his textbook *A Guide to Econometrics*. He is an associate editor of the *Journal of Economic Education* and the *International Journal of Forecasting*. His research interests are in the areas of econometrics and economic education.

Ken McCormick is Professor of Economics at University of Northern Iowa where he teaches macroeconomics, history of economic thought and mathematical economics. His research articles have been published in journals such as *Review of Social Economy, Eastern Economic Journal, Journal of Economic Issues* and *Journal of Economic Education.*

John W. Nevile has retired as Professor of Economics at the University of New South Wales, Sydney, Australia. Currently he is Visiting Professor and Director of the Centre for Applied Economic Research at that university. He is a Fellow of the Academy of Social Sciences in Australia and a past President of the Economic Society of Australia. He has published well over one hundred articles and books on a wide range of topics. His publications have appeared in journals such as the *Economic Journal, Economic Record, Australian Economic Papers, Australian Economic Review, Journal of Post Keynesian Economics* and *Manchester School.*

Bhaskara Rao is Associate Professor of Economics and Director of Postgraduate Studies at the School of Economics, University of New South Wales, Sydney, Australia. He has published papers on macroeconomics and applied econometrics in journals such as the *Economic Journal, Review of Economics and Statistics, Economics Letters, Southern Economic Journal, Australian Economic Papers, Manchester School, Indian Journal of Applied Economics* and *Journal of Quantitative Economics.* He is the co-author of the *Econometrics of Disequilibrium Models* (1990), editor of *Cointegration for the Applied Economist* (1994) and a member of the editorial board of the *Indian Journal of Applied Economics.*

Janet M. Rives is Professor of Economics at University of Northen Iowa. Her research interests include regional economic development, women's labour market behaviour and the economics of gender equity. She has published several research articles in journals such as *Journal of Social Economics, Regional Science Perspectives, Quarterly Review of Economics and Business, Social Science Quarterly* and *Applied Economics.* She is currently co-editing a book of readings titled *The Economics of Gender Inequality: A Global Perspective,* scheduled for publication in 1997.

Peter Sephton is Professor of Economics at the University of New Brunswick. He is the co-author of the Canadian edition of Colander's well known principles of economics textbook. He has been a consultant to the IMF and has held positions at the Bank of Canada and the Ontario Ministry of Treasury and Economics.

Jack Stone is Associate Professor of Economics at Spelman College located in Atlanta, Georgia, USA. He has published articles on firm location theory and the teaching of micro and macroeconomic theory.

Malcolm Treadgold is Professor of Economics at the University of New England, Armidale, Australia. He has held research positions at the Australian National University, and is a former Commonwealth Fellow of St John's College, Cambridge. His research interests are in the fields of macroeconomics, development economics, labour economics and economic history. He is the author of *Bounteous Bestowal: The Economic History of Norfolk Island,* (1988) and *The Economics of Fiji: Performance, Management and Prospects* (1992). He is also a co-author of *A Guide to the Australian Economy: Structure, Performance and Policy* (1994).

1 Introduction

B. Bhaskara Rao

During the last forty years the basic models used to explain the working of the economy and the range of topics discussed – in the introductory and intermediate macroeconomics textbooks – have changed significantly. In the fifties and sixties methodological comparisons between the classical and Keynesian models were popular in the intermediate textbooks. Introductory books used linear consumption functions and the simple 45^0 income-expenditure model to explain the Keynesian multiplier process and the effects of changes in the exogenous variables such as the government expenditure, tax rates etc.

Subsequently the simple partial equilibrium goods market model was expanded and the working of the economy within the general equilibrium framework of $ISLM$ was explained with a variety of four quadrant diagrams. However, its general equilibrium nature was not explicitly and adequately explained. $ISLM$ was also used to explain the differences between the Keynesian and monetarist models and thus bring forward discussions on the methodological issues from the intermediate to introductory textbooks.

The second generation intermediate textbooks assumed that students were familiar with $ISLM$ and some methodological differences between the Keynesian and monetarist models. Therefore they explained the finer theoretical and empirical aspects of the structural equations underlying $ISLM$, such as the consumption-saving function, investment function, demand for money function etc. These developments were seen as providing the missing microeconomic foundations for macroeconomic relationships and the mainstream macroeconomists refined these developments considerably.

Much of the research work in macroeconomics of the fifties and sixties was essentially based on *ISLM*. This activity received a major boost in the early sixties when the Phillips curve was developed. But it also collapsed when it was found that the Phillips curve was highly unstable. However it can be said that, even before this collapse took place, important methodological issues concerning the Keynesian and classical (or Walrasian) models have been neglected by the mainstream macroeconomists and textbook writers. Clower (1965) and Leijonhufvud (1968) were the earliest to highlight these weaknesses and emphasise the need to examine the Keynes versus classics or monetarist debate within a general equilibrium framework. They argued that, while in the Walrasian classical model equilibrium is attained through price adjustments, in the Keynesian system the equilibrating mechanism is quantity adjustment. Consequently, unlike in the Walrasian system, equilibrium in the Keynesian system is not unique and the economy may remain in an underemployment equilibrium with involuntary unemployment for a long period.

The essence of the Clower-Leijonhufvud criticism did not receive the sort of attention it really deserved. Mainstream economists were more critical of the underlying fixprice assumptions of this framework than its general equilibrium implications. However, it did attract the attention of a small group of economists, known as the disequilibrium economists. Subsequently (rather belatedly) Hicks (1979, 1983) offered an important clarification of the nature of his *ISLM*. He noted that *ISLM* was a product of his Walrasianism and it was his way of looking at Keynes through the Walrasian perspective. However while in the Walrasian system all the markets are flexprice markets, in his *ISLM* there is at least one fixprice market. In fact he said that the goods and labour markets are fixprice markets in *ISLM*. Furthermore Hicks was less confident that his *ISLM* adequately captured the essence of the *General Theory*.

At this stage perhaps textbooks should have explained the differences between equilibrium brought through price adjustment (classical/Walrasian) and equilibrium attained through quantity adjustment (Keynesian). The simple microeconomic partial equilibrium demand and supply model and the 45^0 income-expenditure model could have been used to explain these two different adjustment processes respectively. Such an explanation could have been also useful to understand how price signals and quantity signals (through the build-up or depletion of unplanned inventories) induce transactors to modify their economic behaviour in the classical and Keynesian systems. This contrast might have also helped the student to reflect on why, at times, transactors may not have an incentive to adjust prices and therefore adjust quantities.[1] The general equilibrium aspects of the Keynes versus classics debate could have been then explained, for example, with the sort of diagrammatic framework popularised in an earlier generation of textbooks such as Ackley (1961). The *ISLM* model, which is essentially a general equilibrium model with some fixprice markets, could have been then used to explain how real world modern economies, where a large proportion of output transactions are believed to take place in the Keynesian fixprice markets, actually function.[2]

[1] Recent theoretical developments such as the contract and efficiency wage theories, menu costs and near rationality rationalise this very phenomenon.

[2] Implicit in this observation is the belief that in the real world a large proportion of transactions take place in the Keynesian fixprice or sluggish price markets; see Rao (1993a, 1993b, 1994 and 1996) and Rao and Srivastava (1991). Rao (1996) found that about 87.5 per cent of US *GNP* transactions take place in the Keynesian sluggish price markets. New Keynesians use the imperfectly competitive market approach instead of the disequilibrium approach; see Dixon and Rankin (1994) for a survey of this approach.

However, developments in macroeconomics took a different turn. The Clower-Leijonhufvud criticisms and the progress made by disequilibrium economics were seen to be less important. Disequilibrium models were criticised for their fixprice assumption although they only assume that quantity adjustments precede price adjustments and prices are not fixed for ever but may not change sufficiently to clear the markets within the *unit time period.*[3]

Furthermore, estimation of disequilibrium models is more complicated than the estimation of Phillips curves, demand for money functions or consumption equations. Therefore the significance of these developments did not receive much attention. The alternative approach based on imperfectly competitive product and factor markets is even more demanding. For these reasons the $ISLM$ model, which in fact is a fixprice general equilibrium model, seems to have been thought to be adequate for understanding and evaluating rival macroeconomic paradigms viz., fixprice Keynesian and flexprice classical/monetarist models.[4]

The collapse of the Phillips curve and the subsequent stagflation, made worse by the oil shocks, strangely brought the rival schools of macroeconomists much closer. There was an underlying feeling that while the Keynesians are concerned with the demand side of the economy, for the monetarists and the new classical economists the supply side of the economy is the most important relationship. The $ISLM$ model with the expectations augmented Phillips curve did not appeal to the textbook writers partly because it is hard to develop simple diagrams to explain the dynamics of a model with both levels and rates of changes of variables. The most awkward feature of these develop-

[3] This is not to say that disequilibrium framework is adequate to develop modern macroeconomics. But the criticism that this framework is unsatisfactory because it depends entirely on the assumption that wages and prices are fixed is not correct.

[4] See Leijonhufvud (1983) for criticisms of the use of $ISLM$ for this purpose.

ments was that the Keynesians as well as the monetarist and new classical economists have essentially used *ISLM* plus a Phillips curve model to justify their methodological positions. The Phillips curve, a price adjustment equation, was turned upside down and reinterpreted as the aggregate supply curve; see for example Lucas and Rapping (1969). Since an aggregate supply curve was thus invented,[5] all that was needed was an aggregate demand curve to simultaneously determine output and the price level. It seems that some textbook writers have found that a downward sloping relationship between output and price level, that looks like the standard microeconomic demand curve, can be derived from the *ISLM* model and this was quickly renamed as the aggregate demand curve. These developments thus gave birth to the now popular textbook aggregate demand and aggregate supply model (*ADAS*).

Some of the earlier textbooks that have used and popularised *ADAS* are Dornbusch and Fischer (1978), Gordon (1978) and Parkin (1982).[6] Several other textbooks quickly followed their example and adopted *ADAS* as the main textbook model at the introductory and intermediate levels. Virtually all the textbooks took the view that this model is quite general and therefore useful for explaining alternative paradigms such as the Keynesian, monetarist and new classical models. In fact some textbooks imply that the main difference between these alternative models is that while in the Keynesian model the aggregate supply function is highly or perfectly elastic, in the alternative models this

---

[5] Subsequently another version of this curve, derived from the labour market equilibrium condition, has been also used as the aggregate supply curve. This version is popular with the neo classical, monetarist and new classical textbook writers. Both versions of the aggregate supply function give the misleading impression that they are the same as the supply function in microeconomics i.e., the sum of the marginal cost curves of firms in a competitive industry.

[6] Dr Ingo Barens informed that *ADAS* was first introduced by Hansen (1951) and subsequently by McKenna (1955).

elasticity is low or zero. In other words these rival theories were seen as nested models within the more general *ADAS* framework.

However, a small group of post-Keynesian economists took a sceptical view of *ADAS*. But the basis for this scepticism was not clearly documented. One of the earliest critiques of *ADAS* was Rowan (1975). He took the view that the aggregate demand function derived from *ISLM* and used in *ADAS* was not conceptually Keynes' effective demand function. A doubt was thus raised about the suitability of *ADAS* to explain the Keynesian model. Not surprisingly his criticisms were ignored by the mainstream textbook writers. Subsequently an elegant pedagogic version of Rowan's objections and suggested solutions was developed by Hall and Treadgold (1982). A little later Hansen, McCormick and Rives (1985) raised serious doubts on the assumption that the aggregate demand curve is downward sloping in the output-price space. These two contributions are historically important in this debate. The first two chapters in this volume by McCormick and Rives and Hall and Treadgold explain these criticisms and also take into account some recent developments on this controversy.[7]

While these contributions are valuable, it can be said that they did not highlight the need to examine the deficiencies of *ADAS* within the general equilibrium framework, underlying both the *ISLM* and *ADAS* models.[8] Hicks (1983) explained more fully the general equilibrium nature of his *ISLM*. Rao (1991), using these developments, pointed out that there is a serious inconsistency between the assumptions from which the aggregate demand and supply curves are derived in the *ADAS* model. Furthermore neither the

---

[7] Another criticism, similar in scope to Hall and Treadgold (1982), is Rabin and Birch (1982).

[8] It was also felt that the use of the Rowan, Hall and Treadgold effective demand curves in the *ADAS* will lead to the impression that *ADAS* is a partial equilibrium single goods market model which it is not; see Rao (1986).

demand curve nor the supply curve in *ADAS* is conceptually the same as its microeconomic counterpart and the textbook *ADAS* model gives the misleading impression that it is a partial equilibrium goods market model. Colander (1995) subsequently referred to this practice in the textbooks as "dirty pedagogy". It is surprising that these logical deficiencies in the very basic textbook model did not attract the attention of the leading textbook writers and macroeconomists who have been researching on the micro foundations of macroeconomic relationships.

Since Rao (1991) is the first to look at the deficiencies of *ADAS* from a general equilibrium perspective, I have included it, without the usual customary modesty, as the fourth chapter in this volume. Note also that very similar criticisms have been recently made by Barro (1994), Colander (1995), Grieve (1996), Nevile and Rao (1996) and Barens (1997).

The next three chapters by Allen and Stone, Grieve and Kennedy are different in scope. Although the criticisms of *ADAS* by Rao (1991), Colander (1995) and Grieve (1996) are similar, they offer different solutions.[9]

Rao (1991) implicitly suggested that we revert back to *ISLM*, augmented with an expectations augmented Phillips curve. A similar approach is also implicit in the Dornbusch and Fischer version of *ADAS* although, as Grieve has noted, these authors take considerable pains to give the impression that their *ADAS* model is a genuine demand-supply model.

Colander (1995) suggested that the economy's ability to coordinate economic activities should be treated as an additional factor of production and therefore as influencing the position and shape of the aggregate supply curve. On the other hand Grieve (1996) endorsed the Dornbusch and Fischer version of the *ADAS* although he suggests in his contribution to this volume the use of a simpler version of this model in the principles textbooks.

---

[9] Colander, Grieve, McCormick and Rives and Kennedy were not aware of Rao (1991) when they first wrote their papers.

Allen and Stone's chapter is a clear survey of the major developments in this debate up to Colander (1995) and examines several contributions based especially on the general equilibrium perspective. They also explain, more clearly and in some detail, the Colander (1995) model which is somewhat hard to understand in its original form.

In the next chapter Grieve points out, more clearly than any other paper published so far, the logical contradictions between the derivation of the aggregate demand and supply functions. He argues that *ADAS* is over determined and unsuitable as a framework to synthesise the Keynesian and Pigouvian (classical) explanations of employment and unemployment. According to Grieve the two curves in *ADAS* are incompatible since they represent irreconcilably different conceptions of the nature of economic reality.

The lone dissident from these criticisms is Kennedy. While admitting that some textbook derivations of *ADAS* are "dirty pedagogy" he takes the view that the criticism that the assumptions of *ADAS* are inconsistent is incorrect. He suggests that the aggregate demand curve should be termed as the equilibrium goods and money market relationship and likewise the aggregate supply curve as the labour market equilibrium curve; see also Rao (1991) for similar labels for these two relationships. However his support for the retention of *ADAS* in the principles textbooks is based on the outcome of a small survey of his graduate students. These survey results show that a large proportion of his graduate students were unaffected by the "dirty pedagogy" in the textbooks. Similar surveys by others, over the next few years, would be useful to assess the relevance of *ADAS* on a different basis.

The final set of four chapters by Fields and Hart, Colander and Sephton, Nevile and Benassi, Chirco and Colombo suggest various remedies and alternatives to *ADAS*. An important point made by Fields and Hart is that, contrary to the implications of the textbook models, the goods market determines the rate of interest and the price level is determined in the money market. They note the inconsistencies in the *ADAS* model, pointed out in the earlier contributions, but explain these criticisms more clearly with the aid of diagrams and algebra. Following Hall and Treadgold, they also point out the significance of the nature of the supply-side response to changes in demand. Their preferred model has the Lucas type supply function and has been used to illustrate several comparative static results.

The next two chapters by Colander and Sephton and Nevile are somewhat similar in scope but were drafted independently. Both contributions briefly survey the deficiencies of the *ADAS* model and develop simple alternative models that look like the *ADAS* model but are free from its logical inconsistencies. The demand curve in these alternative models is derived from the 45^0 income-expenditure model and not the *ISLM* model. This is reasonable because most central banks nowadays target interest rates instead of the supply of money. Therefore treating the rate of interest as an exogenous variable in the income-expenditure model is meaningful and simplifies the derivation of the aggregate demand function. In both chapters the aggregate demand function is seen as highly inelastic or perfectly inelastic, a point emphasised earlier by McCormick and Rives. There is, however, a difference in the derivation of the aggregate supply functions. Nevile utilises the imperfect competition model and the mark-up price equation with some simplifying assumptions about the elasticities of demand to obtain an aggregate supply relationship. Colander and Sephton derive an aggregate supply path which has roughly the same shape as the typical aggregate supply curve. But this curve has different micro-foundations. It is an empirically based curve that reflects the observed price-setting strategy of real world firms.

In the final essay Benassi, Chirco and Colombo present a very promising and rigourously developed two market macro model of price and output determination. Although a few intermediate textbooks have assumed that the goods and labour markets are imperfectly competitive and explained how output and price are determined within this framework, their attempts have remained somewhat exploratory and at times idiosyncratic. In contrast the Benassi, Chirco and Colombo contribution is one of the clearest expositions of a two market (goods and labour) general equilibrium model. Their contribution will have a significant impact on the expositions of the macro model in the intermediate textbooks if not in the introductory textbooks.

These authors first justify the need to use an imperfectly competitive goods and labour market model, instead of the usual disequilibrium models with sluggish price adjustments and perfect competition assumptions. They then derive what look like the aggregate demand and supply functions, point out their limitations and examine the consequences of nominal and real wage-price rigidities. The assumption that wages and prices are fully flexible in their model gives the standard policy ineffectiveness Walrasian results. In this sense their model is appropriate for nesting rival macroeconomic paradigms and evaluating their relative merits.

Space limitations have prevented us from including other important contributions in this volume. The extensive bibliography is a good guide to the other important contributions on the *ADAS* controversy. Hopefully this volume of essays will make an impact on students, textbook writers and mainstream economists and help them to develop a more satisfactory and logically consistent textbook macroeconomic model.

Finally we have denoted the equations in a chapter sequentially without prefixing the chapter numbers because it simplified typesetting and does not cause any confusion since none of the authors refer to the equations in the other chapters. The table of contents and an exhaustive index will help readers to quickly locate in the text topics of their interest.

2 Aggregate Demand in Principles Textbooks

Ken McCormick and Janet M. Rives

2.1 INTRODUCTION

> Low standards of rigor and sloppiness of thinking have been worse enemies of scientific economics than has been political bias. Schumpeter (1954, p.233).

In 1985 we wrote an article critical of the aggregate demand curve as presented in most principles textbooks (Hansen, McCormick and Rives, 1985). The essence of our argument was that the reasons given for the negative slope of the aggregate demand curve in price level/real *GDP* space were not convincing. Writing in 1997, we note that, with one minor exception, very little has changed.[1]

2.2 CURRENT TEXTBOOK PRESENTATIONS

In our 1985 article, we criticized textbook authors for not drawing a clear conceptual distinction between the aggregate demand curve and a market demand curve. Even though the two demand curves may look alike, the reasons

[1] We want to stress that the discussion in this chapter is limited to the aggregate demand curve as presented in principles textbooks. For excellent discussions of the aggregate demand/aggregate supply model as it relates to the *ISLM* model, see Rao (1991), reprinted in this volume of essays, Barro (1994) and Neville and Rao (1996).

for their negative slopes are quite different. Today we find that most authors have improved their presentations of aggregate demand by making this distinction clear. Authors of current textbooks are also now generally careful to point out that the aggregate demand curve is not simply the sum of all market demand curves.

Not all textbook writers give the same reasons for the aggregate demand curve's negative slope (see Table 2.1). This fact by itself suggests that there is a need to examine the reasons more closely. We have found that current textbooks offer one or more of the following reasons for the negative slope of the aggregate demand curve: (1) the real balance effect, (2) the interest rate effect, (3) the foreign trade effect, (4) the income tax-bracket effect, (5) the property and sales tax effect, and (6) the intertemporal price level effect. With one exception, we will discuss each of these for the case of a decline in the price level, though the logic is symmetrical for the case of a price level increase.

The real balance effect, also known as the wealth effect or the Pigou effect, is a commonly cited reason for the shape of the aggregate demand curve. This explanation contends that, as the price level falls, the real value of money rises, making holders of money wealthier. Their added wealth, in turn, induces them to increase their consumption.

In 1985 we cited evidence that the real balance effect is trivially small. In 1993, using generous assumptions about the propensity to consume out of wealth, James Tobin estimated that a 10 per cent decline in prices would increase spending by 0.06 per cent of *GNP* (Tobin, 1993, p.60). Clearly the real balance effect is much ado about nothing. As Greenwald and Stiglitz put it,

> The enormous attention that the real balance effect has received over the years hardly speaks well for the profession. Quantitatively, it is surely an nth order effect; one calculation put it that, even at the fastest rate at which prices fell in the Great Depression, it would take more than two centuries to restore the

The Aggregate Demand Curve in Principles Texts

	1	2	3	4	5	6	7	8	9	10	11	12	13	14	15	16	17	18	19	20	21	22	23
An *ADAS* model is presented	*	*	*	*	*	*	*	*	*	*	*	*	*	*	*	*	*	*	*	*		*	*
Explicit contrast between the downward slope of individual and aggregate demand curve is made	*		*		*	*		*	*	*	*	*	*	*	*			*			na	*	*
AD derived from the Keynesian cross	*	*	*	*	*	*	*			*	*	*	*	*	*			*		*	na	*	
Explanation given for the negative slope of *AD* are:																							
1. Real balance effect	*	*	*	*	*	*	*	*	*	*	*	*	*	*	*	*	*	*	*	*	na	*	*
2. Interest rate effect:	*	*	*	*	*	*	*	*	*	*	*	*	*	*	*	*	*	*	*	*	na	*	*
a. Stems from effect on money demand	*	*	*	*	*			*	*		*	*	*	*	*		*		*	*	na	*	*
b. Stems from effect on real money supply						*	*			*						*		*			na		
3. Foreign trade effect	*	*	*	*		*		*	*	*	*	*	*	*	*	*	*		*	*	na	*	*
4. Income tax-bracket effect	*																				na		
5. 'Property and sales tax effect	*																				na		
6. Intertemporal price effect						*														*	na		

Notes: 1 Amacher and Ulbrich; 2. Baumol and Blinder; 3. Boyes and Melvin; 4 Byrns and Melvin; 5. Case and Fair; 6. Colander; 7 Ecklund and Tollison; 8. Gottheil; 9. Gwartney and Stroup; 10. Hyman; 11. Lipsey and Courant; 12. Mansfield; 13. McConnell and Bruce; 14. McEachern; 15. Miller; 16. Parkin; 17. Ruffin and Gregory; 18. Samuelson and Nordhaus; 19. Schiffer; 20 Stiglitz; 21. Taylor; 22. Tregarthen and 23. Tucker.

> economy to full employment. And in the short run even its sign is ambiguous, as intertemporal substitution effects may (depending on expectations) more than offset the wealth effects (Greenwald and Stiglitz, 1993, p.36).

We suggest, in the strongest possible terms, that authors of principles texts stop using the real balance effect as an explanation of the negative slope of the aggregate demand curve.

A second common explanation of the aggregate demand curve's negative slope is the interest rate effect, also called the Keynes effect. The interest rate effect suggests that a fall in the price level leads to lower interest rates and, consequently, an increase in real aggregate expenditures. It is worth noting that textbook writers offer two different explanations as to why this happens (see Table 2.1). One group contends that the fall in the price level increases the real money supply. Others argue that the fall in the price level reduces the demand for money. The difference is that the former deals with real money demand and supply while the latter is in terms of nominal money supply and demand. The two approaches are essentially equivalent, though not all textbook authors note explicitly whether they are dealing with nominal or real money demand and supply.

Tobin (1993) cites Chapter 19 of *The General Theory* as the origin of the Keynes effect. In that chapter Keynes makes a list of possible effects of a reduction in nominal wages. The fifth item on the list is the argument that

> The reduction in the wages-bill, accompanied by some reduction in prices and in money-incomes generally, will diminish the need for cash for income and business purposes; and it will therefore reduce *pro tanto* the schedule of liquidity preference for the community as a whole. *Cet. par.* this will reduce the rate of interest and thus prove favourable to investment (Keynes, 1964, p.263, italics in the original).

This is a clear statement of the Keynes effect. Yet Keynes himself had doubts about the Keynes effect. Consider the sentences that immediately follow the passage just cited:

> In this case, however, the effect of expectation concerning the future will be of an opposite tendency to those just considered under (4). For if wages and prices are expected to rise again later on, the favorable reaction will be much less pronounced in the case of long-term loans than in that of short-term loans. If, moreover, the reduction in wages disturbs political confidence by causing popular discontent, the increase in liquidity preference due to this cause may more than offset the release of cash from the active circulation (Keynes, 1964, p.263-4).

Hence, the originator of the Keynes effect placed far less confidence in it than do current principles textbook authors.

The foreign trade effect is a third reason offered in principles textbooks for the negative slope of the aggregate demand curve. This explanation says that, as the domestic price level falls, exports will rise and imports will fall. This happens because the fall in the domestic price level increases the relative price of foreign goods.[2] As long as it is explicitly linked to the assumption of fixed exchange rates, this argument is legitimate. If exchange rates are flexible, the effect will be reduced or eliminated altogether.

The income tax-bracket effect is a fourth reason suggested in one textbook for the aggregate demand curve's negative slope. The argument is that, as prices (and thus nominal incomes) fall, a progressive income tax structure which is not indexed for inflation (or deflation) ensures that some people will pay a lower share of their income in taxes. This happens even if their real income is unchanged, because they will fall into lower tax brackets. The increase in

---

[2] Note that in this case there really is an analogy to a market demand curve in that there is a substitution effect caused by a change in relative prices.

disposable income, in turn, increases consumption spending. What is left out of the textbook discussion, however, is the effect this has on the government. If the government reduces its spending in the face of falling tax collections, then this will offset the increase in consumption spending. If the government maintains its spending by borrowing the additional money, interest rates will rise, counteracting the interest rate effect. In either case, the income tax-bracket effect cannot be used to explain why real spending might rise when the price level falls.

The same text which includes the income tax-bracket argument also presents the property and sales tax effect. To consider this in its most favorable light, we will deviate from our pattern and first consider the case of an increase in the price level This fifth effect allegedly arises from the fact that nominal property and sales tax revenues are not sensitive to price level changes. Hence, real revenues for state and local governments fall as the price level rises. Because most of these governments have a balanced budget requirement, their real spending must also fall. As a result, state and local government spending falls as the price level rises.

There are two distinct problems with this argument. First, recall that the authors' discussion of the income tax-bracket effect focuses on the effect on consumption spending while ignoring the effect on government spending. Yet, their discussion of the property and sales tax effect does just the opposite; government spending is affected but not consumer spending. If a rise in the price level reduces real property tax payments, it may reduce real government spending; but, presumably, the price level rise should also increase consumer spending, if real tax bills decline. (Note that if consumers save the real reduction in their tax bill, interest rates will fall.)

The second problem with the property and sales tax effect is that this is the only one of the six explanations of a downward sloping aggregate demand curve that is not symmetrical. Consider the property and sales tax effect for the case of a decrease in the price level. In this case, real tax revenue will rise. But now, the balanced budget constraint does not come into play. There is, thus, no mechanism to insure that state and local governments will spend the extra real revenue. We cannot argue that spending will rise when the price level falls, even if the converse were true. (And, in any event, the higher real tax bill will reduce consumer spending.)

The sixth reason offered for the negative slope of the aggregate demand curve is the intertemporal price level effect. This effect means that "a fall in the price level, expectations of future prices constant, causes people to switch from future to present consumption" (Colander, 1995, p.171). As stated, this effect would bring about the promised results, namely an increase in real *GDP* demanded as the price level falls. However, it presupposes that a fall in the current price level has no impact on expectations about the future price level. If, as Stiglitz (1993) points out, a fall in the price level leads consumers and firms to expect even lower prices in the future, they may postpone purchases. Thus a falling price level may actually reduce sales. Moreover, this argument highlights a common problem with all six explanations: While, *ceteris paribus,* most of the explanations may be true to at least some degree, they seem to purposefully ignore other effects caused by changes in the price level, not the least of which are changes in expectations resulting from changes in the price level.

2.3 OTHER EFFECTS OF PRICE CHANGES

In their efforts to present reasons why reductions in the price level would increase the amount of real *GDP* demanded, textbook writers seem to have studiously ignored all arguments which suggest that reductions in the price level might have the opposite effect. The desire to give the *AD* curve a negative slope has banished all counter arguments from consideration. We will review some of them here.

One counter argument is that a change in the price level has an effect on the real value of debt. A decline in the price level, for example, increases the real value of debt, a process commonly known as debt deflation. Even though creditors gain the same amount as debtors lose in real terms, the effect on the economy is not neutral if the price decline was not expected. This is because "common sense suggests that debtors have higher spending propensities – that is why they are in debt!" (Tobin, 1993, p 60). Hence debt deflation can lead to a reduction in real spending as the price level falls. Because Fisher (1933) emphasised debt deflation in his analysis of depressions, Tobin suggests that this should be called the "Fisher wealth redistribution effect (not to be confused with other Fisher effects)" (Tobin, 1993, p.60). In Tobin's view, "It is quite possible that this Fisher effect is stronger than the Pigou and Keynes effects combined, particularly when output and employment are low relative to capacity" (Tobin, 1993, p.60).

In a similar vein, Greenwald and Stiglitz (1993) argue that a decline in the price level may have adverse consequences for firms. They discuss factors which influence the risks firms face, noting that "a third important factor is the price level. Since almost all debt is denominated in nominal terms, such changes have large effects on firm real liquidity and real wealth" (Greenwald and Stiglitz, 1993, p.29). A decline in the price level increases the real burden of a firm's debt, with the result that investment might fall. Of the textbooks we surveyed, only Stiglitz (1993, p.834) mentioned this possibility.

Another issue concerns the relationship between changes in the price level and the expected inflation rate. When rising price levels are associated with positive inflationary expectations, the (original) Fisher effect suggests that the nominal interest rate will rise so as to keep the real interest rate constant. The effect is asymmetric, however, because the nominal interest rate is institutionally constrained in the downward direction (i.e., nominal interest rates will not fall below zero). Hence, if falling prices are coupled with expectations of higher rates of deflation, real interest rates could rise.[3] Lower prices could lead to a higher real interest rate, not the lower real interest rate suggested by the Keynes effect.

2.4 ADDITIONAL CONSIDERATIONS

The discussion of expected inflation illustrates an important deficiency of textbook treatments of the aggregate demand curve, namely the failure to address expectations. Mankiw (1990) reminds us that expectations are now a central part of macroeconomics. This holds true regardless of ideology; only the assumptions about how expectations are formed differ. Disciples of Keynes often treat expectations as exogenous or unexplainable.[4] Proponents of rational expectations argue that expectations are largely endogenous. In either case, the effect that a change in the price level will have on expectations depends on the circumstances surrounding it. Given the fact that "expectations ... are quantitatively important determinants of aggregate demand" (King, 1993, p.80), it is perilous to ignore the effect of price level changes on expectations.

An altogether different problem is noted by Colander (1995). The aggregate demand curve, when derived from the Keynesian cross (as is often done, see Table 2.1), contains, in essence, its own supply curve. As Colander puts it,

> The logical problem here is that one cannot derive an *AD* curve from the Keynesian model, because the

---

[3] For example, if the nominal interest rate is 0 per cent and the expected rate of deflation is 1 per cent. the expected real interest rate is 1 per cent. If the expected rate of deflation becomes 3 per cent, the nominal interest rate cannot fall, so the real interest rate rises to 3 per cent.

[4] "In estimating the prospects of investment we must have regard, therefore, to the nerves and hysteria and even the digestions and reactions to the weather of those upon whose spontaneous activity it largely depends" (Keynes, 1964, p.162).

> Keynesian model includes a dynamic interactive effect between supply and demand in the form of the multiplier. The Keynesian model has embodied in it what Robert Clower (1994) calls Hansen's Law – the proposition that demand creates its own supply. This analysis of supply might be totally wrong, but there is no denying that the Keynesian model has assumptions of supply responses in it. As you move along the 45-degree line, supply is changing independently of any change in the wage/price ratio.
>
> Given that the Keynesian model includes assumptions about supply, one cannot logically add another supply analysis to the model unless that other supply analysis is consistent with the Keynesian model assumption about supply (Colander, 1995, p.176).

Colander's analysis exposes the *ADAS* model as the marriage of convenience that it is. The model is fundamentally Keynesian, but it includes a price-adjustment mechanism to make it superficially compatible with neoclassical theory.[5] After all, it is awkward to explain to students in the first part of a course how prices adjust to clear markets in a partial equilibrium setting and then turn around and later suggest that price adjustments have no role to play in a general equilibrium framework.[6] Either price adjustments matter in macroeconomics or they do not, but we cannot pretend to have it both ways. If price adjustments do matter, then the Keynesian supply relationship (Hansen's Law) and its derivative aggregate demand curve must go. If price adjustments do not matter, why construct a model with the price level prominently displayed on the vertical axis?

The aggregate demand/aggregate supply model is a product of the Neoclassical/Keynesian synthesis which has

[5] Colander (1995) was not the first to make this point. Rao (1991) provides an insightful discussion of the problem of adding an *AS* function to an *AD* curve from a Keynesian model.

[6] Such an approach was taken, of course, prior to the advent of the *ADAS* model.

long since collapsed (Romer, 1993; Mankiw, 1990). It is representative of no major current viewpoint. For example, it stresses the role of price level adjustments as the major force in achieving macro-economic equilibrium in a manner that pleases almost no one. New classical theorists contend that "prices continually adjust to equilibrate supply and demand" (Mankiw, 1990, p.1648), and so reject the underlying Keynesian premises of the model. New Keynesians do not believe that price flexibility is even always a good thing, going so far as to argue that "price flexibility contributes to macroeconomic fluctuations and to unemployment" (Greenwald and Stiglitz, 1993, p.26). Advocates of real business cycles object to the emphasis on aggregate demand as a significant source of economic fluctuations.

The aggregate demand and aggregate supply model is a relic of a bygone era. We agree with Barro that "the *AS-AD* model is unsatisfactory and should be abandoned as a teaching tool" (Barro, 1994, p.1).

2.5 THE NEED FOR ALTERNATIVES

If the *ADAS* model is abandoned, what will take its place? David Colander (1995) has offered one alternative. We cannot endorse it, however, because it retains an aggregate demand curve based on the Pigou effect, the Keynes effect, the foreign trade effect and the intertemporal price effect, all reasons we find unconvincing.

Another approach is available in a principles textbook by John Taylor (1995), whose objective is to show

> ··· how the rational expectations assumption and its many intellectual sidekicks, monetary independence, policy rules, credibility, time inconsistency, and the microfoundations of price and wage adjustment, have been integrated into the mainstream macro model of short-term economic fluctuations used by most policymakers in the United States and other countries today (Taylor, 1995, p.xviii).

One striking feature of Taylor's approach is that the aggregate demand relationship is presented in inflation rate/real *GDP* space, rather than price level/real *GDP* space. Hence, the discussion is in terms of variations in the rate of inflation, not the price level.[7] Taylor's aggregate demand/inflation curve has a negative slope because it is derived from a specific monetary policy rule, namely that the central bank raises (short term) real interest rates when the inflation rate exceeds its target value and lowers real interest rates when inflation is below its target. While some might object to this institutionally constrained model, it is consistent with recent economic history, something that cannot be said for the *ADAS* model.

Not everyone may be pleased with Taylor's model. He presents no explicit aggregate supply curve, though he devotes a considerable amount of time to the microfoundations of price adjustments at the firm level before proceeding to the macroeconomic story. Keynesians will be unhappy that long-run equilibrium is reached only at potential *GDP*. Non-Keynesians may object to the fact that the Keynesian cross is retained. Nevertheless, Taylor's model tells a much more believable story than the *ADAS* model. It is, in truth, a little more difficult to teach; but the extra effort is rewarded not only with a better model, but also with a clearer conscience.

Because Taylor's approach will not appeal to everyone and because the *ADAS* model needs to be replaced, there is an opportunity for textbook authors to present models in which they believe.[8] It is, in essence, an opportunity to

---

[7] This solves a pedagogical problem we mentioned in 1987 (Hansen, McCormick and Rives, 1987): How can we reconcile the prediction of the *ADAS* model that the price level falls in response to falling aggregate demand when the price level in the U.S. has not fallen over a one year period since 1955? Taylor's model makes the more palatable prediction that the rate of inflation may decline, not the price level.

[8] In response to our 1985 article we received a letter from *(continued)*

have a fresh start. Abandoning the *ADAS* model of course means that there would no longer be a common model in principles texts, as New Keynesian models will certainly differ from real business cycle models. But how can this be worse than continuing to teach the *ADAS* model which is "logically wrong" (Colander, 1995, p.179)? We encourage passionate supporters of every school of thought to write textbooks from their perspectives, emphasizing whatever they believe to be important. Thoughtful teachers will embrace such fresh approaches to macroeconomics in principles textbooks. They are cognizant of many of the deficiencies in the *ADAS* model and would welcome new ideas. We should not overlook the fact that this change also provides an opportunity for proponents of competing viewpoints to win over a whole new generation of students.

a textbook author. He told us that he agreed with us, "but alas, there are certain things one has to put in a principles text."

3 Aggregate Demand Curves: A Guide to Use and Abuse Revisited*

Peter H. Hall and Malcolm L. Treadgold

3.1 INTRODUCTION

The negative sloped aggregate demand curve showing those combinations of the price level and real output at which the goods and money markets are simultaneously in equilibrium has become a popular analytical tool in introductory and intermediate-level macroeconomic textbooks.[1] It has been widely used in combination with different forms of the aggregate supply function to illustrate the determination of the equilibrium price level and/or real output. At the time of our original paper (Hall and Treadgold (1982)) the by-then-conventional aggregate demand curve had already been subjected to expositional criticisms by at least two writers, Rowan (1975) and Corden (1978), who each offered an alternative construction serving the same ultimate purpose but in a manner which was claimed to be pedagogically superior.

The aims of this chapter are, as they were in our earlier

* The original paper, Hall and Treadgold (1982), was stimulated by discussions with W.M. Corden. Helpful comments at the time of preparing that paper were supplied by D.C. Rowan, J.C. Baldry and B.F. Reece.

[1] The earliest description of this curve that we have found is in Brownlee (1950). The first textbook to employ it appears to have been McKenna (1955).

paper, to examine briefly the nature and use of the conventional aggregate demand curve, to investigate the criticisms made of it, and to evaluate alternatives that have been developed. As before, we focus on insights drawn from Rowan and Corden but also take account (selectively) of more recent developments which have taken place in the debate since 1982. It emerges that the conventional curve, although in itself conceptually valid, has been subjected to widespread misinterpretation and misuse in the textbook literature. The alternatives we consider here do not appear to be so susceptible to these problems, although each in turn possesses its own pedagogic disadvantages.

3.2 THE CONVENTIONAL CURVE

As is well known, the conventional aggregate demand curve is derived by tracing the effects of exogenous price level changes within the usual, negatively-sloped *IS* curve and positively-sloped *LM* curve model of the goods and money markets. An increase in the price level shifts the *LM* curve upwards or to the left (the Keynes effect) and the *IS* curve downwards or to the left (the Pigou effect), thereby implying a reduction in the level of real output at which the goods and money markets are simultaneously in equilibrium. (The rate of interest may of course also change, its direction of movement depending on the relative strengths of the Keynes and Pigou effects.) A decrease in the price level implies the opposite result. The generalised outcome is a negatively sloped curve showing how that volume of real output at which there is an equal volume of aggregate demand varies with the price level.[2]

Figure 3.1 illustrates the use of this curve (*AD*) in the determination of the equilibrium values of the price level

[2] The determinants of the precise shape of the aggregate demand curve are discussed in Gambs (1974, 1975), Havrilesky (1975) and Purvis (1975). However, this discussion, along with a number of other expositions, abstracts from the influence of the Pigou effect.

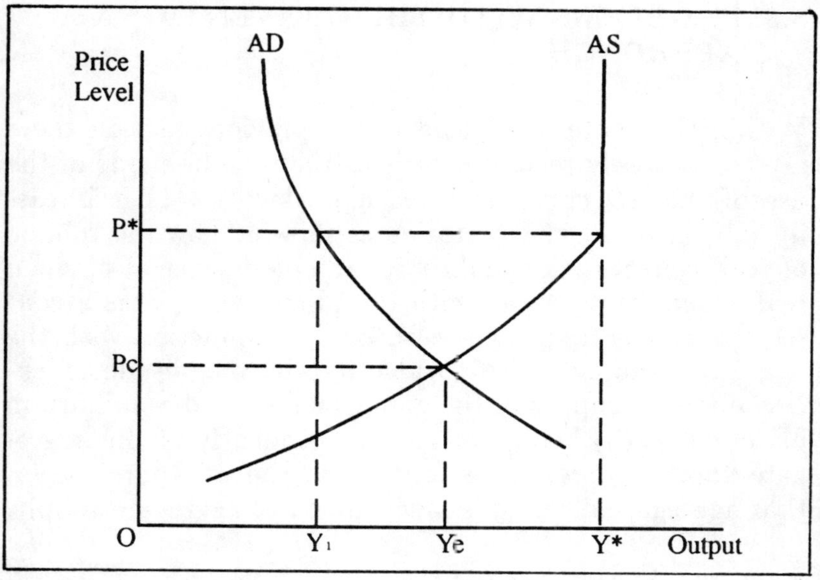

Figure 3.1

and real output. *AD* is shown in this case as intersecting the positively-sloped range of a Keynesian form of the aggregate supply function (*AS*), i.e., one depicting the volume of output supplied varying positively with the price level up to some "full employment" level of output Y^*. The point of intersection identifies the equilibrium price level and output. A shift in either curve changes the magnitudes of both these variables. It should be noted that if *AS* had been constructed on the basis of classical labour market assumptions it would have been a vertical line (i.e., output would have been completely price-inelastic at a full employment level). In these circumstances the forces governing aggregate demand would have influenced only the price level. At the opposite extreme, if *AS* had been assumed perfectly elastic (horizontal) until full employment output was reached, changes in demand would have influenced only output when the economy was operating at less than full employment.

3.3 PROBLEMS WITH THE CONVENTIONAL APPROACH

Within the context outlined in the previous section there are three closely related criticisms that can be made of the use of the *AD* curve as a teaching device: (1) it is easily subject to misinterpretation as showing how the volume of real aggregate demand, in its accepted sense of planned real expenditure, varies with the price level; (2) as a consequence, it is frequently misused in conjunction with the aggregate supply curve to identify the magnitude of excess demand/supply in the goods market at disequilibrium price levels; (3) being derived independently of the aggregate supply curve, it lends itself to the misapprehension that aggregate demand is independent of aggregate supply.

3.3.1 The Volume of Real Aggregate Demand

Consider again Figure 3.1. Only at equilibrium price level Pe will the *AD* curve necessarily measure the volume of real planned expenditure since only at this price level will the actual volume of real output, as governed by the aggregate supply curve, be at that level where there is an equal volume of real planned expenditure. At any other price level the volume of real planned expenditure can be expected to diverge from the *AD* curve. For example, take price level P^*. The *AD* curve indicates that at P^* aggregate demand will be at a level of Y_1 if output is at Y_1. However, on the usual assumption that firms' supply plans are carried out, the *AS* schedule indicates that at price level P^* output actually supplied will be at Y^*. *Ceteris paribus,* consumption demand can be expected to be higher at this latter level of output (income) than at Y_1. At the same time, given the money supply, Y^* will normally imply a higher rate of interest than Y_1, and this is likely to have a depressive effect on investment and possibly consumption. There is no *a priori* reason to expect that these effects will exactly offset each other or, in other words, that aggregate demand will be at

Y_1.[3]

The temptation to describe *AD* as a curve relating real planned expenditure to the price level is nevertheless one to which a number of textbook authors succumbed. This was despite the fact that, in each case, the *AD* curve is derived from the *ISLM* model, and to use Patinkin's (1965) terminology is clearly a market equilibrium curve, as distinct from a true aggregate demand function. The following descriptions of the curve are illustrative.

> This curve shows the level of aggregate demand for real output at various price levels. Boorman and Havrilesky (1972, p.354)

> ... the meaning we will now give to aggregate demand is the level of output (income) demanded at different price levels. Therefore, the aggregate demand function may be thought of as an ordinary schedule of demand for goods and services with respect to price except that it refers to the economy as a whole rather than to an individual market. Dernburg and McDougall (1976, p.184)

> The aggregate demand function is a relationship between the planned level of real spending or demand for goods, and the level of prices, *given* the quantity of money and fiscal policy. Dornbusch and Fischer (1978, p.369).

> *The aggregate demand curve* depicts the quantity of national income, or net national product, that would

[3] See Rowan (1975), pp.397-8. It is possible, of course, to assume that in the face of a deficiency/excess of demand at any disequilibrium price level firms may fail to carry out their supply plans with the result that actual output diverges from the output level identified by the *AS* schedule. However, in the absence of complete and sustained rigidity of prices, there is no basis for assuming the divergence to be precisely such as to entail actual output shifting to the level identified by the *AD* curve. Hence, there is still no basis for expecting this curve to show aggregate demand at any disequilibrium price level.

> be *purchased* at each general price level. Glahe (1977, p.13).
>
> The aggregate demand curve represents the amount of national income that is purchased at each price level. Makin (1975, p.266).
>
> The demand curve is defined as a schedule which relates the quantities of real income (output) that will be demanded at various price levels. Zahn (1975, p.118).

In fairness to all these authors, it must be observed that elsewhere in each text either there appeared a further, more accurate description of the nature of the *AD* curve[4] or alternatively its true properties might easily have been inferred from the method of derivation. However, over-simplified summary statements of the above type are fundamentally inaccurate and, to foreshadow the second criticism, appear to encourage misuse of the curve.

3.3.2 The Measurement of Excess Demand/Supply

Given that the level of real planned expenditure may, and indeed probably will, diverge from the *AD* curve at any price level other than that at which the *AD* curve intersects the *AS* curve, it follows that the horizontal distance between the curves at such a disequilibrium price level cannot be identified *a priori* as a measure of aggregate excess demand/supply.[5] Thus, in terms of Figure 3.1, the horizontal distance Y_1Y^* indicates by how much output supplied at price level P^* exceeds the level of output at which aggregate demand and supply are brought into equilibrium at that price level. It does not show by how much output supplied exceeds the level of demand that will prevail when the price level is P^*, which is of course the usual interpretation

[4] For example, see Dornbusch and Fischer (1978, p.371) and Glahe (1977, pp.201-4).

[5] See Rowan (1975), pp.397-8

of excess supply. That the two gaps are likely to differ can easily be seen once it is recalled that output (income) affects demand. A level of output greater than that hypothetical level on the *AD* curve can accordingly be expected to entail a volume of demand different from that implied by the *AD* curve and hence a level of excess supply different from Y_1Y^*. Corresponding arguments apply to the identification of excess demand at price levels below *Pe*.

Notwithstanding these arguments, a considerable number of macroeconomic textbooks mistakenly identified excess demand/supply at any given disequilibrium price level as the horizontal distance between the *ISLM*-derived aggregate demand curve and the aggregate supply curve. (A detailed list of references may be found in our original paper, p.40.) Admittedly, a careful reading of at least one of these works, Branson (1979, pp.127-128, 133, 167), revealed that in this context the term "excess demand" was being used to identify the excess of the amount of output that would be demanded at some disequilibrium price level, if goods and money markets were in equilibrium, over the amount of output producers wish to supply at that price level. However, no attempt was made to point out, let alone justify, this major departure from commonly accepted usage.

3.3.3 Interdependence of Aggregate Demand and Supply

This criticism has two strands, both based essentially on the fact that the *AD* curve is derived independently of aggregate supply conditions. The first strand is that because of this derivation, diagrams such as Figure 3.1 encourage the false impression that aggregate demand responds to price level changes in a manner which is entirely independent of the influence of these changes on aggregate supply. In fact, given the direct and indirect influences of output (income) levels on aggregate demand, any price-induced change in aggregate supply will in turn affect aggregate demand. In short, "a student may be too easily led into treating general equilibrium analysis in the same way as partial equilibrium analysis" (Rowan, 1975, p.399).

The second strand stems from the recognition by Corden (1978) that aggregate demand may also be affected by autonomous or parametric shifts in the aggregate supply function, or by the outcome of the model, if for example, income distribution is consequently changed in a manner which alters the aggregate propensity to consume and/or profit expectations (and hence investment). Such "feedback effects" will require adjustments to the position of the *AD* curve.[6] However, since that curve is usually constructed without reference to the variables underlying the aggregate supply curve, let alone the outcome of the model, users of the simple *ADAS* model of price level and output determination may well, we suggest, tend to ignore or overlook these effects.

The interdependence between aggregate supply and aggregate demand has been emphasised in more recent literature under the general heading of "aggregate-demand externalities", as, for example, in Mankiw (1992). The feedback effect here is through the real money balances effect. When any subset of all firms cuts product prices, the average price level falls and the value of real balances rises. As the *LM* curve consequently shifts outwards, demand for the products of *all* firms increases. The aggregate demand externality arises in the form of additional demand for output stimulated by the increase in real balances. This sort of argument has appeared in the context of New Keynesian analysis which has striven to explain sticky wage and price adjustments in the presence of menu costs and coordination failure; see Mankiw (1985), Cooper and John (1988), Ball and Romer (1991). It is not our purpose here to enter into that discussion but merely to observe that

---

[6] Corden (1978) does not specifically mention effects other than a change in income distribution. However, price expectations and international competitiveness are two further channels through which shifts in the aggregate supply function may affect the *AD* curve.

these developments indicate the potential importance of yet another channel for interdependence.

3.4. TWO ALTERNATIVES

3.4.1 Rowan's Curve

Awareness of shortcomings in the conventional analysis prompted Rowan (1975) to construct an entirely different type of aggregate demand schedule, which is of considerable interest, not only for its analytical advantages, but also because it stands in direct line of descent from *The General Theory* of Keynes (1936).[7] Interdependence between aggregate demand and aggregate supply is a feature of Keynes' model which is of particular interest here. Weintraub (1957) (and, later, Davidson and Smolensky (1964)), maintained the emphasis on this interdependence. From the point of view of our discussion, Weintraub's central contribution is to have derived a "demand-outlay" function in price-quantity space which builds upon the discussion of aggregate demand in books III and IV of *The General Theory.* Rowan follows on in this tradition.

Rowan's basic model (1975, pp.394-5) builds on the same demand-side assumptions as the conventional *ISLM* anal-

[7] Discussion in this chapter ignores the naive version of the aggregate demand function in the Keynesian tradition, represented in the so-called "Keynes cross" diagram familiar to all first year undergraduates. In this treatment, which throws no light on the determination of the price level, a 45 degree line from the origin relates values of aggregate output and income on the horizontal axis to equal values of planned aggregate expenditure on the vertical axis. Superimposed on this line is an aggregate demand schedule comprising a consumption function, relating planned consumption demand to aggregate income, and a vertically added autonomous planned investment function. Given that this approach (deliberately) eschews behavioural considerations on the supply side, ignores the money market and says nothing about the determinants of investment demand, it is clearly ill-fitted for anything but the most simple of analyses.

ysis, except that the Pigou effect is ignored. The model is very simple and derives D, real aggregate demand, as follows:

$$D \equiv (C_p + I_p) \tag{1}$$

$$C_p = c(Y) \qquad 0 < c' < 1 \tag{2}$$

$$I_p = i(r) \qquad i' < 0 \tag{3}$$

$$M^d = L(r, PY) \qquad L_r < 0,\ L_{PY} > 0 \tag{4}$$

$$M^s = \overline{M} \tag{5}$$

$$M^d = M^s \tag{6}$$

The notation is standard, the subscript (p) indicating planned magnitudes. Simple manipulation and substitution then yields:

$$r = L'(PY, \overline{M}) \tag{7}$$

$$D = c(Y) + i(L'(PY, \overline{M})) \tag{8}$$

Now Y, real output supplied and income thereby generated, can be shown to be a function of the price level if the model is extended to the supply side on the assumptions:

$$Y = f(K, N) \qquad f_K,\ f_N > 0;\ f_{KK},\ f_{NN} < 0 \tag{9}$$

$$Pf_N = W \tag{10}$$

$$K = \overline{K} \tag{11}$$

Profit maximising behaviour and a competitive goods market are implied by (10), where W is the money wage. Since K is given, at $\overline{K}$, and (9) is twice differentiable, $f_N = g(Y)$. Thus:

$$Pg(Y) = W$$

$$\text{or} \quad Y = h(P, W) \tag{12}$$

If W is taken as given, (12) reduces to:

$$Y = S_1(P) \tag{13}$$

$$\text{or} \quad PY = PS_1(P) \tag{13a}$$

These are forms of the aggregate supply function and can be incorporated in (8) to give D or PD as a function of P, given specified values of the money wage and nominal money stock, i.e.,:

$$D = c(S_1(P)) + i(L'(PS_1(P), \overline{M})) \tag{14}$$

$$\text{or} \quad PD = P_c(S_1(P)) + Pi(L'(PS_1(P), \overline{M})) \tag{14a}$$

In price level-real output space, (13) represents the aggregate supply schedule and (14) the aggregate demand schedule which, as the structure of the equation shows, must be derived interdependently with the supply function. The dependence of aggregate demand on the supply side is logically entailed by use of the *ISLM* model, since the consumption and demand for money functions (equations (2) and (4)) both have Y as an argument – real income generated by real output supplied. This dependence occurs irrespective of the particular form of the aggregate supply function used in the full *ADAS* framework. Thus, although we recognise that the particular specification of the *AS* schedule in our original paper now looks decidedly dated, this in no way undermines the force of the entirely general claim that aggregate demand and supply are interdependent.[8] In Figure 3.2 the two schedules are represented by the lines *DD* and *AS*. Their point of intersection yields equilibrium values for the price level and real output.

The properties of Rowan's aggregate demand schedule, *DD*, and its relation to the *AS* curve can be described intuitively in terms of this figure; see Rowan (1975, pp.361-6).

---

[8] We are chided by Fields and Hart (1990, p.680: fn.6) for using a Keynesian "kinked" aggregate supply curve but in their own analysis they call only for the use of "some reasonable theory of aggregate supply" (p.678). We have no quarrel with their use of a perfectly standard, more modern "Lucas-type" function incorporating price expectations. But there is nothing unreasonable about our specification and it makes the general point just as effectively.

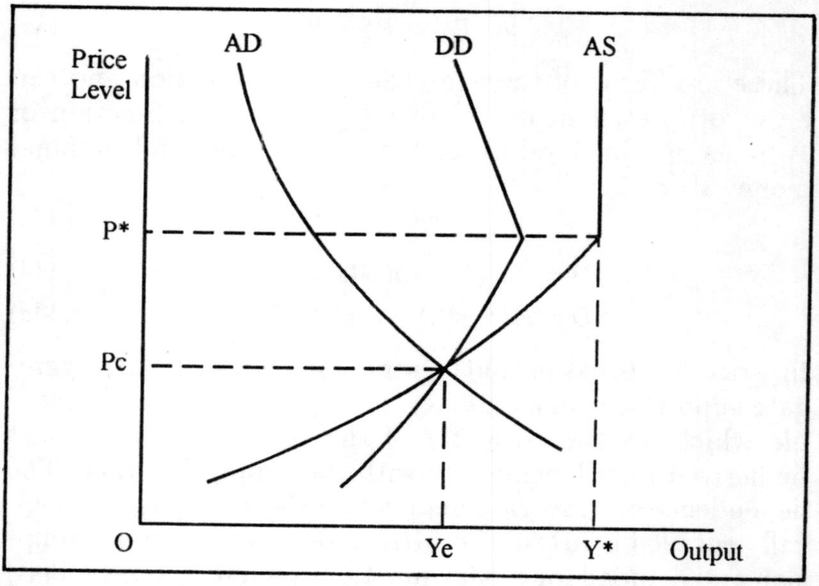

Figure 3.2

Starting at a very low price level where output supplied is correspondingly low, we may expect aggregate demand to exceed output or aggregate supply if there is an autonomous component in consumption demand. Moreover, excess demand will be increased by the fact that the combination of a low price level and a low level of real output will mean a relatively small demand for nominal money balances, a consequently low rate of interest, and hence a relatively high level of investment demand.

As the price level rises, consumption demand will increase less rapidly than aggregate supply, given a marginal propensity to consume of less than one. At the same time, the rising level of money income will expand the demand for nominal money balances, thus raising the rate of interest and depressing investment demand. Therefore aggregate demand will increase at less rapid rate than aggregate supply. This of course implies that the *DD* curve has a steeper slope than the *AS* curve and will eventually intersect it.

Indeed, at some sufficiently high price level, the DD curve will kink back or reverse its slope. The maximum price level at which this will occur is that which induces a full-employment level of aggregate supply. Any increase above this price level cannot induce an increase in consumption demand because real income can rise no further. However, a price level increase will still induce a further rise in the rate of interest and hence a fall in investment. Consequently, aggregate demand must fall and the DD curve bends backward to the left. Depending on parameter values, this reversal of slope could of course occur at a lower price level than that associated with a full-employment level of aggregate supply. Furthermore, the chances of such an occurrence would be enhanced if the Pigou effect were admitted into the analysis. These points seem to have been overlooked by Fields and Hart (1990) who accuse us of concluding that the portion of the DD curve below Y^* is unambiguously upward-sloping (p.680:fn 6).

It will already be apparent that Rowan's approach (unlike that of the conventional AD curve which, for comparison, is also shown in Figure 3.2) correctly identifies real aggregate demand and hence excess demand or supply at disequilibrium price levels. In addition, it makes quite clear that the response of aggregate demand to price level changes will not be independent of the response of aggregate supply to these changes. In fact, to take an extreme case which is not explicitly explored by Rowan, if his Keynesian or positively-sloped version of the aggregate supply curve is replaced by a classical or vertical aggregate supply curve, any positively-sloped range of Rowan's aggregate demand curve disappears and that curve must become negatively-sloped throughout. This change occurs because a classical supply curve implies a level of real output (income) which is invariant with respect to the price level. Under these conditions it becomes impossible for the consumption component of real planned expenditure to vary positively with the price level, and increases in the latter can serve only to depress demand through rate of interest and (possibly)

Pigou effects.[9]

At the other extreme, if the *AS* curve is specified in excessively crude Keynesian terms as horizontal or infinitely elastic at some given price level up to a full employment level of output, then it is quite possible that Rowan's aggregate demand curve will also possess an infinitely elastic range at that same price level. This may occur because the *AS* curve now implies a range of possible outputs consistent with the given price level rather than merely one unique level. The consequence is that the equilibrium level of output may be indeterminate in terms of the Rowan model (although it may still be identified by use of the negatively-sloped *ISLM*-derived aggregate demand curve). This may be considered an expositional disadvantage. However, it should be pointed out that as long as the price level is assumed given, there is, of course, no need to show the determination of equilibrium output in price level-real output space. It can be determined quite satisfactorily in terms of the *ISLM* model alone.

A perhaps more serious difficulty with Rowan's aggregate demand curve is that although it will shift in reaction to parametric shifts in the aggregate supply curve (e.g., in the case of the positively-sloped Keynesian version of the curve, as a result of an autonomous increase in money wages), these reactions stem solely from the effects of the parametric shifts on aggregate real output supplied at a given price level (or, putting it around the other way, on the supply

[9] In our original paper we argued that with a vertical aggregate supply curve, it was possible, but would be "freakish coincidence", for the associated *DD* curve to coincide with the conventional *AD* curve. As the analysis of Fields and Hart (1990, p.679) indicates, however, the two curves would never coincide (except at their points of intersection with the aggregate supply curve). In fact, *DD* would always be steeper than *AD*. This is so because the multiplier process that reinforces the direct (interest-induced) impact of a price change on investment demand in the conventional (*AD*) approach is necessarily absent when real output and income are long-run constants.

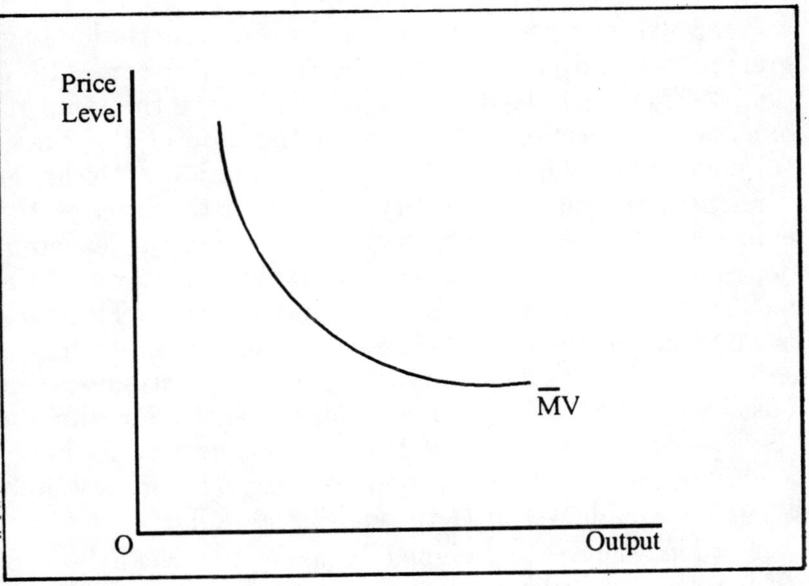

Figure 3.3

price of a given level of real output). As in the case of the conventional *AD* curve, channels for the operation of the type of feedback effects Corden appears to have in mind are not specified. Indeed, Rowan assumes income distribution constant (1975, p.379n).

3.4.2 Corden's Constant-MV Curve

When Corden (1978) introduced his own alternative version of the aggregate demand schedule, he described it as a constant *MV* curve, where *MV* is the level of money expenditure, *M* the supply of money, and *V* the income velocity of circulation. This curve is also drawn in price level-real output space. It shows in the form of a rectangular hyperbola all those combinations of real aggregate demand and the price level which represent a constant level of aggregate nominal demand; see Figure 3.3. The latter is assumed to be determined by demand management policy.

Corden's MV curve should not be confused with what

was termed in some texts the classical (or neoclassical) aggregate demand curve; see, for example, McKenna (1977, pp.272-274). Admittedly the two curves have the same geometrical properties. However, in the case of the classical curve (which is derived from the equation of exchange version of the quantity theory of money) the level of MV embodies the assumption that V is a short run constant depending on payment habits, industrial structure and the nature and practices of financial institutions. Thus MV is an endogenous variable solely dependent on M in the short run. By contrast, Corden specifically recognises the possibility of variations in V. Consequently, for him the (policy-determined) level of MV does not necessarily imply a unique level of M and, moreover, changes in MV may occur independently of M through fiscal policy.

Corden's curve is designed to assist in his analysis of "the roles of aggregate demand management and ⋯ real and money wage levels in determining employment" (Corden, 1978, p.159) under various forms of price and wage rigidity/flexibility. For this analysis he rejects the use of the conventional $ISLM$ derived aggregate demand function on what are essentially the previously discussed grounds that this function may be subject to change in response to changes in the aggregate supply function or the outcome of the model. As a replacement, his own curve embodies the assumption of a given, policy-determined level of money expenditure, with the so-called feedback effects eliminated, or rather compensated for, by "the busy manipulations" of the monetary authority which adjusts M "in order to offset these feedback effects on V" (Corden, 1978, p.174).

Corden's MV curve has played a role in the analysis of proposals for nominal income targeting; see, for example, Argy (1992). Otherwise, so far as we are aware, it has not been widely adopted in the exposition of macroeconomic theory. This may reflect several disadvantages. First, because observation of private sector behaviour on the demand side of the economy is ruled out by construction, the MV curve has severe pedagogic limitations in any context wider than that specified by Corden. It is not only unrealistic to assume that policy-makers can and will hold *MV* constant, but in addition such assumptions suppress any information about the other forces contributing to aggregate demand.

Secondly, in the very nature of the *MV* schedule, wealth effects could arise as a result of demand management policies. These effects might, in turn, bring about further shifts in planned real demand. This would be the case if increasing (decreasing) wealth were assumed to have a positive (negative) influence on consumption demand and the demand for real balances. Suppose, for example, that an expansionary bond-financed fiscal policy were used to maintain the economy on some given *MV* curve in the face of feedback effects of the kind already noted. Economic agents, unless ultra-rational, would perceive an increase in their net wealth, which would raise their consumption demand, but reduce investment demand as the interest rate rose in response to a greater demand for real balances. Unless these two effects exactly cancelled, real aggregate demand would ultimately change. It could be argued in reply that (1) Corden's gifted policymakers could, by assumption, deal with wealth effects as efficiently as all their other tasks; (2) such effects can be discounted on theoretical grounds; (3) such effects are, empirically, likely to be insignificant; (4) this point is only bringing in new complexities through the back door. Whether any or all of these are considered acceptable rejoinders, the question should at least be addressed.

Thirdly, even within Corden's own terms of reference, the principle of Occam's Razor leads to the question of whether it is necessary to construct a new type of aggregate demand curve when, granting the abilities he is prepared to confer upon policymakers, the conventional curve could be modified to meet his objections to it. In particular, given that Corden's approach can be interpreted as ascribing to policymakers the capacity to manage real aggregate demand in such a way that, irrespective of the price level, total money expenditure remains constant, it would seem no less implausible to ascribe to them the capacity to manage real aggregate demand in such a way that full supply/demand equilibrium always occurred at some point on the conventional *AD* schedule defined by the initial parameters.

3.5 CONCLUSION

It may be useful to attempt a summary assessment of the relative pedagogic advantages of the three aggregate demand functions that have been discussed in detail above: the conventional *AD* curve, Rowan's curve and Corden's constant *MV* curve. To this end, it is helpful to distinguish between their uses in positive and normative contexts.

For positive analysis concerned with developing in a static framework a basic understanding of the forces governing the behaviour of aggregate demand, Corden's constant *MV* curve is of little use. The over-riding reason is, of course, its lack of private sector behavioural content or rather the suppression of it. In effect, Corden's explanation of the volume of real aggregate demand at any price level reduces to the statement that the volume of demand is simply the level of money expenditure decided upon by policymakers deflated by that price level. For different reasons already discussed, the conventional *AD* curve also leaves much to be desired. Although built on explicit assumptions about the forces determining private (as well as public) demand, it does not in fact illustrate the actual behaviour of real aggregate demand with respect to the price level, and it fosters the misapprehension that aggregate demand and aggregate supply are independent. As we have noted in this revised version of our paper, the importance of interdependence has been increasingly recognised and understood since our original paper appeared.

This leaves Rowan's curve as the most useful concept in a positive context. It embraces essentially all the underlying behavioural assumptions of the conventional *AD* curve; but in addition it genuinely tracks real demand in the face of price level variations and, moreover, in a way which explicitly takes into account an important form of dependence on aggregate supply. Admittedly, the feedback effects which justifiably worry Corden are not specified in the analysis. However, in view of the basic emphasis in Rowan's approach on interdependence, the chances of them being recognised by the student seem considerably greater in this milieu than in the case of the *AD* curve which is derived entirely without reference to aggregate supply.

For normative analysis directed at the selection of a level of demand appropriate for the attainment of some policy goal (or goals), our assessment is rather different. Subject to the feasibility of Corden's assumption that those responsible for demand management are able to achieve and sustain any level of money expenditure they choose, his curve seems to be *prima facie* the most useful concept. Not only is it expositionally very simple, but it also has the desirable properties of identifying accurately real aggregate demand at any price level and providing a built-in adjustment for feedback effects. Nevertheless, on the last point, the suggestion has already been made that the conventional *AD* curve mode of analysis could in principle be modified to incorporate policy responses which neutralise feedback effects; and that same is true of Rowan's curve which (along with Corden's curve) possesses the advantage of showing real aggregate demand at each price level rather than just at the equilibrium price level.

4 What is the Matter with Aggregate Demand and Supply?*

B. Bhaskara Rao

4.1 INTRODUCTION

The aggregate demand and supply model has now replaced the *ISLM* model as the main textbook macroeconomic model. Yet somehow the aggregate demand and supply model does not seem to do what a good model is supposed to do. Furthermore some of its present textbook versions unfortunately leave the misleading impression that the basic methodological differences between the Keynesian and the neo classical macroeconomic models can be reduced simply to a difference between the elasticities of the aggregate supply functions in these models.[1]

The outline of this chapter is as follows. Section 4.2 gives an outline the structure of the model from which the aggregate demand and supply functions are derived in a large number of textbooks. This is followed by an examination of the nature of the assumptions of the *ISLM* model because, in almost all the textbooks, the aggregate demand function is derived from it. Next in sections 4.3 and 4.4 we

* Moderately edited version of Rao (1991).

[1] See Dornbusch and Fischer (1984) p.402 and Parkin (1982) pp.363-364. It is precisely for a somewhat similar reason Leijonhufvud(1983) has scrutinised the *ISLM* model and pointed out that the well-known debate between the Keynesians and the monetarists ignored the fundamental methodological differences between their models and diverted attention to less important issues about the relative magnitudes of the elasticities of the demand for money and the investment functions.

shall examine two popular versions of the aggregate demand and supply model and point out some confusions in their exposition and inconsistencies between the assumptions underlying the derivation of the aggregate supply function and the *ISLM* model. Some suggestions to overcome these inconsistencies and confusions are also given in these sections. Finally the conclusions of this chapter and their implications for the teaching of macroeconomics are summarised in section 4.5.

4.2 AGGREGATE DEMAND, SUPPLY AND THE ISLM MODEL

The aggregate demand and supply model is deceptively similar to the conventional demand and supply model in microeconomics and liberally uses the Walrasian terminology with which most students are familiar. In virtually all textbooks the aggregate demand curve is derived from the *ISLM* model without any significant attempt to explain the nature of this model and its assumptions. The aggregate demand curve is then combined with an aggregate supply curve to determine the level of aggregate output and the price level, simultaneously, within an equilibrium framework. However, with the exception of Dornbusch and Fischer (1984),[2] the aggregate supply function is derived from the profit maximisation assumption of the firms. Even though Dornbusch and Fischer apparently derive their aggregate supply function from a set of more realistic assumptions the theoretical underpinings of their supply function are not made clear.

Before we examine these models it is important to understand the structure of the model from which the aggregate demand and supply functions are derived in the majority of the textbooks and especially the nature of the *ISLM* model from which the aggregate demand function is

[2] References to textbooks are not updated because there are no significant differences in the discussion on the aggregate demand and supply model in the earlier and current editions.

derived. The remainder of this section is concerned with these aspects.

To conserve space we shall not use an elaborate diagrammatic approach.[3] Instead we shall use the algebraic approach based on the two sector closed economy *ISLM* model and a simple labour market.[4] These simplifications, however, do not affect the main conclusions of this chapter. The structural equations from which the aggregate demand and supply functions are derived in several textbooks are as follows:

$$Y = C + I \tag{1}$$

$$C = C(Y) \qquad 0 < C_y < 1 \tag{2}$$

$$I = I(r) \qquad I_r < 0 \tag{3}$$

$$M^d = P.L(Y, r) \quad Lr < 0, L_y > 0 \tag{4}$$

$$M^s = M^* \tag{5}$$

$$M^d = M^s \tag{6}$$

$$Y = f(K^*, N) \quad f_k,\ f_n > 0,\ f_{kk},\ f_{nn} < 0 \tag{7}$$

$$P.f_n = W^* \tag{8}$$

---

[3] By far the clearest and the best diagrammatic exposition of this type of model, based predominantly on the neo classical assumptions, is given in Parkin (1982). There are various other textbooks which explain the aggregate demand and supply model, using the neo classical and/or the Keynesian approaches with which most readers are familiar. To conserve space we shall not list all of them here. Readers may refer to Hansen et.al., (1985) and Hall and Treadgold (1982) for references to several macroeconomics textbooks. However, Barro (1984) departs from all other textbooks in its exposition of both the neo classical and the Keynesian models and is immune from most of our criticisms. But it should be noted that this book is mainly concerned with the exposition of the structure of the neo classical and new classical models. Of the 550 pages in this book only 25 pages are devoted to the Keynesian model.

[4] See Hall and Treadgold (1982), reprinted in this volume, for an excellent algebraic exposition of the aggregate demand and supply model.

where Y = output, C = consumption, I = investment, r = the rate of interest, M^d = demand for money, M^s = supply of money, M^* = exogenously determined money stock, K^* = exogenously given capital stock, N = employment, W^* = money wage rate which is exogenous and P = price level. The first and second order derivatives of these functions are denoted in the standard way. For example C_y is the marginal propensity to consume, f_{nn} is the second order derivative of Y with respect to N etc.

Equations (1) to (6) are the standard equations in the two sector closed economy $ISLM$ model. The goods and money market equilibrium conditions, given by (1) and (6), yield the IS and LM curves respectively. Since there will be three unknowns in these two equations viz., Y, r and P, the aggregate demand equation can be seen as a semi-reduced form equation and can be expressed as:

$$Y = Y(P, M^*) \tag{9}$$

It can be easily shown that $Y_m > 0$ and $Y_p < 0$.[5] Therefore we have a downward sloping curve between P and Y for a given level of M.

The short-run aggregate production function with the usual properties and the marginal productivity condition are given by (7) and (8) respectively. Therefore if firms maximise profits, the marginal productivity condition is also their labour demand function. To simplify exposition the money wage rate is assumed to be exogenous and the labour supply function is suppressed. Hence the variable, N, is the level of employment. Equations (7) and (8) yield a semi-reduced form equation for Y which can be expressed as:

$$Y = h(P, W^*) \tag{10}$$

It can be shown that $h_p > 0$ as $(dW/W) < (dP/P)$ and $h_w < 0$. Therefore, for a given money wage rate, (10) yields a positive relationship between Y and P.

---

[5] These restrictions can be derived from the equations for the IS and LM curves and by using the restrictions on the partial derivatives of (1) to (6).

Since the relationships between Y and P, implied by (9) and (10), resemble the microeconomic demand and supply curves respectively, these two relationships are labelled by textbooks as the aggregate demand and supply functions respectively and the usual equilibrium condition is added to explain the simultaneous determination of aggregate output and price level. Thus the textbook aggregate demand and supply model can be said to be formulated as:

$$Y^d = Y(P, M^*) \qquad Y_p < 0,\ Y_m > 0 \tag{11}$$

$$Y^s = h(P, W*) \qquad h_p > 0,\ h_w < 0 \tag{12}$$

$$Y^d = Y^s \tag{13}$$

This simple model can be further extended by adding the labour supply function. A distinction between the short and long-run versions of this model can be made by introducing price expectations into the labour supply function. Such an extended model is used, in several textbooks, to explain the short and long-run dynamics of output and price level or the dynamics of unemployment and inflation and also to illustrate, for example, the implications of the rational expectations hypothesis, the effects of adverse supply shocks etc. However, it should be noted that the three equation static model in equations (11) to (13) is the foundation on which such extensions are based. We shall argue later that this foundation is weak and unsatisfactory.

So far known criticisms of the aggregate demand and supply model have been concerned with the aggregate demand function. Hansen et.al., (1985) pointed out that there are conceptual differences between the aggregate demand function and its microeconomic counterpart. They also argued that if the additional channels through which the price level impinges on aggregate demand are taken into account, *a priori*, its slope may be indeterminate.[6] Next, follow-

[6] A simple explanation is as follows. Suppose a rise in the price level leads to a depreciation of the domestic currency. If the Marshall–Lerner condition holds then net exports will increase. To preserve the downward slope of the aggregate demand function the *(continued)*

ing Rowan (1975), Hall and Treadgold (1982) have argued that in the derivation of the aggregate demand function its dependence on aggregate supply has been ignored. If this dependence is taken into account, the aggregate demand function should be upward sloping up to the full employment level. While these criticisms draw attention to some of the weaknesses of the aggregate demand and supply model, they do not show an adequate appreciation of the general equilibrium nature of the *ISLM* model from which the aggregate demand curve is derived. The aggregate demand and supply model gives the misleading impression that it is analysing only the goods market in isolation of the money, bond and labour markets. These criticisms also ignore the overall consistency of the assumptions underlying the derivation of the aggregate demand function with those of the aggregate supply function. It is important, therefore, to understand the nature of the *ISLM* model from which the aggregate demand function is derived and then its consistency with the profit maximisation assumption from which the aggregate supply function is derived.

Hicks explained, as early as 1979 and more explicitly in 1983, the nature of his *ISLM* model and its usefulness and limitations as a framework to understand the Keynesian income determination model.[7] He says that the *ISLM* model was a product of his Walrasianism, at the time it was

---

fall in the domestic component of aggregate demand should be larger than the increase in net exports.

[7] The scope of this chapter does not allow for a full consideration of the limitations of the *ISLM* model. The issues involved here are concerned with the methodology of model construction when both the flow and stock variables are present in the model. In general the unit time needed for equilibrium of the flow variables is much shorter than for the stock variables. Since the *IS* curve is based on the flow variables and the *LM* curve is based on the stock variables the time units underlying these two relationships are different.

Solow (1984) defends the *ISLM* model by pointing out that Keynes himself overcame such a problem by assuming that in a unit period the changes in stock variables caused by changes *(continued)*

developed; and it is his way of representing the Keynesian three way exchange on a two dimensional diagram. The three markets are, as in Keynes, the goods, money and the bond markets and the three main concepts used to explain the three way exchange are the marginal efficiency of capital, the consumption function and the liquidity preference. Note that the labour market has been ignored. Therefore, according to Hicks, the *ISLM* model can be seen as a simple Walrasian general equilibrium model with only three markets and two relative prices viz., the price of goods and the price of bonds which is the reciprocal of the rate of interest. Because of the Walras law, if two markets are in equilibrium the third market must be also in equilibrium. Therefore the three way exchange can be understood by analyzing any of the two markets. Hicks ignored the bond market. His *ISLM* model, therefore, analyses the conditions under which the goods and the money markets can be in equilibrium.

There is, however, one important difference between the *ISLM* model and the Walrasian model. It is that while in the Walrasian model all markets are flexprice, or *P* markets in Hicks' terminology, in the *ISLM* model the bond and money markets are *P* markets and the goods market is a fixprice or, in Hicks' terminology, a *Q* market. It is in this sense the *ISLM* model is novel and departs from the Walrasian tradition.

Once the fixprice assumption is introduced into the Walrasian system its nature and conclusions change.[8] In contrast to the Walrasian system where all the demand

---

in the flow variables are negligibly small and therefore can be ignored. Recall that in the *ISLM* model the consequences of changes in the capital stock have been ignored. Therefore a model consisting of both flow and stock variables can be first analysed for flow equilibrium by ignoring the equilibrium in the stock variables. Next it can be reanalysed for stock equilibrium by ignoring this time the flow equilibrium. Reader should refer to the aforesaid works for a fuller understanding of the issues.

[8] Walrasian economists often dismiss the fixprice assumption as arbitrary. However, Benassy (1986, p.3) observes that the *(continued)*

and supply functions depend on the relative prices and initial endowments, in the fixprice systems these relationships depend only on the relative prices in the P markets, initial endowments and, instead of the relative prices in the Q markets, on the quantities actually traded in these markets. The latter are given by the minimum of demand and supplies in the Q markets. In the Walrasian system adjustments toward equilibrium which is both unique and stable take place through price adjustments. But in the fixprice models such adjustments take place through quantity adjustments. Although stable equilibrium points exist in these models they are not unique and are distinguished from the unique Walrasian equilibrium by calling them Dreze equilibria. Finally the Walrasian equilibrium is consistent with the Pareto optimum which in the present context can be said to be the full employment equilibrium and the system always attains the full employment equilibrium through price adjustments and the free inter play of market forces. However, in the Q market system such mechanisms are absent and the economy may remain in a stable under employment

---

fixprice non-Walrasian models are not anti-Walrasian. On the contrary they apply the methods of analysis that have been so successful in the Walrasian theory under more general assumptions. According to the modern disequilibrium economists as well as some leading general equilibrium theorists such as Arrow (1981, p.141-2) a weak point in the Walrasian model is that market clearing is taken as an axiom and not derived from any valid microeconomic analysis of price making behaviour.

Furthermore it is not necessary to assume that the price level is fixed as a constant in the fixprice models although such an assumption is often made to simplify exposition and explain how the system can attain a non-Walrasian stable equilibrium through quantity rather than price adjustments. The fixprice assumption can be easily replaced with the more realistic assumption that the price level is not sufficiently flexible to ensure that the market clears within the unit time period; see Rao and Srivastava (1991). It is for this reason Benassy claims that the fixprice models are more general.

equilibrium for prolonged periods. It is in these respects the Hicksian *ISLM* model successfully explains the general nature of Keynes' General Theory and the existence of equilibrium at less than full employment.[9] A comparison of the simpler variant of the *ISLM* model in which the aggregate demand function is combined with the 45^0 line, with the standard Walrasian demand-supply model makes clear how the fixprice and flexprice models adjust towards equilibrium through quantity and price adjustments respectively; for an explanation of the working of the fixprice disequilibrium models see Srivastava and Rao (1990), Levacic and Rebmann (1982).

The aforesaid differences between the Walrasian and Keynesian models is totally eschewed by some modern day Keynesians and many textbook writers by uncritically embracing the aggregate demand and supply paradigm. However, Hall and Treadgold (1982) and Rabin and Birch (1982) have suggested modifications to the textbook aggregate demand and supply model. They argue that the aggregate demand function based on the *ISLM* model is not really the effective demand function on which Keynes placed so much emphasis. Therefore they derive an alternative aggregate demand function, sometimes also known as the Rowan (1975) demand function, from the textbook aggregate demand and supply model.

However, in spite of their good intentions this alternative aggregate demand function does not exist in the Keynesian state characterised by excess supply conditions in both the goods and labour markets. Their modifications are

[9] Needless to say several post Keynesians claim that Keynes cannot be couched into the Walrasian framework. They believe that Keynes was not interested in the problems of a pure exchange economy devoid of production, distribution and growth problems. Therefore Keynes' tradition is classical rather than marginalist in nature. For this reason post Keynesians are sceptical about the usefulness of the *ISLM* framework and classify the *ISLM* Keynesians as the bastard Keynesians.

based on extending the original three market *ISLM* model to include a fourth market viz., the labour market. It is implicitly assumed that while the labour market is a fixprice market, the goods, money and bond markets are all flexprice markets. In the absence of this implicit assumption there will not be any formal difference between the Walrasian flexprice model and the Keynesian aggregate demand and supply model. Such a procedure seems to be legitimate but creates further problems, and as Hicks has pointed out in the following passage, Keynes himself appears to have thought in terms of such a system. To understand Hicks' passage it is useful to assume that the four markets are A (labour), B (goods), C (bonds) and X (money) where the last market is ignored through Walras' law; and D_a and P_a are the demand for and the price of labour etc., Now consider what Hicks said:

> One could construct a model in which only the market for labour was a fixprice market, and in which not only the rate of interest but also the price (or price level) of finished products was flexible. That would fit very exactly into the scheme that has just been outlined, with demand-supply equations determining D_a (employment) and the two flexible prices P_b, P_c. *It is possible that Keynes himself sometimes thought in terms of that sort of model* (see, for example, Keynes, 1936, ch.21), *but it cannot be this that ISLM is supposed to represent.* For Y is taken to be an index not only of employment, but also of output, so the prices of products also are supposed to be fixed in terms of the standard; and it is hard to see how that can be justified unless the prices of products are derived from the wage of labour by some mark-up rule. But if that is so we have not one, but two, fixprice markets. Hicks (1983, p.54, my italics).

Thus Hicks clearly points out the difficulties involved in using an *ad hoc* approach in which the labour market is a fixprice market but the goods market is a flexprice market. The link between employment and output cannot be easily severed unless the length of the unit time period is extended to enable capital formation to take place and/or some implausible assumptions are made about the degree of substitutabilty between labour and capital. A second problem with the Hall-Treadgold and Rabin-Birch extension is that it ignores the significance of spillover effects between the fixprice labour market and the flexprice goods market. If the labour market is in a state of excess supply, households cannot sell all the labour they plan to sell. Therefore their effective demand for goods will be less than their notional demand and the former is now constrained by the actual level of employment and not by the price level in the goods market. Therefore it is inappropriate now to assume that firms will plan to produce and also actually produce their notional profit maximising outputs. Actual output is given by the effective demand for output. If it is realised that in the *ISLM* model output is determined by the effective demand for goods and the aforesaid spillover effect provides the missing microeconomic rationale for the Keynesian consumption function, then the aggregate demand function derived from the *ISLM* model is in fact the effective and not the notional demand function. Therefore the Rowan-Hall-Treadgold and Rabin-Birch extension is based on a serious omission of the inter market relationships in the fixprice general equilibrium systems.

Finally the Rowan-Hall-Treadgold and Rabin-Birch extension ignores the fact that *ISLM* is a three market general equilibrium model and the cruder textbook versions of the model give the misleading impression that not only the price level is determined by the interaction of the demand and supply forces in the goods market but adjustments in the goods market towards the equilibrium take place through the Walrasian price adjustments rather than the Keynesian quantity adjustments. The latter is totally inconsistent with what has been taught in the introductory macroeconomics courses with the simpler versions of the

ISLM model within the 45^0 framework and there is hardly any empirical support for the former explanation of price determination in the industrial countries.[10]

The aforesaid nature and implications of the Hicksian *ISLM* model are not explicitly recognised in the current textbook explanations of the aggregate demand and supply model. We shall now examine two popular versions of the textbook model.

4.3 THE NEO CLASSICAL VERSION

The neo classical version of the aggregate demand and supply model is the more popular version. Although it uses the aggregate demand function derived from the *ISLM* model it does not address the issues raised in the previous section. Ideally while the aggregate demand and supply model should have been a two dimensional representation of the Hicksian four way exchange process, the neo classical version leaves the impression that it is a straightforward *P* market Walrasian demand and supply model of only the goods market. It is not known from the discussion of this model which of its markets are assumed to be *Q* markets and which are *P* markets, although it is clear that its main objective is also to explain the four way Hicksian rather

---

[10] We are grateful to one of the referees for pointing out that the aggregate demand and supply model implicitly asserts the patently ridiculous idea that the macroeconomy adjusts to equilibrium by means of price adjustments, both positive and negative. The referee goes further and notes that in the U.S. the *CPI* hasn't declined over a year-long period since 1955. We wish to add to these observations that in the U.K. the change in the *GDP* deflator was never negative between 1950 and 1986. In an interesting study Alogoskoufis and Pissarides (1983) found that the U.K. *GDP* deflator hardly adjusts by 25 % towards its equilibrium value within a year.

Some recent work by Rao and Srivastava (1991), Rao (1993, 1996) also shows that price adjustments in the U.S. and U.K. economies are highly sluggish and as much as 87% of *GNP* transactions in the U.S. economy take place in the Keynesian markets.

than the Walrasian exchange process. However, since the aggregate demand relationship in this model is derived from Hicks' *ISLM* model it can be said that at least the goods market is a Q market. Furthermore the goods market is in an excess supply state and, therefore, output is determined by the demand for output.

Hicks' explanation makes clear that when the goods market is a Q market, irrespective of whether the labour market is a P or Q market, the demand for labour should depend on the demand for goods or output. It follows from this that the marginal productivity condition, given by (8), in which there is no role for the demand for output, cannot be the labour demand function. Therefore, the aggregate supply function given by (10) and derived from the marginal productivity based labour demand function is inconsistent with the assumptions underlying the aggregate demand function derived from the *ISLM* model.

Needless to say this inconsistency is a major source of confusion in understanding the working of the neo classical aggregate demand and supply model. In a typical macroeconomics course students are taught, in the first few weeks, how output is determined by aggregate demand within the 45^0 line framework and then how output and the rate of interest are simultaneously determined within the *ISLM* framework. In both models the price level is assumed to be exogenously determined, independent of the excess demand rate in the goods market. Thus the goods market is assumed to be a Q market with an excess supply. Later on, the students are taught to unlearn all of this and understand once again how the price level and output are simultaneously determined by the intersection of the aggregate demand and aggregate supply functions. The intelligent student is left to ponder how the level of output, that was already determined in the *ISLM* model, can once again be determined by the aggregate demand and aggregate supply functions, given that the aggregate demand function in this model is derived from the *ISLM* model. This difficulty has been already overcome by some textbook writers by relegating, to the appendix, the links between the aggregate demand function and the *ISLM* model and by pretending, in the main text, that the aggregate demand function is actually derived by aggregating the micro demand functions.

A further weakness of this model lies in the process through which an increase in the demand for goods is assumed to lead to an increase in the demand for labour and hence in the levels of output and employment. An increase in the demand for goods is assumed to increase the price of goods i.e., the goods market is now assumed to be a P market. Therefore the demand for labour, drawn in the money wage-employment space, is assumed to shift up leading to an increase in employment and output. This process implies that a reduction in the real wage rate is essential for an increase in employment and output. It does not allow for the possibility, implicit in the *ISLM* model, that firms can expand output and employment when the demand for output increases. Whether or not goods prices increase depends on the behaviour of the unit costs of production and not on the excess demand in the goods market.

There are also other weaknesses in this model. For example this model cannot explain the observed pro-cyclical changes in the real wage rate or the counter cyclical changes in the share of wages. In fact it implies that the real wage rate is counter cyclical and the wage share is pro-cyclical. Furthermore the labour demand function, based on the profit maximisation assumption, implies that it is highly elastic with respect to the real wage rate. For example if the production function is Cobb-Douglas this elasticity is given by the reciprocal of the share of profits. Needless to say there is hardly any empirical support for this implication; see Solow (1980) for some critical comments on the use of the marginal product of labour as the demand for labour in the Keynesian model.

Let us consider now how some of these limitations of the neo classical aggregate demand and supply model can be overcome. There are two possibilities. If the basic assumption of this model is that all the real world markets are

P markets, it should adopt the standard Walrasian general equilibrium tradition and derive the demand and supply functions from the utility and profit maximisation assumptions. In this case there is no place for the aggregate demand function based on the *ISLM* model. The demand and supply functions should depend on the relative prices and the initial endowments of the agents. It is somewhat puzzling, therefore, to note that some textbooks use the *ISLM* based aggregate demand function to explain the implications of the rational expectations hypothesis even though in the theoretical work on this hypothesis the standard Walrasian demand functions are used; see Levacic and Rebmann (1982, p.369 fn.1).

The existence of unemployment in such Walrasian models can be explained in the standard way, as shown for example by Lucas and Rapping (1969), by introducing some elements of temporary disequilibrium. However, until there is an adequate and unequivocal empirical support for the aggregate demand and supply model based on the strict Walrasian tradition, such a model is unlikely to be treated more than as a theoretical construct.

Another alternative is to abandon the pure Walrasian tradition and introduce into the model some important Keynesian and Hicksian features. In such an approach one should start with the explicit assumption that, in the real world, while some markets are P markets there are other important markets, notably the labour and goods markets, that are Q markets. The *ISLM* model, if extended with adequate awareness about the nature of its assumptions, can explain the Hicksian four way exchange process. The contradiction between the Q market assumption for the goods market and the profit maximisation assumption underlying the aggregate supply relationship can be overcome by deriving the labour demand function from the cost minimisation hypothesis. However, to describe the resultant upward sloping relationship between output and the price level as the aggregate supply function will be misleading because it is well known that when firms are demand constrained there is no unique relationship between the quantity supplied and the price level. It would be more appropriate to treat such a model as a two dimensional representation of the Hicksian four way exchange process. In particular it should be emphasised that it is not a straight forward representation of the Walrasian goods market in which output and the price level are simultaneously determined by the intersection of the so called aggregate demand and supply relationships. A somewhat simplified version, based on these lines, has been already developed by Dornbusch and Fischer (1978, 1984). Therefore we shall examine their model in the following section.

4.4 THE KEYNESIAN APPROACH

Dornbusch and Fischer do not make explicit that the goods market in the *ISLM* part of the model is a *Q* market. Nor do they clearly explain the theoretical basis for their labour demand function. In fact they claim that the positive relationship between output and the price level that they derive from their labour demand function and wage-price equations is conceptually a supply curve and at times try to assure the reader that some of their conclusions are consistent with the implications of the competitive theory of firm and the classical labour demand function; see Dornbusch and Fischer (1984, p.398, fn.12). Therefore one gets the impression that their model is also Walrasian in spirit.

In spite of such an impression the Dornbusch and Fischer model is a simpler version based on the Keynesian and Hicksian features rather than the Walrasian *P* market framework. The aggregate demand function is derived in this model from the *ISLM* model and the aggregate supply function differs significantly from the neo classical version.

The Hicks-Keynesian nature of this model is partly obscured by insufficient clarifications about the nature of assumptions underlying the Dornbusch and Fischer aggregate supply function. Moreover, at times, Dornbusch and Fischer (p.384) also give the impression that the structure of their model is essentially the same as the neo classical model with some transitory disequilibrium features implying that the assumption that wages and prices are fully flexible is replaced in their model with the assumption that wage-price adjustments are sluggish in the short-run. If this observation is correct then the aggregate supply function in the Dornbusch and Fischer model can also be said to be derived from (7) and (8) where the equilibrium condition (13), perhaps, is replaced with some dynamic price-quantity adjustment equations, for example such as the ones suggested by Chow (1977).

But, subsequently Dornbusch and Fischer (1984, p.391) clearly explain the limitations of the labour demand function based on the marginal productivity theory. In particular they emphasise the inability of the marginal productivity condition to explain the observed relative stability or the mild pro-cyclical nature of the real wage rate. But they take the view that this limitation can be overcome by recognising that firms do not fully utilise the capital stock at all levels of output. Therefore they assume that marginal productivity is relatively less variable since the ratio of the utilised capital per worker is stable over the cycle. Thus the impression one gets from all this is that Dornbusch and Fischer have also derived their labour demand function from the profit maximisation assumption with a modification that capacity utilisation is an additional variable in the production function.

However, the final labour demand function used by Dornbusch and Fischer is different although it is not obvious from their exposition how it has been derived from their earlier discussion on the importance of the capacity utilisation rate. If Dornbusch and Fischer explicitly recognised that in the $ISLM$ model the goods market is a Q market, then their subsequent assumptions that, in the short-run, technology does not permit a lot of capital-labour substitution (p.391) and that there are constant returns should have enabled them to express the production function as:

$$Y = \alpha N \tag{14}$$

where α is a positive constant. From this the labour demand function can be derived from the constrained profit maximisation assumption by inverting the production function to give:

$$N = (1/\alpha)Y \qquad (15)$$

This labour demand function is the same as the one used by Dornbusch and Fischer but makes clear the nature of the assumptions from which it can be derived. Alternatively a similar labour demand function can be also derived from the cost minimisation hypothesis, implied by the Q market nature of the goods market, with the further assumption that in the short-run the elasticity of substitution between labour and capital is zero. In both methods firms are constrained by the demand for output from hiring labour up to the point of equality between the marginal product and the real wage rate.[11] While in the aforesaid alternative method this is made explicit, the Dornbusch and Fischer exposition unfortunately obscures these aspects.

The model consisting of (11), (14) and (15) is not complete and the latter pair of equations do not yield an upward sloping relationship between output and price level. If the price level is assumed to be determined by exogenous factors and a labour supply function is added to the model it can be used to determine output, employment and unemployment. Textbook models based on these lines were common before the aggregate demand and supply paradigm became popular. Some of these earlier models explained wage-price determination separately with a simple Phillips curve and a mark-up price equation. One limitation of these earlier approaches was that they have ignored the two way links

[11] Barro (1984), following Barro and Grossman (1971), also uses the sales constrained labour demand function to explain the Keynesian model but treats the Keynesian model as a special case of the disequilibrium model. Sinclair (1983) and Levacic and Rebmann (1982) use the sales constrained labour demand function to explain the disequilibrium model but use the neo classical labour demand function to explain the Keynesian model.

between the goods and the labour markets and allowed for only a one way relationship from the former to the latter. This is not an entirely unrealistic approach because producers do not quickly adjust prices. In contrast the aggregate demand and supply model emphasises the two way relationship between the goods and the labour markets.

Dornbusch and Fischer achieve the two-way integration between the goods and the labour markets by assuming, in the Keynes-Hicks tradition, that the price level is set by producers, as a mark-up on the unit costs;[12] and use a simple Phillips curve to determine the rate of change of

---

[12] Although Dornbusch and Fischer use current unit costs in their price equation, it is possible to assume that producers use normal unit costs to set prices. In this case it is not necessary to assume that profit margins are pro-cyclical to explain the observed counter-cyclical behaviour of the wage share but the constant returns production function (14) should be replaced with the usual diminishing returns function.

In Barro's Keynesian model the rate of change in the price level is determined by the excess demand rate in the goods market. This type of neo classical approach is popular in the empirical work on the disequilibrium labour markets. It is also possible to assume in Barro's Keynesian model that prices are set by producers as a mark up on unit costs. In this case a neo classical wage adjustment equation and a mark up equation should be added to the disequilibrium model.

However, an important limitation of adding a neo classical price (or wage) adjustment equation to the general disequilibrium model is that it is not obvious how notional excess demands can induce price adjustments. Such models also imply that involuntary unemployment can be eliminated through market induced wage-price adjustment and therefore call for policies to improve the efficiency of the market mechanisms. These policy implications are at odds with the main thrust of the theoretical work in disequilibrium economics and with much of what a typical Keynesian economist believes. In the typical Keynesian model wage-price determination is treated as exogenous, irrespective of whether satisfactory rationalisations to make this consistent with the microeconomic foundations exist; see Blinder (1987 and Akerlof and Yellen (1987) for a general methodological defense of *(continued)*

wages. The unemployment variable in the Phillips curve is linked with output through the labour demand function and exogenously defined full employment labour supply and full employment output. It is also possible to link these markets with Okun's law. It is not important to examine here the technical aspects of the derivation of the Dornbusch and Fischer aggregate supply curve which is:

$$P_t = P_{t-1}\left(1 + \eta \frac{Y - Y^*}{Y^*}\right) \qquad \eta > 0 \tag{16}$$

where Y^* is the full employment output and η is parameter from the Phillips curve. It can be seen that (16) implies a positive relationship between the price level and output. Even though Dornbusch and Fischer (p.400) argue that (16) is conceptually a supply curve it cannot be a supply curve because such an animal may not exist in a model where firms are demand constrained.

It is, therefore, important to understand the meaning and usefulness of this upward sloping relationship between output and the price level. Two interpretations seem to be possible. First, if the labour market is a P market then this relationship represents the combinations of Y and P along which the labour market would be in equilibrium. But it should be kept in mind that the demand for labour depends on the demand for output and not on the real wage rate. Therefore the so called aggregate demand function in fact is the goods and money market equilibrium condition and the aggregate supply function is actually the labour market equilibrium condition. These two sets of equilibrium conditions help us understand the Hicksian four way exchange process in the two dimensional space. Alternatively, if the labour market is assumed to be a mix of both the P and Q characteristics, i.e., the wage rate is assumed to respond sluggishly to the excess demand rate in the labour market but not fully to ensure equilibrium within the unit time

---

such an approach. If the Dornbusch and Fischer approach to wage-price determination is seen in this light it can be said that their approach is free from the limitations of the Barro model.

period, the positive relationship between Y and P is a wage-price reaction function or simply a variant of the Phillips curve in which the unemployment rate is replaced with the full employment output gap variable. This latter interpretation implies that the output-inflation dynamics can be also explained with the Phillips curve.[13]

4.5 CONCLUSIONS

In this chapter we have shown that in the textbook versions of aggregate demand and supply model there are certain confusions in the exposition and inconsistencies in the assumptions. These weaknesses can be attributed to their neglect of the nature of the goods market in the *ISLM* part of the model and its implications for the derivation of the labour demand and the aggregate supply functions. This neglect seems to have also led to the belief that the main difference between the neo classical and the Keynesian versions of the aggregate demand and supply model is that while in the former wages and prices adjust rapidly to clear the markets such adjustments are sluggish in the latter. Therefore the aggregate supply function in the neo classical version is less elastic than in the Keynesian version. This chapter implies that this distinction is tenuous because conceptually there is no supply function in a model where

---

[13] In fact Dornbusch and Fischer (1984) use the Phillips curve, instead of their aggregate demand and supply model (as they have done in the first two editions of their textbook), to explain the inflation-output dynamics.

The Phillips curve based aggregate supply function can be also interpreted as the labour market equilibrium condition if one takes Solow's view of equilibrium in the labour market. Solow (1984, p.18) says that "The trained intuition writes: Supply = Demand. That is an excessively narrow notion of Equilibrium. What we really mean by equilibrium in the labour market is a set of wage and employment conventions that no party to the transaction feels impelled to take direct action to change. Price-mediated market-clearing is one concept of equilibrium, but only one and an extreme one at that."

the aggregate demand function is derived from the *ISLM* model. It is suggested that a distinction between the neo classical and the Keynesian macro models should be based on whether the model follows the pure Walrasian general equilibrium tradition or the Hicksian tradition. Finally it is argued that it is inappropriate and confusing to call the downward and upward sloping relationships between output and the price level as the aggregate demand and aggregate supply functions respectively. While the so called aggregate demand function is actually the goods and money market equilibrium condition, the aggregate supply function is the labour market equilibrium condition or simply a variant of the Phillips curve if the labour market is a disequilibrium market.

These conclusions imply that perhaps we should resurrect the *ISLM* model, the Phillips curve, mark-up price equation and the Okun law as the main textbook macroeconomic paradigm; see for example Rao (1992).

5 Walrasian, Non-Walrasian and Post-Walrasian Perspectives on the ADAS Model: Theoretical and Pedagogical Implications

Ralph C. Allen and Jack H. Stone

5.1 INTRODUCTION

There is now a considerable professional literature focused on the logical and methodological problems of the "traditional" aggregate demand and aggregate supply ($ADAS$) model. The literature argues that both demand and supply behavior are embedded in the aggregate demand curve, as derived from the $ISLM$ analysis; consequently, the aggregate demand curve is not a demand curve as commonly understood by economists. Exacerbating this problem is that the supply behavior underlying this aggregate demand curve is often inconsistent with the supply behavior used to derive the corresponding aggregate supply curve; Fields and Hart (1990, p.678). One result of this inconsistent behavior is two different levels of income and supply at each disequilibrium price level.

In an attempt to remedy these problems, Henry and Woodfield (1985), Dalziel (1987), Colander (1995), and Colander and Sephton (1996) employ models that derive aggregate demand based on a fixed level of aggregate income. In addition, Rowan (1975), Hall and Treadgold (1982), and Fields and Hart (1990) have proposed new models that "macroise" aggregate supply and demand by linking a supply generated income to the analysis which develops aggregate demand. Dutt and Skott (1996) and Allen and Stone

(1993, p.255) suggest a Marshallian approach to the *ADAS* model that begins with a real supply level and uses the *ISLM* framework to determine the price level that clears the commodity market. Each method eliminates the conventional model's concept of an "equilibrium" level of real income determined by the demand curve analysis independently of firm behavior embodied in the aggregate supply curve. However, inconsistencies remain even in these alternative models; Rao (1986; 1991), Nevile and Rao (1996), Smyth (1989), and Allen and Stone (1993).

In this chapter, it is argued that the fundamental reason for these problems is that the traditional *ADAS* framework adopts mixed sets of coordination environments, some of which are mutually inconsistent. This chapter develops the institutional environments underlying the *ISLM* derived aggregate demand curve and the classical and Keynesian aggregate supply curve – specifically, the presence or absence of an auctioneer to assure market coordination. The inconsistencies arising from these environmental mixes are presented. Then the proposed alternatives to the traditional *ADAS* framework are analysed to determine whether they remove these inconsistent environments. It is argued that many of the proposed alternative models suffer from the same environmental inconsistencies as the traditional *ADAS* model. Finally, David Colander's (1995) "coordination" *ADAS* model, which incorporates income adjustment mechanisms in both the demand and the supply model, is analysed. While the Colander model removes the environmental inconsistencies present in the traditional *ADAS* model, Colander's coordination approach requires a reorientation in economic analysis that may be difficult for the instructional community.

5.2 INSTITUTIONAL ENVIRONMENT

In a Walrasian world, an auctioneer calls out resource prices expressed in terms of quantities of specific present and future commodities. Given these barter prices, economic agents solve the appropriate optimization problem and prepare contracts corresponding to their optimal notional levels. By these contracts, households offer specific resource services to firms in exchange for specific quantities of present and future commodities, and firms offer specific present or future commodities to households in exchange for specific quantities of productive resources.

These exchange contracts are transmitted to the auctioneer who aggregates contracts. If one or more markets fail to clear (total bid contracts are not matched to total ask contracts), the auctioneer prohibits any transactions from being carried out and calls out a revised set of prices. Only when a set of prices is established that clears all markets will the auctioneer allow contract transactions to actually be carried out.

The result of this coordination is a unique and full (notional) employment level of production and sales. The barter of resource services for commodities and the coordinating price-setting actions of the auctioneer determines real variables and removes the possibility of non-notional exchange.[1]

While there is no role for money in determining real variables, a unit of account could be chosen to establish an arbitrary price and wage level.

The long-run, vertical or classical aggregate supply curve is equivalent to a barter Walrasian model in which the supply of labour directly constitutes the demand for commodi-

---

[1] As usually presented, this Walrasian model is simplified to include only one resource (labour), and a single, currently consumable commodity. Wage rates are expressed in commodity units, and commodity supply is determined simultaneously with labour market equilibrium. The exchange of current resources for future commodities occurs first by an exchange of resources for current commodities and then by an exchange of unconsumed current commodities (savings) for a claim on future commodities (investment). This simplification reduces the number of commodities and prices needed and creates an explicit interest rate.

ties; thus equilibrium in one market implies equilibrium in the other. This Walrasian model does not require a separate demand curve to determine real output, for by Say's Law, demand equals supply in this environment.[2]

In the Walrasian model, an auctioneer operates in all markets. However, in the case of the positive-sloping Keynesian aggregate supply curve, the auctioneer, while continuing to function in the commodity market, fails to function in the labour market. Prices are expressed in nominal terms, and it is usually assumed that nominal wages are fixed and excess labour supply exists. Although workers are not operating on their notional supply curves, the commodity market auctioneer assures that firms are. Specifically, as the auctioneer raises the commodity price level, firms expand production to their notional levels and workers are willing, even at lower real wages, to supply the additional services. For the Keynesian supply curve case, the auctioneer is no longer setting real wages to equate the demand and supply of labour. Therefore, in contrast to the Walrasian model, this absence of a labour market coordinating mechanism requires the development of a separate, income-constrained aggregate demand curve.

5.3 INSTITUTIONAL ENVIRONMENT BEHIND ISLM

To develop a separate, income-constrained aggregate demand curve, an *ISLM* analysis is traditionally employed. In this *ISLM* model, in contrast to the environment of the classical and Keynesian aggregate supply curves, money is explicitly used as a medium of exchange and a store of value. In addition, in contrast to the Keynesian supply environment, the auctioneer is removed from both the labour and the commodity markets. Removing the labour and commodity market auctioneer leaves the economy devoid of a

[2] Some textbooks derive from the equation of exchange a "classical" demand curve. This demand curve determines, however, only the price level and not real output.

coordinating institution which sets market-clearing product and resource prices. Without the auctioneer, individual agents must establish the market and set their own prices. Contracts must be accepted (or rejected) without knowledge of whether the trading prices are market clearing.

Given that money acts as a store of value in the *ISLM* model, a household's offer of resources and a firm's offer of commodities can be demands for money, not demands for commodities and resources, respectively. In a monetary environment without an auctioneer, households that purchase commodities, firms that hire resources, and investors that undertake capital formation do so without offsetting resource and commodity sale contracts and thus without knowing whether their notional plans will be ultimately realised. Without the auctioneer to reset prices and coordinate notional plans, agents, when faced with actual sales constraints, must themselves decide whether to reset prices or to incorporate sales constraints at existing prices into their behavioral decisions.

Without the auctioneer in the labour and commodity markets, it is usually assumed that the nominal wage rate and commodity price level are downwardly rigid. Consequently, there is persistent excess labour and commodity supply. However, the *ISLM* model assumes that an auctioneer continues to adjust the interest rate to clear the money market, but this interest rate does not assure that savings is equal to investment.

Persistent excess supply in both the labour and commodity markets results in households being income-constrained and firms being sales-constrained. The constrained income level, rather than real wages, now enters the household demand function to determine the level of consumption. Likewise, the constrained level of sales now replaces the real wage rate in the labour demand function.

Textbooks develop this *ISLM* based aggregate demand curve by determining the "equilibrium" level of aggregate demand, aggregate supply and income for each price level. This equilibrium level of income results from the interaction of sales-constrained firms, which adjust production to realised sales at set prices, and households, which face the employment and income constraints imposed by firms. The resulting aggregate demand curve is the series of price level and commodity/money market equilibrium states that result from this institutional environment. The *ISLM* model that generates this relationship is a closed model – both demand and supply behavior are included.[3]

5.4 INCONSISTENCIES IN ADAS AND PROPOSED ALTERNATIVES

Incorporating both the *ISLM* based aggregate demand curve and the Keynesian aggregate supply curve in one model implies that firms (and, for the classical aggregate supply curve case, firms and households) are operating in two inconsistent institutional environments. The aggregate demand curve environment incorporates sales and income constraints; but, in the Keynesian aggregate supply curve case, firms (and for the classical aggregate supply curve case, also households) assume that their realised sales will be equal to the notional quantities at the given price (and wage) level. There are several manifestations of this inconsistency. The aggregate demand curve analysis derives an "equilibrium" level of income independent of the level of income read off the aggregate supply curve analysis. Thus two different levels of income exist at each disequilibrium price level. In addition, for price levels below equilibrium, the aggregate demand environment implies sales constraints are operating even when excess commodity demand is indicated by the overall *ADAS* model.

[3] Perhaps a more fundamental objection to the aggregate demand model is that the aggregate demand curve is not really a demand curve at all. Since at every point along the aggregate demand curve, output (that is, the amount of goods and services supplied) is equal to aggregate demand, it may be more appropriate to call it an "aggregate equilibrium curve"; Colander (1995), and Rabin and Birch (1982, p.236)

Textbook authors gloss over these inconsistencies by adding an auctioneer to adjust the price level in the commodity market to produce a single market clearing output and income level. This technique determines the price level at which income read off the aggregate supply curve would be the same as the equilibrium quantity in the *ISLM* based aggregate demand model. This introduction of an auctioneer to clear the commodity market does not, however, unify the sales-constrained aggregate demand model with the notional firm behavior in either the classical or Keynesian aggregate supply environment. For the classical aggregate supply curve case, it also does not resolve why money is an integral part of the aggregate demand model but not an essential part of the institutional environment of the classical aggregate supply model. More critically, an income-constrained aggregate demand model is inherently in conflict with the notional demand and supply behavior underlying the classical aggregate supply environment.

Most attempts to remove the analytical problems associated with the traditional *ADAS* analysis do not attempt to address the institutional environment issue directly, but instead try to treat the manifestations of these inconsistent environments by removing the impact of the supply adjustments from the aggregate demand curve. Henry and Woodfield (1985), and Dalziel (1987), simply fix the income used in the aggregate demand analysis. The aggregate demand curve is derived by allowing changes in the price level to have an impact on aggregate demand, at the specified constant income level, through the Pigou and Keynes effects. As a result, the *ISLM* behavioral framework remains intact, but the income multiplier is removed from the analysis. Since aggregate demand does not necessarily equal the level of fixed income from which it is derived, this fixed-income model removes the concept of an "equilibrium" income determined by the demand analysis.

These authors then add either a classical or Keynesian aggregate supply curve to the analysis. As a result, two manifestations of inconsistent environments appear. First, with the aggregate supply curve added to the model, two different income levels still exist at each disequilibrium price level. One is fixed and determined by some (unprescribed) act of history or expectations; and one is determined by the aggregate supply analysis. Second, if the fixed level of income also represents the actual level of supply that period, then two levels of supply exist at each disequilibrium price level. These two supply levels create the possibility of two, possibly opposing, price level behaviors – one responding to excess demand or supply as determined by the fixed supply level and one responding to excess demand or supply as determined by the aggregate supply curve. These manifestations are the result of the continued mixing of notional firm behavior in the supply curve environment and a sales-constrained demand curve environment.

Rowan (1975), Hall and Treadgold (1982), and Fields and Hart (1990), propose a macroised model that removes the ambiguity as to the correct level of supply and income at a given disequilibrium price by employing in the aggregate demand analysis the income from the aggregate supply curve at that price level. Therefore, as the price level changes, aggregate demand changes through the Pigou and Keynes effects and through the effect that the price level has on aggregate supply. Combining commodity supply and demand, the auctioneer adjusts commodity prices to ensure that actual exchanges are executed only at market clearing prices.

In this macroised model firms are behaving notionally in both the aggregate demand and supply analysis. The sales-constrained firm behavior, which exists in the *ISLM* based aggregate demand analysis and which causes conflicts with notional firm behavior in both the classical and Keynesian aggregate supply curve case, is removed. However, for the Keynesian supply curve case, this model does use the odd environmental assumption of an auctioneer mechanism which clears all markets except the labour market. The labour market is in persistent excess supply, and labour incorporates income constraints into their demand behavior.

On the other hand, if a classical aggregate supply curve is employed, the inconsistency in labour market behavior, notional in the classical aggregate supply analysis but income-constrained in the aggregate demand analysis, remains.

Dutt and Skott (1996) and Allen and Stone (1993) have suggested a Marshallian interpretation to the *ADAS* model. Beginning with an expected price level, firms determine their notional level of supply and produce a fixed, market-period level of income and output. Consistent with the analysis of Henry and Woodfield (1985) and Dalziel (1987), this fixed income level is used to derive the aggregate demand curve and to determine the price level that equates quantity demanded to the fixed, market-period level of supply. The result is a demand-determined, market-clearing price level in each market period.[4]

In this Marshallian model, sales-constrained firm behavior is removed from the aggregate demand analysis eliminating the inconsistency with notional firm behavior in the classical and Keynesian aggregate supply cases. If a Keynesian aggregate supply curve is employed, the odd environmental assumption of an auctioneer mechanism to clear all markets except the labour market is used. However, if a classical aggregate supply curve is employed, the environmental inconsistency exists in the labour market as it did for the macroised model. In either case, when explaining macroeconomic behavior to a student, is the assumption of market clearing price variations in each market period empirically and institutionally relevant?[5]

---

[4] If the market-period price exceeds (is less than) the reservation supply price, as determined by the notional aggregate supply curve at that level of output, firms adjust price expectations and thus the following market-period level of supply and income upward (downward). Assumptions concerning how firms adjust price expectations and supply to disequilibrium prices allows several stories to be told concerning the path of price and real income movements in this Marshallian model.

[5] Dutt and Scott (1996) argue that, in addition to the *(continued)*

5.5 POST-WALRASIAN COORDINATION IN ADAS

Stripping the Walrasian model of the auctioneer mechanism removes the coordination of notional quantities in the labour market with the corresponding notional quantities in the commodity market. In such an environment, David Colander (1995) argues that economic agents themselves choose prices and output levels that are likely to result in macro coordination failures that affect production and income.

A macro coordination failure occurs when mutual gains, attainable from a feasible all-around change in agent behavior, are not realised because no individual agent has an incentive to deviate from his/her current behavior. The above definition of coordination failure implies that there are multiple, stable, aggregate production equilibriums, each associated with a different degree of coordination.

Colander's (1995) argument is that coordinating institutions are needed to affect firms' expectations of demand and thus the probability of realised sales. For example, without these coordinating institutions, managers may perceive that the probability of making a sale is a function of the general level of activity in the economy.[6] If each manager expects little economic activity and thus a low probability of sales success, then each manager will reduce production and sales activities. In this environment, no firm has the incentive to expand production and sales activities. Since there is no market to adjust expectations to their optimal

---

Marshallian *ADAS* model, several other frameworks can be used to derive an *ADAS* model without the inconsistencies in the *ISLM* derived *ADAS* model. However, each of the *ADAS* models ultimately employ an auctioneer to price clear the commodity market. Dutt and Skott (1996, p.17) note that creating an internally consistent model does not necessarily generate an empirically realistic model.

[6] This belief is reflected in managerial interest in macroeconomic forecasting.

level, the collective impact is a self fulfilling low level of economic activity.[7]

However, if an institution, e.g., the Federal Reserve, could coordinate expectations so that firms expect higher sales activities, then a higher sustainable level of macroeconomic activity could be attained from the efforts generated by these coordinated expectations. In the Colander analysis, an improvement in the coordination of business-sector sales expectations increases expected profitability, which in turn creates incentives to increase production from any given level of resource use.[8] Conceptually, resources that are "employed" but "standing around" are utilised more intensively. As a result of the increased production and expected profitability, owners increase investment demand, and as members of the household sector they increase their consumption.[9] As expectations are fulfilled and ac-

---

[7] Colander (1995, p.182) suggests that the public good nature of macroeconomic expectation is a reason for the failure of private markets to provide expectation coordination and is thus a justification for centralised action.

[8] Colander's (1995) specific proposal involves the introduction of a coordination variable, X, into the production function that underlies the supply side of the *ADAS* analysis

$$Q = f(K, L, X)$$

where K and L are resources used in production. As macroeconomic coordination becomes more effective, firms expect higher macroeconomic activity, and thus they increase the level of output from a given employment level. In effect, a coordination improvement will affect aggregate output by shifting the production function upward.

[9] An alternative coordination method which generates multiple equilibriums is suggested by Roger McCain (1996) who incorporates the coordination variable into the investment function instead of the production function. McCain assumes that the expected return on investment undertaken by any firm depends on the investment strategy employed by the remaining firms in the economy. Depending on the strategies chosen, different expenditure levels and thus equilibriums could exist.

tual sales occur, income increases, additional employment may occur, and a second increase in demand may result from these income flows. These changes may again alter expected demand and thus production. In the Colander analysis, changes in production and demand are employed in a dynamic adjustment story in which the interdependencies between the two are emphasised.

How does Colander's proposed supply relationship affect the model and the geometry underlying the $ADAS$ analysis? Colander has not specified a formal model; however, the following framework reflects his analysis.

First, the standard $ISLM$ based aggregate demand curve is replaced by an aggregate demand curve derived from a fixed income level, Y^s, incorporating both the Pigou and Keynes effects. That is:

$$
\begin{aligned}
C &= C(Y^s, r, M/P) \\
I &= I(r, Y^s) \\
Y^d &= C + I \\
M^d &= M^d(Y^d, r) \\
M^s &= M/P \\
M^d &= M^s
\end{aligned}
$$

where C, I, Y^d, r P, M, M^d, and M^s are the actual level of consumption, investment, total demand, interest rate, prices, money balances, money demand and money supply, respectively. In Colander's model, the use of a fixed income level, Y^s, in the demand framework removes the supply inconsistencies associated with the $ISLM$ derived aggregate demand framework and is similar to solutions proposed by Henry and Woodfield (1985) and Dalziel (1987). As a result, the income multiplier effect is removed from the aggregate demand model; and the aggregate demand curve, whose slope now depends only on the strength of the Pigou and Keynes effects, becomes more vertical.

Second, Colander (1995, p.185) employs a vertical, "effective aggregate supply" curve, Y^s, which is controlled by firms' expectations, Y^e, of aggregate economic activity which are in turn affected by actual demand, Y^d, and macroeconomic coordination, X:

$$Y^s = Y^s(Y^e(X, Y^d)).$$

At equilibrium, effective aggregate supply, Y^s, is equal to aggregate demand, Y^d. Conceptually, different levels of coordination, X, result in different expectations of aggregate economic activity and thus produce different equilibrium levels of production and income.[10]

While the price level is a component of the formal model, price level changes are not an integral part of Colander's (1995, p.183) analysis. Colander believes that, in a economy with contracts expressed in nominal terms, such price (or wage) level adjustments would be disruptive, rather than coordinating. As a result, institutions resist these disruptive price level adjustments. Instead, a change in coordination alters expected income and, therefore, causes both the effective aggregate supply and the aggregate demand curve to shift, further altering expectations, i.e.,$\Delta X \Rightarrow \Delta Y^e \Rightarrow \Delta Y^s \Rightarrow \Delta Y^d \Rightarrow \Delta Y^e$. Therefore, expected and actual income changes are used in his model as the integrating link from aggregate supply to aggregate demand. Based upon his concept that supply changes affect the economy through their link to expected income, Colander accepts the label "supply-side Keynesian".

Do multiple equilibrium actually exist in the Colander model? That is, is the increase in aggregate demand resulting from improved coordination adequate to sustain a higher equilibrium level of production and income? A mechanism (endorsed by Colander in a personal conversation) which can produce an appropriate increase in demand and thus multiple equilibriums is Say's Law. If financial markets are coordinating savings and investment such

[10] Formally, Colander's supply function is also a function of capital, K, and labour, L. However, he treats both as fixed, leaving coordination as the principle factor to bring about equilibrium.

that any savings generating by the coordination-induced expansion of production will be absorbed by investment, $\Delta Y^s - \Delta C(\Delta Y^s, r, M/P) = \Delta I(r, \Delta Y^s)$, the increase in supply and the resulting demand are equal.

However, in the Colander model, if savings initially exceeds investment, the coordination of investment with savings does not result from a downward interest rate adjustment. Not only does Colander not support the price adjustment mechanism; but, in this formalised Colander model, increases in aggregate demand resulting from improved coordination would tend to raise – not lower – interest rates. The coordination of investment with savings results from expectation-induced efforts by the financial sector to generate the investment necessary to absorb the additional savings created at the higher equilibrium level of production and income.

The Colander model removes the inconsistencies, in the traditional *ADAS* model, by developing non-notional, constrained behavior in both the aggregate demand and the aggregate supply analysis. The model, therefore, provides a logically consistent contrast to the notional Walrasian model. The difficulty with using the model as an instructional tool is that the institutional details of this macrocoordination process have not been developed. For example, what are the mechanisms by which institutions such as the Federal Reserve coordinate macroeconomic expectations? Colander is calling for a research agenda in this regard, but it is far from the stage of development needed by the instructional community. In addition, Colander's assumption of a fixed labour force alters the traditional focus of changes in employment over the business cycle – a potential source of discomfort for the instructional community.

5.6 CONCLUSION

As indicated in the introduction, there is now a considerable literature on the logical and methodological problems associated with the *ADAS* model as well as suggestions for remedying these problems. The present authors believe that, although professional economists have become intensely interested in these problems, a critical issue is the pedagogical implications of this literature. Specifically, what pedagogical reform (if any) does this literature suggest at both the principles and intermediate macroeconomics course levels?

The authors of this chapter believe that it is very important to examine the market environments implied by the various components of the traditional and alternative *ADAS* models. Specifically, firm decision making under constrained demand conditions is different than under conditions in which an auctioneer ensures that firms plans' are realised. The world becomes more complex and the coordination of economic activity is made more difficult when a centralised auctioneer is removed from the model.

This suggestion implies that students should be disabused of the idea that there is only one monolithic model with a "right answer" in favor of the notion that there are different models with different conclusions. This comparative approach would emphasise the controversies in the profession over macroeconomic issues and hopefully contribute to the student's ability to evaluate various approaches (in particular, the critical assumptions underlying each).[11] Although a comparative approach emphasizing controversy and focusing particularly on the different assumptions underlying the controversy (and specifically identifying them as assumptions) risks making the discipline appear to be a Tower of Babel, it may be consistent with good pedagogy as well as intellectual integrity.

[11] This suggestion is consistent with that made by Mosely and Wolf (1992).

6 The ADAS Model: Two into One Won't Go*

Roy H. Grieve

6.1 INTRODUCTION

It has for some time been the almost universal fashion, amongst authors of intermediate macroeconomics textbooks, to employ the aggregate demand and aggregate supply (*ADAS*) model to explain the determination of aggregate output and the price level. Perusal of a representative selection of such texts reveals that most – all but three out of fifteen surveyed – make use of a version, or versions, of *ADAS*.[1] Recently however dissident voices have been raised in criticism of the propriety of relying on the *ADAS* construction. Among those who have drawn attention to the inherent inconsistency of the standard model are Rao (1991), Barro and Grilli (1994), Colander (1995, 1996), Nevile and Rao (1996) and Grieve (1996). Colander,

---

* I am grateful to Eric Rahim for valuable discussion of various drafts on the subject of *ADAS*.

[1] The texts examined were: Abel and Bernanke (1996), Barro (1990), Barro and Grilli (1994), Barron et. al., (1989), Branson (1989), Brown (1995), Burda and Wyplosz (1993), Dornbusch and Fischer (1994), Froyen (1993), Gordon (1993), Levacic and Rebman (1982), Mankiew (1994), Miller and Pulsinelli (1986), Parkin and Bade (1982) and Sachs and Larrain (1993); of these the only exceptions not using *ADAS* were Barro (1990), Barro and Grilli (1994) and (introducing but not endorsing the model) Dornbusch and Fischer (1994).

for one, does not mince words (1995, p.170): "*ADAS* does not fulfil the minimum requirement of a model: logical consistency. Its component parts are derived from models that reflect different, and inconsistent models of the economy." This chapter seeks to set the problem of the *ADAS* model in the context of the development of macro theory.

6.2 THE TEXTBOOK MODEL

In the typical textbook treatment, when the exposition moves beyond the fix-price world of the Keynesian cross and *ISLM*, the familiar story is that, within the economy, the volume of output and the price level are simultaneously determined at the point of intersection of the *AD* and *AS* schedules. The negatively-sloped *AD* curve, with quantities of output corresponding to *ISLM* equilibrium at different price levels, *ceteris paribus,* is said to represent the value of effective demand as a function of prices. In deriving the positively-sloped short run *AS* schedule it is supposed that expenditure changes affect commodity prices, but when prices change, money wages – whether because of misperceptions or rigidities – are slow to respond. The real terms on which labour is supplied are thus understood to alter so that, with this shift of the labour supply curve, a change in employment, and consequently of output, occurs. In this way price level changes are believed to induce, at least in the short term, changes in the level of activity. In the longer run, as misperceptions are corrected, or inflexibilities relaxed, the labour supply curve returns to its original position, yielding a vertical long run *AS* curve.

Our concern is with the inconsistency of the two halves of the model – inconsistency arising from the essential incompatibility of the theoretical conceptions from which the *AD* and *AS* curves are respectively derived. The peculiarity of the construction is that the treatment of the demand side is Keynesian in character, while that of the supply side is pre-Keynesian or classical.

It is surprising that the *ADAS* model has held sway for

so long in the textbook world; the fact that there is something fundamentally wrong with it ought not to have been too difficult to spot. Consider the sort of account commonly presented. Imagine, for instance, an economy initially at full employment, and that this equilibrium state is upset by a sharp fall in spending. Assume (unrealistically, but in accord with convention) a downward-sloping marginal product of labour schedule (which, in textbook terms, is described as the labour demand function). Experiencing a contraction of sales, firms cut production and employment and move down their short-run supply curves, reducing prices as they do so. If we assume that money wages remain unchanged, real wages will rise as employment falls. Suppose that prices fall by 2 per cent and that employment is down by 10 per cent. In terms of *ADAS*, the interpretation of this situation is that the *AD* curve has shifted and moved the point of equilibrium leftwards along the short-run *AS* curve. The rationalisation offered for the change of output in response to the change in spending is that, as labour is effectively asking for a higher real wage, the conditions of labour supply have altered; as a result, in the labour market the new intersection of labour supply and demand schedules implies a lower level of employment, and correspondingly in the commodity markets, a smaller volume of output.

How can this unemployment problem be resolved? In classical terms, as implicit in the *AS* curve, the demand for labour is a function of the real wage; if workers eventually respond to the fall in commodity prices by accepting a 2 per cent cut in money wages, the original real wage would be restored, and so also should be the original level of employment. But the model includes, along with the short-run *AS* curve, the downward sloping *AD* schedule; it may be asked, with reference to aggregate demand, how far prices have to fall to counteract the (approximately) 10 per cent fall in demand which has taken place. The position and slope of the *AD* curve imply that a far greater fall in prices than the 2 per cent which has already occurred is required to restore demand to the full employment level. The model is evidently self-contradictory – it embodies two different explanations of how the level of employment is determined and (if the price level is not that at which *AD* and *AS* intersect) offers two different indications of what employment will be – as corresponding to the classical theory underlying the *AS* curve and as corresponding to the Keynesian theory represented by the *AD* curve.

The internal inconsistency, the over-determinacy, of the *ADAS* model is effectively obscured by the way in which the subsequent dynamics of adjustment are typically treated. The scenario is that, as the economy moves back to full employment (as it is confidently expected to do), changes in the real wage and in the price level take place simultaneously; Gordon (1993), for example, describes a stage by stage adjustment process of money wages chasing prices in a wage-price spiral. It is understood that, as this process works itself out, diminishing returns being assumed, money wages gradually recover their original relationship to commodity prices as output goes back to its "natural" level.

Whatever is intended, this story doesnt reconcile the two theories of employment: it only serves to disguise the fact that the Keynesian theory falls out of the picture, so that the conclusion reached is, by default, an essentially classical one. In describing the adjustment process, attention is concentrated on the response of the workforce to the unemployment which has emerged. Given the belief that the workers will correct their expectational errors (you can't fool all of the people all of the time) or that the passage of time ultimately allows for relaxation of institutional constraints on wage changes, it is taken for granted that the initial change in effective conditions of labour supply is in due course reversed. The understanding is apparently that labour is in a position, by correcting its initially inadequate response to the disturbance experienced, to re-establish in the labour market the conditions required for full employment. That is the crux of the matter – the presumption that labour, by revising the terms on which it is willing to work, is able to bring about its desired labour market situation; if that is the guaranteed outcome, there is no room for aggregate demand as an independent determinant of employment – the only role left to demand is to set the price level. We are in this way brought, despite the model being in part derived from *ISLM*, to the pre-Keynesian conclusion that employment is determined by the conditions of labour supply, and prices by the volume of spending.

Seen in these terms, fluctuations in employment are essentially a supply side problem: aggregate demand may alter, but output and employment would not be affected if the initial supply side response, particularly that of labour, were the proper one. If the economy happens not to be operating at the "natural rate of employment", this analysis focuses attention on the behaviour of the workforce: the solution to the problem is held to lie in the correction of misperceptions or in renegotiation of an inappropriate wage rate. Nothing of great difficulty, that is to say, seems to be involved in re-establishing employment at the "natural" rate. In recession conditions, there is apparently no need for a change of outlook among potential buyers – no need for recovery of business confidence or regeneration among consumers of the feel-good factor. Since the deviation of employment from its normal equilibrium level is explained by factors said to be responsible for the temporarily non-vertical slope of the *AS* curve, when these causes cease to operate, unemployment will necessarily have returned to the "natural" rate. As demand for labour and output are understood to correspond to the intersection of the marginal product of labour and labour supply schedules, the necessary implication (as regards comparative statics equilibria) is that the price level automatically accommodates itself to variations in the volume of monetary spending.

To teach the above story invites less than desirable consequences. For one thing, it can hardly promote clear understanding to go from expounding (through the income-expenditure and *ISLM* models) the proposition that employment depends on real planned expenditure to the contention that the terms of labour supply are the key determinant of employment. For another, the message emerging from this theoretical confusion is that, even if account is taken of the Keynesian theory of effective demand, modern macroeconomics carries the practical implication that the economy does, of itself, readily tend to be a "natural" state of full employment; if that were so, there could be nothing particularly dangerous or socially costly in a government deliberately creating (supposedly temporary) unemployment in order to "squeeze inflation out of the system".

6.3 TWO THEORIES, ONE MODEL: NO GO

If we subject the conventional *ADAS* model to closer inspection, the nature of its peculiar duality becomes apparent. Far from it being the case that the two schedules together determine a unique equilibrium, each in itself represents a self-contained theory of the relationship between the price level and levels of output and employment; if we focus on either curve, the other is redundant.

With respect to the *AD* curve, both Rao (1991) and Colander (1995, 1996) have observed that, while it may be described or defined as being analogous to a micro demand curve, it is in fact, as conventionally derived from *ISLM*, not really a demand curve at all. Since what this curve shows in relation to price are levels of income corresponding to *ISLM* equilibrium, the *AD* curve is actually a locus of points of equality of aggregate demand and aggregate supply. Rao (1991, p.276) identifies it as the equilibrium condition of the goods, bond and money markets; Colander (1995, p.175) suggests the designation "aggregate equilibrium curve". It is obvious that a curve of this nature cannot be used along with an independent aggregate supply schedule to form a tenable *ADAS* model. An equivalent situation exists with respect to the supposed supply-side. The *AS* curve is evidently based on a pre-Keynesian understanding of the functioning of the labour market. The significant characteristic of that pre-Keynesian analysis is that the labour market is treated in exactly the same terms as the market for any final commodity – as if it was of no consequence whether the subject under consideration was the market for, say, Scotch pies (or peanuts) rather than the market for labour services. It is supposed that in the labour market price and quantity are (in diagrammatic terms) determined by intersection of demand and supply schedules of the usual sort; labour demand and supply are both taken to be functions of the real wage. Changes in the level of employment must then be attributed to movement of one or other curve: in the short run, with the marginal product of labour (labour demand) curve fixed in position in accordance with the given technological conditions, it is only through movement of the labour supply curve that employment can alter.

But to account in these terms for fluctuations of employment is to ignore the special nature of the labour market: the presumption that a shift of the labour supply curve is a necessary and sufficient condition for employment to change completely neglects the fact that demand for labour is *derived* demand, depending on the demand for output. If short run variations in employment could always be explained by changes in conditions of labour supply, it would have to be the case that the volume of planned demand automatically matched the labour supply situation: on all occasions, demand would need to be just what was required to take up the output associated with the employment given by intersection of the marginal product of labour and labour supply schedules. In other words, the conventional neoclassical representation of the labour market depends for its validity on the assumption that aggregate demand is "tame" – or that supply really does create its own demand. An aggregate supply curve based on these neoclassical foundations therefore depicts, as a function of the price level, quantities of output which are matched by an equal volume of effective demand. That is to say, with aggregate demand equal to aggregate supply at all points along the curve, we have a second goods market "aggregate equilibrium curve".

It makes no sense to put the two "aggregate equilibrium curves" together: the conventional *ADAS* model is an attempt to combine the incompatible. The terms of this model's rejection by Barro and Grilli (1994, p.428) are worth quoting:

> The main problem with the *AS-AD* framework is that the various pieces of the analysis are contradictory. The *AD* curve reflects the underlying *IS/LM* model … The *AS* curve assumes that producers (and workers) can sell their desired quantities at the going price, P. That is why the quantity supplied rises when P increases relative to P^e (the expected price level). This set-up is inconsistent with the Keynesian idea – present in the *IS/LM* model and therefore in the *AD* curve – that producers and workers are constrained by aggregate demand in their ability to sell goods and services.

6.4 THE ROOT OF THE PROBLEM

We have then the extraordinary situation that the typical modern macro textbook presents to its readers a model which embodies at the same time – as supposedly complementary elements – the Keynesian theory of demand and employment (or at least a version of it) together with the classical theory of employment – which was the specific target of Keynes's attack in the *General Theory.* That such a situation can come about can only be attributed to failure – even after 60 years – by the majority of textbook authors to appreciate the nature of Keynes's break with neoclassical orthodoxy.

Keynes, as is well known, directed his critical fire particularly at Pigou's 1933 *Theory of Unemployment* – the work he identified (Keynes, 1936, p.279) as constituting the classical theory in its "most formidable presentment". The conception of the relationship between the goods and labour markets which in the current textbook literature underlies the *AS* curve is essentially that which informed Pigou's theory of employment. Pigou believed – just as do contemporary textbook authors – that employment is determined in the labour market at the point of intersection of the demand and supply schedules. If, as in the slump years of the 1930s, a substantial disparity existed between the number of people in employment and the number desirous of work, the diagnosis – and the solution – of the problem, according to Pigou (1933, p.256), was simple: the real wage was too high, and a reduction would secure increased labour demand. In other words, Pigou and the textbook authors share the interpretation that, in explaining the level of employment it is to the terms on which labour is offered for employment that we must look.

In Pigou's case however this treatment of the labour market is accompanied by the further presumption that aggregate (planned) demand can be relied upon to take up whatever output is produced by the quantity of labour corresponding to the intersection of the conventional labour demand and supply schedules. In Pigou's two-sector model, a reduction in real wages leads to increased employment in the wage-goods industry and a larger surplus of that industry's output over its own requirements; this greater surplus of wage-goods is available to support increased employment in the non-wage-goods sector. Pigou's critical assumption, essential for the *logical* justification of his contention that lower wages would guarantee more employment (the *validity* of that assumption is of course another matter) was that an increase in the demand for non-wage-goods, sufficient to absorb all the extra employment made possible, would then automatically materialise:

> If the real wage rate is reduced in wage-goods industries, a powerful reaction is set up for an expansion in the demand for labour in the non-wage-good industries ··· It is certain that in practice the reaction (on employment) will be substantial. (Pigou, 1933, p.73).

The point is that while Pigou and the majority of

present-day textbook authors apparently subscribe to the same theory of employment – focusing attention on the terms of labour supply – these same textbook authors are not supposed, given their acceptance of a Keynesian-type AD function, to go along with Pigou's evident belief that supply does indeed create its own demand: the Pigouvian-neoclassical treatment of the labour market demands for its logical validity adherence to Say's Law.

What the textbook authors have failed to appreciate is that Keynes's treatment of the labour market was radically different from that of Pigou. Despite its continuing popularity in the textbooks the Pigouvian/neoclassical model of the labour market is inappropriate when, as in Keynesian theory, aggregate demand is taken to be an independent parameter of the system. Keynes recognised that as the demand for labour is derived demand, the situation in the labour market essentially depends on the prevailing state of affairs in the goods markets. While there may be indirect (unreliable) feed-back from the labour to the goods markets, the fundamental causal relationship runs from the demand for commodities to the demand for labour; see Pasinetti (1974, pp.42-45). Given that understanding of the linkage between the goods and labour markets, and appreciating that, in consequence, the going level of employment need not correspond to the intersection of the marginal product of labour and labour supply curves, it follows that the downward-sloping MPN schedule cannot be described as the "labour demand schedule": it should more properly be termed an "employment-real wage" or "price-determined real wage" schedule. With employment set in accordance with the demand for output, the real wage is determined by the level of employment, and not *vice versa* (Keynes 1936, p.30). It is then possible to conceive (in diagrammatic terms) of a gap between the quantity of labour actually demanded and the quantity available for employment – available on terms consistent with its employment. That, of course, is the point of Keynes's famously obscure definition of involuntary unemployment (Keynes 1936, p.15) –

that such a gap may exist, and can be closed as demand for labour increases relative to the given supply.

In Keynes's theory any increase of real wages accompanying a reduction of employment is an incidental, and trivial, consequence of the fall in activity – categorically, *not its cause.* It is not that the labour supply curve shifts: with involuntary unemployment, labour is off its supply curve. Had Keynes at the time of writing been aware that the inverse relationship between employment and real wages postulated in the *General Theory* was not consistent with the observable facts, he would not have felt obliged to introduce what has turned out to be a source of subsequent misunderstanding; if, in accordance with his later (1939) remarks, the occurrence of involuntary unemployment had been dissociated from wage changes, it would have been unambiguously obvious that employment depended on aggregate demand.

6.5 CONCLUSION

The textbook *AS* curve, derived from a Pigouvian conception of the working of the labour market, cannot be combined with a schedule representing aggregate demand as an independent determinant of output and employment. *The two curves are incompatible – they represent irreconcilably different conceptions of the nature of economic reality.* If we wish to employ a consistent model of a classical (Say's Law) type, we must drop the *AD* part of the model; correspondingly – and one would hope more probably – if we desire to have a logically coherent model of Keynesian character, we must abandon the conventional *AS* curve.

The familiar *ADAS* textbook model is comprised of components that simply do not fit together; it is high time that its deficiencies were much more widely recognised by those engaged in the teaching of macroeconomics. As a "powerful instrument of miseducation" this "jerry-built" construction must be put aside.

6.6 POSTSCRIPT

While the conventional *ADAS* model ought to be abandoned forthwith, a model superficially similar, but in reality essentially different, may be of pedagogic value – if handled with care; see Grieve (1996). The intended role of *ADAS* has been to advance the textbook analysis beyond the fix-price *ISLM* model. That objective may be achieved, and the problems of the *ADAS* model avoided, by use of an "aggregate output/price level" (*AO*/*PP*) model which depicts the interaction of the equilibrium level of output and the price level. This construction combines Colander's "aggregate equilibrium curve" with a schedule showing the level of prices as a function of output (not output as a function of price). The slope of this price level curve would comprehend, as appropriate, the relationship between output and marginal cost, mark-up variation, and the effect of labour market conditions (tightness or slackness) on money wages. Not being derived from the neoclassical model of the labour market, the *PP* curve would not associate price level changes with changes in labour supply. A model of this type may in fact be found in one well-known macro text – see Dornbusch and Fischer, (1994) – although, curiously, the authors take considerable pains to disguise the difference of their model from the conventional textbook *ADAS* .

7 Defending ADAS: A Perspective on the ADAS Controversy

Peter Kennedy

7.1 INTRODUCTION

The aggregate demand and supply (*ADAS*) diagram has been a hot topic recently. Journal articles have appeared with provocative titles such as "What is the Matter with Aggregate Demand and Aggregate Supply" (Rao, 1991) and "The Use and Abuse of Aggregate Demand and Supply Functions" (Nevile and Rao, 1996). Emotive language such as "dirty pedagogy" has been used to describe its textbook use, and dramatic accusations of internal inconsistency have sought to destroy its credibility. As a modest contributor to this debate (Kennedy, 1996) and an author of textbooks employing the *ADAS* diagram (Kennedy, 1984, 1997) I seek in this chapter to provide some perspective on this controversy along with a personal view of its status. I begin with a discussion of why the *ADAS* diagram rose to prominence.

7.2 THE RISE OF ADAS

By the early 1980s the aggregate demand and supply diagram had supplanted the 45^0 diagram and the *ISLM* diagram as the expository diagram of choice in introductory and intermediate macroeconomics textbooks. There were four main reasons why this happened.

1. Supply-side shocks such as the OPEC price increases of the 1970s were not easily analysed using

the old diagrams. Economists were embarassed that their textbook models could offer no easy way of illustrating for students the impact on the economy of supply-side shocks and the policy prescriptions they implied. A more explicit modeling of the supply side of the economy was needed, along with a clearer vision of how it was incorporated into textbook expository diagrams.

2. High inflation rates characterizing the 1970s forced economics instructors to pay more attention to the overall price level, a variable hidden from sight in the old models. The *ISLM* diagram chooses to picture the interest rate and bury the price level; by burying the interest rate and picturing the price level the same model in the form of an *AD* curve directs more attention to the price level.

3. The advent of supply-side economics as a strong political force made it desirable to find some easy way of contrasting this view with traditional views. The supply dimension of the *ISLM* diagram is divorced from the *IS* and *LM* curves themselves, being bound up in a supplementary labour market diagram/analysis. By consolidating this supply dimension into an aggregate supply curve, the *ADAS* diagram offered a means of expositing supply-siders' views in a form that could readily be contrasted with traditional views.

4. The *ADAS* diagram seemed to offer economists a means of extending microeconomic supply and demand diagrams to the macroeconomic context, creating a pedagogically appealing link between microeconomic and macroeconomic analysis. Because supply and demand curves are the foundations of economic analysis, this was a seductive argument.

The first three of these arguments are cogent. The *ISLM* diagram did make it difficult to *see* the impact of a supply-side shock, what was happening to the price level was hidden from view, and supply-siders views were not easily portrayed on this diagram. The *ADAS* diagram allowed supply-side shocks to affect the diagram directly through shifts in the *AS* curve, the price level came into the open, and supply-side views could be portrayed via the *AS* curve. In all these respects introduction of the *ADAS* diagram was successful. Generations of students were taught that the supply side of the macro economy is as important as the demand side, and that the price level (and by extension inflation) is in many respects of more interest than the interest rate.

These first three reasons for introducing the *ADAS* diagram are not controversial, since it is evident that in these three respects the profession has benefited from viewing the macroeconomy in this way. The current controversy surrounding yhe use of *ADAS* diagram for pedagogical purposes, as evidenced for example by Colander (1995) and Nevile and Rao (1996), is associated with the fourth reason given above. In a nutshell, it is claimed that the *ADAS* model is internally inconsistent and in addition gives rise to misleading and confusing expositions of the operation of the macroeconomy, unnecessarily inhibiting student understanding.

7.3 NO INTERNAL INCONSISTENCY

Before discussing the complaint that the *ADAS* diagram produces misleading and confusing expositions, a complaint that has some substance, I will dispose of the incorrect claim that the *ADAS* diagram is internally inconsistent. The essence of the claim of internal inconsistency is that the *AD* curve has embedded in it at each price level a horizontal aggregate supply curve so that it doesn't make sense to introduce another aggregate supply curve. Both Nevile and Rao (p.198) and Colander (p.176) articulate this clearly. The error in this thinking comes from a misinterpretation of the *AS* and *AD* curves.

The *AS* and *AD* curves are what economists call market

equilibrium curves which consist of combinations of values of the variables measured on the axes that create equilibrium in some market or markets. The *AD* curve is defined as combinations of price and income for which the goods and services market and the money market are in simultaneous equilibrium. (Walras law implies that the bond market is also in equilibrium.) In open economies this is extended to incorporate international sector equilibrium. The *AS* curve is defined as combinations of price and income for which the labour market is in equilibrium. A distinction is drawn between short and long run equilibrium giving rise to short and long run *AS* curves. The market equilibrium interpretation of the *AD* curve is commonplace, but the labour market equilibrium interpretation of the *AS* curve is not widely appreciated. Independent expositions of this view can be found in Pesek and Saving (1967, pp.7-8), Kennedy (1984, p.283) and Rao (1991, pp.275-276).

These curves imply no causality of any kind. Given a price level one finds the corresponding point on the *AD* curve by asking what income level would have to be matched with this price level for equilibrium to be maintained in the goods and services and the money markets. No supply curve is involved: The *AD* curve does not implicitly have imbedded in it at each price a horizontal supply curve to explain how the economy gets to the equilibrium income level because no such explanation is required in the context of equilibrium curves. Consequently, no inconsistency arises when the *AS* curve is introduced. How could respected economists have misinterpreted the fundamental nature of the *ADAS* diagram? Two possible reasons come to mind.

1. Most equilibrium curves in economic analysis have on their axes variables which affect but do not themselves represent the supply or demand side of a market. In the *ADAS* diagram, however, one of the variables on the axes is income, the level of aggregate supply. This introduces a potential source of confu-

sion - as the level of this variable is varied to trace out the equilibrium curve, this variation could be misinterpreted as an actual supply response.

2. The labour market is ignored in the early stages of most textbook developments of the *IS* and *LM* curves. In this beginning version of the *ISLM* model, income is determined by appending to the *IS* and *LM* curves an assumption that the economy reacts (via a "horizontal supply curve") to increase aggregate supply to match whatever aggregate demand is produced by the intersection of the *IS* and *LM* curves. When moving to the *ADAS* diagram, which consolidates the *IS* and *LM* curves, it could easily be forgotten that the horizontal supply curve was not a part of the *IS* and *LM* curves themselves.

7.4 ADAS CAN BE CONFUSING

Let me turn now to the claim that the *ADAS* diagram can be misleading or confusing. The fourth reason given earlier for the adoption of the *ADAS* diagram was that it appeared to offer economists a means of extending microeconomic demand and supply diagrams to the macroeconomic context, creating a pedagogically appealing link between microeconomic and macroeconomic analysis. Unfortunately, the *AS* and *AD* curves are fundamentally different from microeconomic supply and demand curves. The *AS* and *AD* curves are equilibrium curves reflecting combinations of price and income that create equilibrium in particular markets. Given a price level, a microeconomic demand curve can be used to tell us what will be the demand for that product, and a microeconomic supply curve can tell us what will be the supply of that product. But given a price level the *AD* curve cannot tell us what will be aggregate demand for goods and services, and the *AS* curve cannot tell us what will be aggregate supply of goods and services. The *AD* curve tells us only what income level would have to prevail for there to be simultaneous equilibrium in the goods and services market and the money market if that price level were to hold. And the *AS* curve tells us only what income level would have to prevail for there to be equilibrium in the labour market if that price level were to hold.

This lack of correspondence between the microeconomic and macroeconomic curves can be pedagogically disruptive. Textbooks cannot correctly refer to the *AS* curve as telling us what aggregate output would be supplied for a given price, and cannot correctly interpret the difference between the *AD* and *AS* curves as the level of excess aggregate demand, for example. It seems as though students' familiarity with microeconomic supply and demand analysis cannot be exploited.

How do textbook authors deal with this problem? Remarkably, most authors ignore this problem and treat the *AS* and *AD* curves as though they can be defined and interpreted just like their microeconomic counterparts! This is not done by mistake – these authors know that they are not defining and using the *AS* and *AD* curves correctly. They do this deliberately, in the belief that more important macroeconomic concepts will be better understood if students are shielded from these technical details. Colander (1995) has termed this phenomenon "dirty pedagogy".

This is a straightforward application of economic cost-benefit analysis, but to my knowledge there exists no empirical evidence one way or the other on this matter. The fact that a majority of textbook authors have consciously chosen to gloss over the technical differences between the aggregate and microeconomic curves offers some indirect evidence on this issue, but it would be nice to have some student opinion.

In a modest effort to address this issue I surveyed 21 economics graduate students who had had at least two semesters of graduate study, including a graduate course in macroeconomics. This is a "convenience" sample with a small sample size and so should not be taken too seriously, but I believe the results are indicative. Graduate students were chosen because of Colander's belief (p.174) that it would be the better students who might have trouble with the unexplained differences. The survey questionaire is reproduced in the Appendix.

The first question on the survey asked students if their undergraduate text had glossed over the difference between the *AS* and *AD* curves and their microeconomic counterparts, i.e., used dirty pedagogy. The second question asked if they believed that their learning was helped, hindered or unaffected by the character of their textbook exposition. Of the 17 students whose textbook used dirty pedagogy, 12 felt their learning was unaffected, 3 felt that it was hindered and 2 felt that it was helped. Of the 4 students whose textbooks did not use dirty pedagogy, 3 felt their learning was unaffected and 1 felt that it was hindered.

Of the very good students (i.e., potential graduate students) whom Colander believes might be affected by dirty pedagogy, most are unaffected. (It should be noted, though, that if Colander is correct the students whose understanding was hindered may have switched to another major and thus be selected out of this sample!) A small number are helped and a small number hindered. The written comments explaining why they were helped or hindered proved not to be of value. An uncharitable intepretation of these comments is that those who were helped or hindered could not say why. Of the small number of students in the sample who were not exposed to dirty pedagogy, no one claims to have been helped by this.

I conclude from these results that there are very, very few good students whose learning is hindered by dirty pedagogy, and these are offset by a roughly equal number of good students whose learning is helped. Furthermore, there is nothing to suggest that switching away from dirty pedagogy will help these students' learning. Looking just at the very good students, I find the case for abandoning dirty pedagogy less than convincing. In contrast, my casual experience with the vast majority of students suggests that these less able students are not harmed by dirty pedagogy, and that forcing these students to wrestle with the distinction between the macro and micro supply and demand curves is disruptive to their understanding of more-important dimensions of macroeconomics.

7.5 DYNAMICS

The *ADAS* model as written out in most textbooks is a comparative static model with no explicit dynamics in its algebraic formulation, as illustrated for example by Rao (1991, p.266). Consequently, the *AS* and *AD* curves simply reflect potential equilibria associated with these algebraic equations. But the interesting macroeconomic issues, schools of thought, policy implications, empirical results are much more closely associated with dynamics attached to this model than with its equilibrium representation. Consequently, the actual use of the *ADAS* diagram in macroeconomic analysis is as a foundation to which different dynamic specifications are added, in an effort to analyse as realistically as possible the actual behavior of the macroeconomy. Colander refers to this as "storytelling".

A typical such story begins with the economy in full long run equilibrium and then it is subjected to a shock such as an increase in government spending. The *AD* curve shifts to the right creating a situation in which the economy's actual position is off the new *AD* curve, implying a disequilibrium. This creates forces for change, but not necessarily forces that push the economy quickly and smoothly to a new equilibrium. The money, bond and foreign exchange markets are usually assumed to clear very quickly, so being off the *AD* curve is thought to correspond to excess demand disequilibrium in the goods and services market (a disequilibrium whose current magnitude is not accurately pictured by the gap between *AS* and *AD* at the prevailing price, because the rightward shift of *AD* incorporates the multiplier phenomenon). The excess demand causes the price level to rise, disrupting equilibrium in the labour market. A story is now told about how the labour market reacts to this disequilibrium, involving information problems causing misperceptions about the real wage, and implicit or explicit contracts inhibiting wage flexibility. These short run phenomena cause the economy to slide up the short run *AS* curve and at the same time shift this curve upwards as wages and price level expectations change. Since the short run *AS* curve is designed to reflect possible short run equilibria in the labour market, it is usually postulated to shift so as always to capture the economy's actual position; in the long run the economy returns to the long run *AS* curve, typically drawn as a vertical line at the natural rate of unemployment. Complications such as hysterisis could shift the long run *AS* curve, but it remains such that whenever the economy is off this curve there should be a disequilibrium somewhere which will cause further change. The art of storytelling is to articulate these disequilibrium forces in a convincing fashion. Competing schools of thought tell these stories in different ways, the New Classicals by emphasizing information problems and the New Keynesians by stressing price and wage rigidities, for example.

These dynamic specifications are not easy to formulate. Judgements must be made on issues such as price-adjusting versus quantity-adjusting markets, notional versus actual demands, temporary versus permanent equilibria, speed of multiplier operation and modeling of expectations. The role of the *ADAS* diagram is to serve as a common foundation to facilitate exposition and comparison of dynamic specifications. If it does not serve this function as well as an alternative, it should be supplanted by that alternative. Complaints about the *ADAS* diagram should be viewed from this perspective.

The recent controversy about *ADAS*, as in Colander (1995) and in Nevile and Rao (1996) for example, is focused primarily on dynamics and so complains not about the foundation *ADAS* model but rather about ways in which that model has been extended to incorporate different dynamic specifications. It may be that the *ADAS* model is not the best foundation to use for this purpose, and the alternatives offered by these critics, such as Colander's involving the "co-ordination-augmented production function," look interesting. But to date these alternatives seem to me to be too complicated to be useful for lower-level textbook exposition; I predict the *ADAS* diagram will continue its reign as the textbook favorite. I also predict that the expectations-augmented Phillips curve will continue its reign as the curve of choice for expositing the infamous inflation and unemployment trade-off. This prediction flows from, and reinforces, the previous prediction: the expectations augmented Phillips curve, and its long run version, vertical at the natural rate of unemployment, are isomorphic to the short and long run *AS* curves, with the inflation rate rather than the price level on the vertical axis.

7.6 CONCLUSION

When I was first introduced to *AD* and *AS* curves my reaction was that they were too complicated to use as a vehicle for expositing macroeconomics to undergraduate students. Then when I learned that textbooks were adopting this diagram while leading students to believe they could be interpreted in the same way we interpret microeconomic curves, I was appalled. This was wrong, I thought, and therefore should not be done! As an economist I should have known better than to react this way. Telling little white lies can be the right thing to do if the benefits outweigh the costs. I am forever grateful that in high school I was taught Euclidean geometry rather than a more-correct geometry that incorporates the curvature of the earth. And so I have come to believe that *AS* and *AD* curves are suitable for undergraduate textbooks.

Appendix to Chapter 7: Survey Instrument

The *ADAS* diagram is a popular means of teaching macroeconomic phenomena. The *AS* and *AD* curves are "equilibrium curves," the former consisting of combinations of price and income corresponding to equilibrium in the labour market and the latter consisting of combinations of price and income corresponding to simultaneous equilibrium in the money and the goods and services markets. As such, they cannot legitimately be treated as though they are similar to microeconomic supply and demand curves.

But most textbooks do treat these curves as though they are similar to microeconomic curves, for example by measuring excess demand as the difference between *AD* and *AS*, or by defining the *AS* curve as giving the output an economy will produce for each price level. Textbook authors are fully aware that they are "cheating" by doing this, but defend it on the grounds that teaching students the technically-correct interpretation of the *AS* and *AD* curves inhibits their learning of more-important macroeconomic concepts. This phenomenon has been termed "dirty pedagogy".

I ask you now to look back on your own experience as an undergraduate student learning principles of macroeconomics and intermediate macroeconomics.

1. Did your textbooks "gloss over" the conceptual difference between the *AS* and *AD* curves and their microeconomic counterparts?

Yes...... go to question 2a

No...... go to question 2b

2a. Do you believe that your learning of macroeconomics was helped, hindered or unaffected by this glossing over?

Helped...... Hindered...... Unaffected......

2b. Do you believe that your learning of macroeconomics was helped, hindered or unaffected by your textbook not glossing over these differences?

Helped...... Hindered...... Unaffected......

3. If your answer to question 2a or 2b was "helped" or "hindered," please provide an example to explain your answer.

8 Theoretical Inconsistencies in the ADAS Model: Can the Model be Rehabilitated?*

T. Windsor Fields and William R. Hart

8.1 INTRODUCTION

The aggregate demand and aggregate supply model is the dominant pedagogical device in virtually all intermediate macroeconomic textbooks. Central to this textbook model is the conventional aggregate demand (AD) curve derived from the $ISLM$ framework. Price-induced changes in the real money supply shift the LM curve along an unchanging IS curve (absent a real balance effect) and map out levels of output at which aggregate demand and real output are equal. The resulting AD curve is then paired with an aggregate supply (AS) curve, derived from the labour market and a production function, to determine the equilibrium price level and rate of output.[1]

* We would like to thank Ingo Barens, Robert Clower, David Colander, George Davis, Kirk Elwood, Richard Moody, and Michael Parkin for helpful comments on earlier drafts of this chapter. Any remaining errors are our own.

[1] Most of the leading macroeconomic textbooks employ this approach, which we refer to as the "textbook" model. These texts include Abel and Bernanke (1994), Dornbusch and Fischer (1994), Froyen (1993), Gordon (1993), Hall and Taylor (1993), and Mankiw (1994). The conventional AD curve in the textbooks is *(continued)*

We argue in this chapter that the textbook *ADAS* model is internally inconsistent in at least two important respects.[2] First, the textbook *AD* curve is not a true demand curve but rather a "market equilibrium" curve derived under the assumption that output supplied is perfectly elastic with respect to changes in demand. Clearly, the behavioral response of firms implicit in this derivation is inconsistent with the behavioral response implied by a vertical (long run) or upward-sloping (short run) *AS* curve when the goods market is out of equilibrium.

The second inconsistency is that the textbook *ADAS* model appears to demonstrate, via partial equilibrium analysis, that the price level is determined in the goods market while the interest rate is determined in the money market. In fact, something approaching the opposite is true.[3] The textbook equation for aggregate demand, for example, indicates very clearly that, absent a real balance effect, the quantity of goods demanded is independent of the price level. And while the quantity of goods supplied may depend on the price level in the short run, it is fully independent of price in the long run. The implication of this pair of facts is that the price level plays no role, in the long run, in equilibrating the goods market. It is, in fact, the interest rate, not the price level, that clears the goods market in

based on the "Keynes' effect (described above). There are, however, several alternative justifications for a downward-sloping *AD* curve. Some textbook authors, for example, refer to the real balance effect on consumption spending as the price level falls. Others rely on the terms of trade effect on net exports (implicitly or explicitly holding the exchange rate constant) to motivate a negatively-sloped *AD* curve. Some authors use all three effects. What we refer to in this chapter as the "conventional" *AD* is derived exclusively using the Keynes effect.

[2] Hall and Treadgold (1982) and Rabin and Birch (1982) were among the earliest critics of the textbook *ADAS* model. More recent attacks include Barro (1994), Clower (1993, 1994), Colander (1993, 1995), Fields and Hart (1990), Nevile and Rao (1996) and Rao (1991).

[3] Among intermediate macroeconomic theory textbooks, a significant exception to this inconsistency is Barro (1993).

the textbook model, although one would be hard pressed to find this stated explicitly in the leading texts. Conversely, it is not difficult to show, in a general equilibrium context, that it is the price level, not the interest rate, which clears the money market.

We organise this chapter as follows. Section 2 provides a brief overview of the textbook *ADAS* model. Because our primary focus is on the textbook *ADAS* model and not on the various competing (short run) theories of aggregate supply, the analysis is carried out using the classical (or long run) *ADAS* model in which wages and prices are flexible and economic agents have perfect information. The classical model is common to virtually all macroeconomic textbooks, and it's use allows us to avoid numerous complications which only serve to detract from our primary objective. In section 3, we examine the conventional *AD* curve and show that it is internally inconsistent with the classical *AS* curve and, by logical extension, with all textbook *AS* curves. We then respecify the *AD* to eliminate this inconsistency and contrast the respecified curve with the conventional curve. An important difference between the two is that output supplied is a shift parameter in the respecified *AD* curve but not in the conventional *AD* curve. In section 4, we pair our respecified *AD* curve with the classical *AS* curve to form a theoretically consistent *ADAS* model and consider the usefulness of this model as a pedagogical device. Section 5 briefly addresses the complications that arise when the *AD* curve is derived to be consistent with an upward-sloping (short run) *AS* curve. Finally, in section 6 we show that, contrary to the impression given by the textbook *ADAS* model, the interest rate is determined in the goods market while the price level is determined in the money market. We present an alternative, "Barro-like", *ADAS* model consistent with this point of view and compare the general equilibrium properties of the two approaches. It turns out that the two approaches yield identical general equilibrium results. What is dissimilar in the two approaches, however, is that each implies a different "story" of the economy's adjustment from one general equilibrium to another following a disturbance. We discuss this difference and conclude that the textbook *ADAS* model may be pedagogically defensible because it tells a better, or more convincing, story.

8.2 THE TEXTBOOK ADAS MODEL

The conventional *AS* curve implied by the classical model is vertical at the natural level of output y_1^* because employment and, hence, output supplied are independent of the price level in the long run (and in the short run as well in the classical model). Algebraically, the classical *AS* curve can be expressed as:

$$y^s = y_1^* \tag{1}$$

The textbook aggregate demand curve is a downward-sloping function of the price level and is derived from the following standard *ISLM* model:

$$y^d = c(y^s) + i(r) + g \tag{2}$$

$$(M/P) = m^d(y^s, r) \tag{3}$$

where y^s is aggregate supply (all of which ultimately accrues to households in the form of income), y^d is aggregate demand, r is the interest rate, g is government purchases of goods and services, M is the nominal money supply, and P is the price level. Desired real consumption and investment expenditures are represented by $c(y^s)$ and $i(r)$, respectively, while $m^d(y^s, r)$ is the demand for real money balances. The response of aggregate demand to a change in price (i.e., the *AD* curve) is derived by totally differentiating equations (2) and (3) with respect to P, solving equation (3) for dr/dP and substituting the result into equation (2). This yields:

$$\frac{dy^d}{dP} = \frac{\partial c}{\partial y^s}\left[\frac{dy^s}{dP}\right] - \frac{\partial m^d}{\partial y^s}\left[\frac{\partial i/\partial r}{\partial m^d/\partial r}\right]\left[\frac{dy^s}{dP}\right] - \left[\frac{\partial i/\partial r}{\partial m^d/\partial r}\right]\left[\frac{M}{P^2}\right] \tag{4}$$

It is helpful to think of equation (4) as a generic AD curve awaiting some assumption regarding the response of aggregate supply to a change in P. The conventional AD curve is really a specialised version of equation (4) in which it is assumed that output supplied is perfectly elastic with respect to aggregate demand. Thus, the assumption underlying the conventional AD curve is that $dy^s/dP = dy^d/dP$.[4] Substituting this result into equation (4) and solving for dy^d/dP yields the slope of the conventional AD curve:

$$\frac{dy^d}{dP} = \frac{-\left[\dfrac{\partial i/\partial r}{\partial m^d/\partial r}\right]\left[\dfrac{M}{P^2}\right]}{(1-\partial c/\partial y^s)+\left[\dfrac{\partial m^d}{\partial y^s}\right]\left[\dfrac{\partial i/\partial r}{\partial m^d/\partial r}\right]} \tag{5}$$

which is unambiguously negative.[5]

When the AD curve is paired with its companion AS curve, we see, in Figure 8.1, that there is only one price level, P_1, at which the goods market will be in equilibrium. At a price higher than P_1, there is an excess supply of goods which causes the price level to fall. The fall in price results in a movement down the AD curve until equilibrium is restored at P_1. Just the opposite occurs if the price level is

[4] Perfect elasticity of aggregate output supplied with respect to aggregate output demanded, or "demand creates its own supply," is what Clower (1993) has referred to as "Hansen's Law." More generally, this assumption underlies the Keynesian "multiplier" process.

[5] The intuition behind this result is straightforward. A decrease in the price level raises the real money supply and creates an excess supply of money balances at the initial interest rate. This causes the interest rate to decline which raises the investment component of aggregate demand. The numerator of equation (5) captures this direct effect. The direct effect is then augmented by the multiplier process as captured by the denominator of equation (5). Specifically, consumption expenditures respond positively to the assumed increase in aggregate supply (i.e., real income) which, after some crowding out through the money market, serves to further increase aggregate demand.

too low. Thus, according to the textbook *ADAS* model, the price level falls when there is excess supply of goods and rises when there is an excess demand for goods. That is, the price level is seen as the variable which adjusts to equilibrate the goods market.

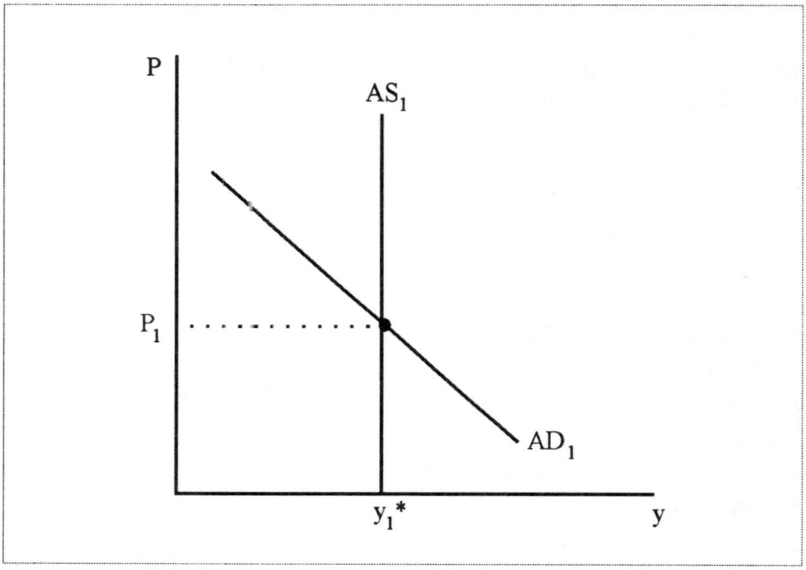

Figure 8.1

8.3 THE AGGREGATE DEMAND CURVE [6]

Equation (4) forcefully illustrates the dependence of aggregate demand on the supply side of the economy. In light of this dependence, the *AD* curve should be derived in a manner consistent with the supply response embedded in the *AS* curve with which it is eventually paired. Clearly the conventional *AD* curve, as captured by equation (5), does not meet this consistency test. The classical *AS* curve,

[6] Some of the analysis presented in this section draws from Fields and Hart (1990).

equation (1), indicates that output supplied is equal to y_1^* at every price. The conventional *AD* curve, by contrast, is derived under the assumption that output supplied is perfectly elastic with respect to output demanded at every price, i.e., $dy^s/dP = dy^d/dP$ in equation (4). But this necessarily implies that output supplied rises in response to a decrease in the price level and falls in response to an increase in the price level. Obviously, this is a serious inconsistency. A decrease in the price level cannot cause real output to remain unchanged (as implied by the classical *AS* curve) and rise (as implied by the conventional *AD* curve) at the same time![7]

What is missing in the derivation of the conventional *AD* curve is proper consideration of the role played by aggregate supply when the goods market is out of equilibrium. To derive an *AD* curve that is consistent with the supply side of the economy in the classical model, we propose an alternative, or respecified, *AD* curve that is based on the supply response implied by the classical *AS* curve. Since this *AS* curve is vertical the relevant supply response is $dy^s/dP = 0$ which, when substituted into equation (4), yields the slope of the *AD* curve implied by the classical model:

$$\frac{dy^d}{dP} = -\left[\frac{\partial i/\partial r}{\partial m^d/\partial r}\right]\left[\frac{M}{P^2}\right] < 0 \qquad (6)$$

With output supplied, hence household income, constant at every price, the response of aggregate demand to a change in price is limited to the direct (interest-induced) impact on investment expenditures. This impact effect is identical to the numerator of equation (5). Comparing equation (6) with equation (5), it is clear that our respecified *AD*

[7] Notice that this inconsistency cannot be removed by postulating a positively-sloped *AS* curve (e.g., one of the several varieties of the "Lucas-type" short run *AS* curves). In this case, a rise in *P* (or at least an unexpected rise in P) causes output supplied to be higher. At the same time, the conventional *AD* curve assumes that output supplied is lower.

curve is steeper than the conventional AD curve.[8] Intuitively, this is because the multiplier process that reinforces the direct effect of a change in price in the conventional AD curve is necessarily absent in the respecified AD curve. In the discussion that follows, we consider some of the major differences between the two AD curves.

First, it should be evident that the conventional AD curve is not a "true" aggregate demand curve. Instead, it is a curve that shows what aggregate supply *would have to be* at every price in order to make aggregate demand equal real output. And since the number of goods demanded is different at every price, it follows that output supplied varies along the conventional AD curve. This is in direct contrast to our respecified AD curve along which aggregate supply is constant (at y_1^*) at all points along the curve. Therefore, a primary difference between a properly specified AD curve and the conventional AD curve is that output is a shift parameter in the former but not the latter. An increase in y^* raises household income and causes consumption to rise by the marginal propensity to consume times the increase in y^*. Other things the same, this increases aggregate demand at every price and shifts the respecified AD curve to the right. At the same time, the increase in y^* raises the demand for money, thereby creating an excess demand for money balances. This raises the interest rate in the money market and causes investment demand to fall. *Ceteris paribus,* this lowers aggregate demand at every price and shifts the respecified AD curve left. Because we do not know *a priori* which effect is larger (in absolute value), the shift in AD is ambiguous. If, as seems reasonable, we assume that the rise in consumption is greater than the decline in investment then the net effect of a rise in y^* will be to shift the respecified AD curve to the right.

Another important difference between the two AD curves lies in the effect of changes in g and M. A change in g or

[8] This assumes that the basic multiplier, given by the denominator of equation (5), is greater than 1.0 in the conventional case.

M will shift both curves in the horizontal direction, but the magnitude of the shifts are quite different. For example, a bond-financed increase in g shifts the respecified AD curve to the right by the change in g. There is no multiplier effect because output supplied (and therefore household income) is constant. By contrast, with the conventional AD curve the shift is:

$$\left\{1/\left[\left(1-\partial c/\partial y^s\right)+\frac{\partial i/\partial r}{\partial m^d/\partial r}\left(\partial m^d/\partial y^s\right)\right]\right\}\, dg$$

or the change in g times the multiplier. Similarly, an increase in M shifts the respecified AD curve horizontally by only:

$$\left[\frac{\partial i/\partial r}{\partial m^d/\partial r}\right]\left[\frac{dM}{P}\right]$$

whereas in the conventional case the shift is:

$$\left\{\left[\frac{\partial i/\partial r}{\partial m^d/\partial r}\right]/\left(1-\partial c/\partial y^s\right)+\frac{\partial i/\partial r}{\partial m^d/\partial r}\left(\partial m^d/\partial y^s\right)\right]\right\}\left[\frac{dM}{P}\right].$$

In both cases the horizontal shifts are smaller using the respecified AD curve because, unlike the conventional AD curve, it incorporates the appropriate supply response – namely, that output supplied is constant at y^*.

Finally, the textbook $ADAS$ model does not give the correct measure of excess demand or supply when the goods market is out of equilibrium. To illustrate, consider Figure 8.2 in which the conventional AD curve, AD_C, and the respecified AD curve, AD_R, are paired with the classical AS curve. Both AD_C and AD_R must intersect the AS curve at the same price level, P_1 in this case, since AD_R assumes $y^s = y_1^*$ throughout and the point at which AD_C crosses the AS curve must be the point on AD_C at which output supplied is assumed to be y_1^*.

At a price level below P_1, say P_0, the excess demand for goods (EDG) is $y_2 - y_1^*$ according to the respecified AD curve, whereas with the conventional AD curve the EDG is $y_3 - y_1^*$. However, $y_3 - y_1^*$ is not the correct measure of EDG. Because the conventional AD curve assumes that output responds

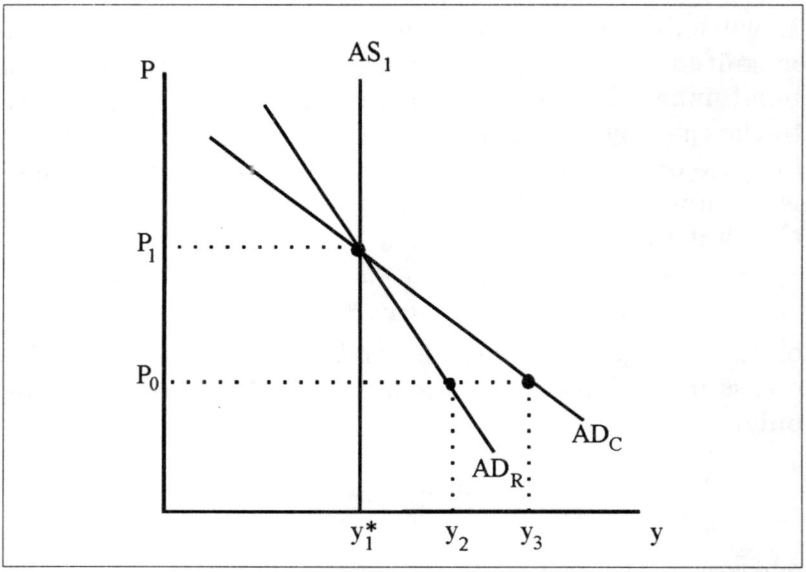

Figure 8.2

passively to demand, y_3 is the number of goods demanded when output supplied is also equal to y_3. Thus the distance $y_3 - y_1^*$ does not show by how much the level of output at which the quantity of goods demanded exceeds the quantity supplied at P_0. Instead, $y_3 - y_1^*$ shows by how much the level of output at which the quantity of goods demanded equals the quantity supplied at P_0 exceeds y_1^*. By contrast, the distance $y_2 - y_1^*$ is a correct measure of EDG at P_0 since y_2 is the number of goods demanded at P_0 given real income y_1^*.[9]

8.4 A THEORETICALLY CONSISTENT ADAS MODEL

Figure 8.3A, illustrates a theoretically consistent *ADAS* model.[10] The aggregate supply curve (AS_1) is vertical at

---

[9] This point has been made earlier by Rabin and Birch (1982).

[10] There have been other attempts to derive theoretically *(continued)*

natural output y_1^*. The aggregate demand curve is derived to be consistent with the supply-side response implied by AS_1 (i.e., $dy^s/dP = 0$). As a reminder that output is constant at y_1^* at all points along the curve, the aggregate demand curve is labeled $AD_1(y_1^*)$. Goods market equilibrium occurs at point A where the price level is P_1 and output is y_1^*. Figure 8.3B depicts the textbook version of the money market. Given the nominal money supply M_1 (exogenously determined) and price level P_1, the money supply curve is vertical at (M_1/P_1). The money demand curve is a downward-sloping function of the interest rate and is derived by holding output constant, at y_1^* in this case, and plotting the inverse relationship between real money demand and the interest rate. Equilibrium is at point A where the interest rate is r_1. The curves are drawn such that this initial equilibrium in the money market is consistent with the goods market.

We believe that this internally consistent *ADAS* model is superior to the textbook *ADAS* model in at least three important respects. First, the dynamic adjustment in response to a demand-side shock is theoretically consistent in this model since the excess demands and supplies are properly measured. This is not the case with the textbook *ADAS* model. We saw earlier, for example, that an increase in the money supply implies a rightward shift in the conventional

---

consistent *ADAS* models. Hall and Treadgold (1982) use a "kinked" or "backward L" aggregate supply curve to generate the output responses to a change in the price level. The result is an unusual demand curve that has short run characteristics below y_1^* and long run characteristics at y_1^*. Fields and Hart (1990) derive the short run *AD* curve that is implied by a Lucas-type short run *AS* curve. Under this assumption there are an infinite number of short run *AD* curves, each associated with a different expected price level. More recently, Colander (1995) attempts to rehabilitate the textbook model by deriving an *AS* curve that is consistent with the conventional (Keynesian-type) *AD* curve. All of this work stands in direct contrast to Barro (1994), who argues that the textbook *ADAS* model is beyond rehabilitation and should be abandoned.

AD curve equal to:

$$\left\{\left[\frac{\partial i/\partial r}{\partial m^d/\partial r}\right]/\left[\left(1-\partial c/\partial y^s\right)+\frac{\partial i/\partial r}{\partial m^d/\partial r}\left(\partial m^d/\partial y^s\right)\right]\right\}\left[\frac{dM}{P}\right]$$

whereas in the respecified *AD* curve the shift is only

$$\left[\frac{\partial i/\partial r}{\partial m^d/\partial r}\right]\left[\frac{dM}{P}\right].$$

Since output is fixed at y_1^*, the impact effect implied by the textbook *ADAS* model is obviously incorrect. But this means that the dynamic adjustment path implied by the standard textbook *ADAS* model is quantitatively incorrect as well.

Second, the respecified model is internally consistent in its treatment of demand and supply shocks. Again, this is not the case with the textbook *ADAS* model. It is no wonder that students typically are baffled by the textbook *ADAS* model when told that a change in income (output) shifts the *AS* curve but not the *AD* curve. In this regard, we have found the respecified model to be an easier framework for students to understand. By way of illustration, consider the effect of a supply-side disturbance – say a positive technology shock that shifts (and rotates) the short run production function upwards and raises natural output. Figure 8.4 reproduces the goods and money market from Figures 8.3A and 8.3B. The initial general equilibrium position for the economy corresponds to the set of points labeled *A*. A positive technology shock raises output from y_1^* to y_2^* and shifts the aggregate supply curve from AS_1 to AS_2. The rise in y^* also raises household income (by the change in y^*) and causes consumption expenditures to increase by the marginal propensity to consume (*mpc*) times the increase in household income. Other things the same, this shifts the (respecified) *AD* curve right. Of course, other things are not the same because the rise in y^* also raises the demand for money. This shifts the money demand curve right to $m^d(y_2^*)$, creates an excess demand for money balances, and causes

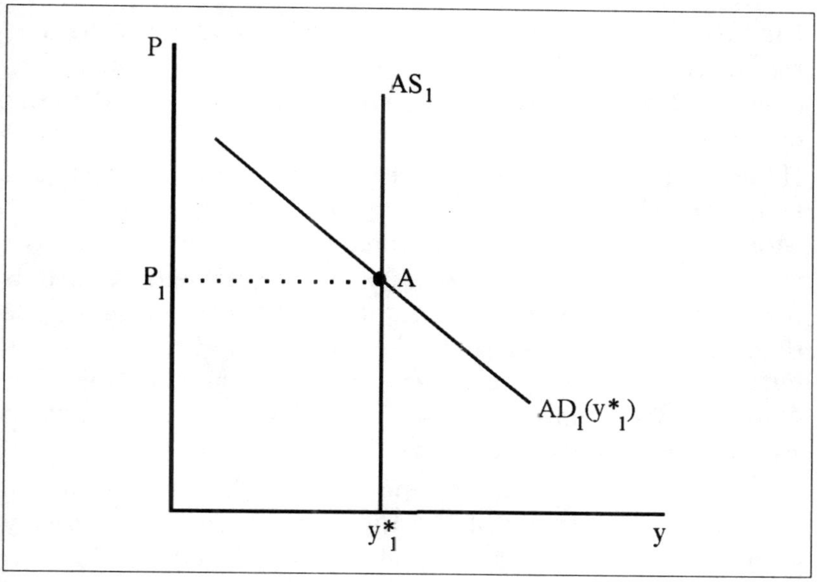

Figure 8.3A

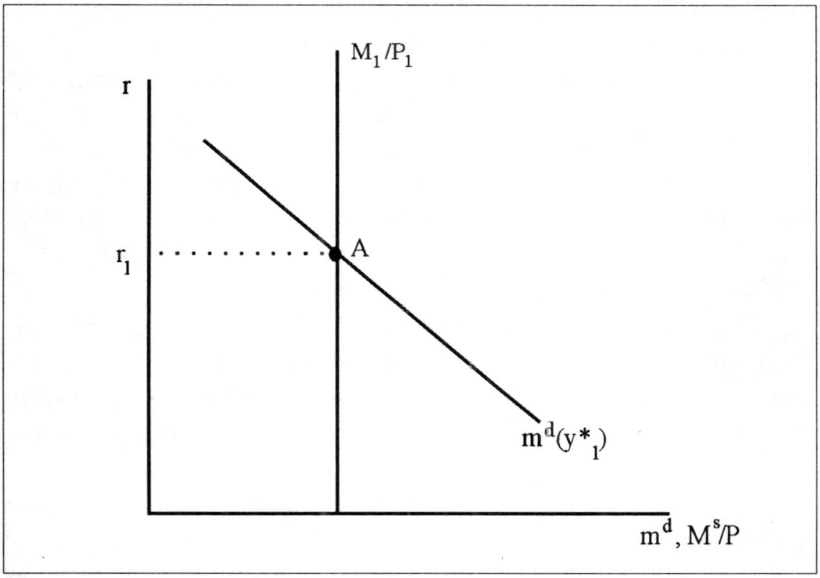

Figure 8.3B

the interest rate to rise (temporarily) to r_2 at point B. The rise in the interest rate then causes investment demand to decline. *Ceteris paribus,* this shifts the aggregate demand curve to the left.

If $\Delta c > |\Delta i|$, and we assume that it is, the net effect is a rightward shift in the aggregate demand curve to $AD_2(y_2^*)$. Moreover, since consumption demand rises by less that the rise in y^* (because the $mpc < 1$) and investment falls, it is necessarily the case that the rightward shift in the aggregate demand curve is less than the rightward shift in the AS curve. The result is an excess supply in the goods market equal to $y_2^* - y_2$ that causes the price level to fall from P_1 to P_0 where equilibrium is restored at point C.[11]

Returning to the money market, the decline in price to P_0 increases the real money supply, which shifts the money supply curve right to M_1/P_0, and causes the equilibrium interest rate to fall to r_0 at point C. How can we be sure of this result? In the new general equilibrium, the total demand for goods must equal the higher level of output y_2^*. Since consumption demand does not rise by the full amount of the increase in aggregate supply and since government spending is unchanged, investment must rise to pick up the slack. But this will only happen if the equilibrium interest rate falls (which is exactly what happens as the price level declines). In fact, the interest rate in the final general equilibrium (r_0) must be lower than the interest rate in the initial equilibrium (r_1) so long as $mpc < 1$.

Third, it is comparatively easy to incorporate more realistic (and sophisticated) theories of the components of aggregate demand into the respecified model and to examine alternative views of the effects of various economic shocks.

[11] The perceptive reader will notice that the conventional AD curve passes through points A and C in Figure 8.4A. Consequently, the textbook $ADAS$ model implies the same general equilibrium result as the respecified model. Our contention, however, is that the failure of the conventional AD curve to shift in response to a change in income when the mpc is clearly nonzero is very confusing to students.

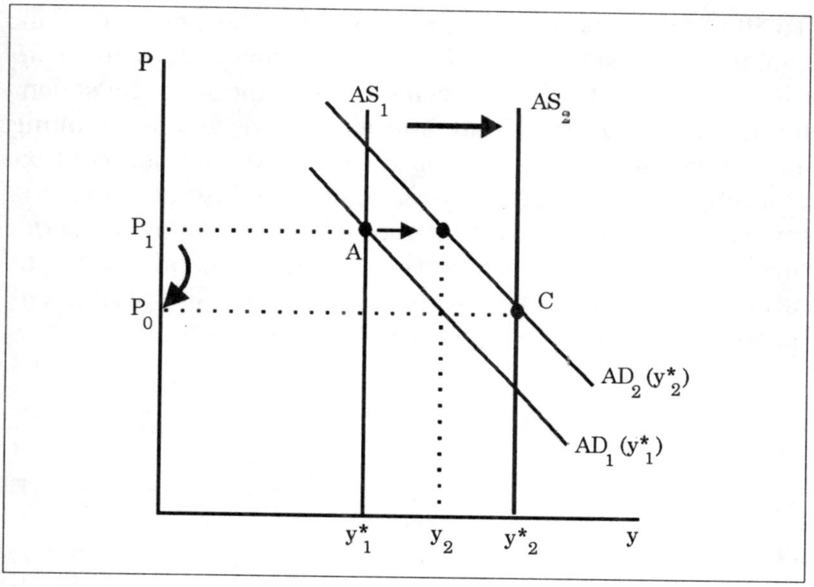

Figure 8.4A

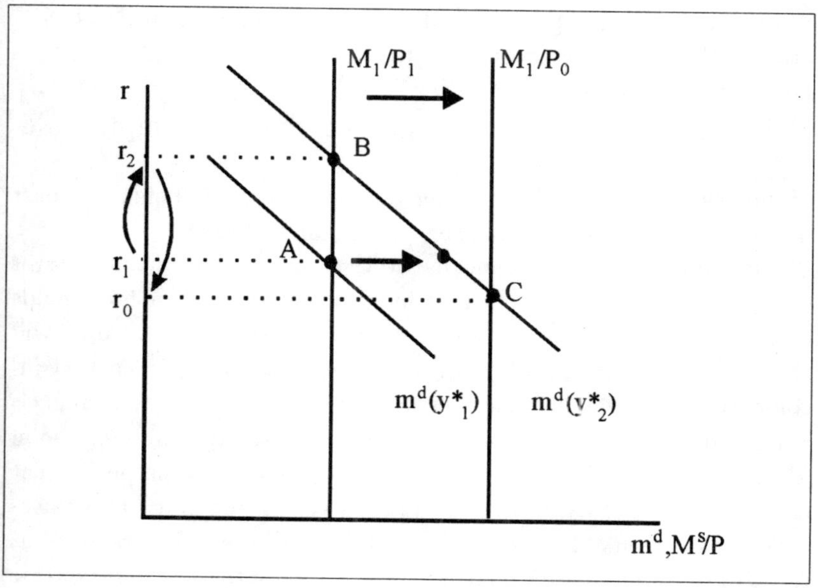

Figure 8.4B

To illustrate but one example consider the permanent income hypothesis (PIH). It is straightforward to incorporate the PIH into the respecified $ADAS$ model. The salient feature of the PIH is that households are forward looking and make their consumption decisions within the context of a long run planning horizon that takes into account current and expected future income. Permanent income is defined as the level of income that could be sustained indefinitely given lifetime resources. Mathematically, permanent income can be derived from the following formula:

$$y_t^* + \frac{y_{t+1}^*}{(1+r)} + \frac{y_{t+2}^*}{(1+r)^2} + \cdots + \frac{y_{t+n}^*}{(1+r)^n} = y_p + \frac{y_p}{(1+r)} + \frac{y_p}{(1+r)^2} + \cdots + \frac{y_p}{(1+r)^n} \quad (7)$$

where y_t^* is income in period t, y_{t+i}^* is expected income in period $t+i$, and y_p is permanent income as of period t.[12] The LHS of equation (7) is the present value of lifetime resources. Thus, permanent income is the (hypothetical) constant income stream having the same present value as the expected income stream.[13]

What effect does the assumption that consumption de-

---

[12] For simplicity, we are ignoring the fact that households pay part of their income to the government in the form of taxes.

[13] Of course, this does not mean that permanent income never changes. If, for example, current income changes and/or households revise their estimates of future income, then permanent income will change accordingly. In addition, the effect of a change in current income on permanent income will depend on whether that change is perceived to be permanent or temporary. For example, an increase in y_t^* of, say, one unit that is perceived by households to be permanent raises each term on the LHS of equation (7) by one unit. This raises permanent income by one unit as well. If, however, the rise in y_t^* is temporary (a one-period increase say) then only the first term on the LHS of equation (7) rises. In this case permanent income rises, but by substantially less than one unit because the temporary increase in income is spread out over the household's lifetime.

pends on permanent income have on the respecified *AD* curve? The answer is that it has no effect on the slope, but the shift parameter becomes permanent income instead of y_t^*. Since the *AD* curve is still derived in a manner that is consistent with the supply response implied by the classical *AS* curve, it follows that the effect of a change in price on the quantity of goods demanded is still limited to its impact on investment demand. Permanent income now replaces y_t^*, however, as the shift parameter in the respecified *AD* curve, implying that a change in y_t^* will shift the respecified *AD* curve only to the extent that it affects permanent income.

Suppose we are willing to assume, as a first approximation, that the marginal propensity to consume out of permanent income, denoted $mpc(y_p)$, is equal to 1. Given this, a one unit increase in current income that is expected to be permanent raises consumption by one unit and shifts the *AD* curve to the right by one unit. If, however, the one-unit increase in current income is expected to be temporary, then consumption will rise and the *AD* curve will shift right by less than one unit, perhaps by much less than one unit. In this way students are led to consider that changes in current income can have very different effects on aggregate demand depending on how households view the permanence of the change. An extension of this approach to fiscal policy and the differential impacts of permanent and temporary changes in taxes is straightforward.

Let's now reconsider the macroeconomic consequences of a supply-side shock when consumption depends on permanent income rather than current income. In Figure 8.5A the economy is initially in general equilibrium at the set of points marked *A*. Suppose that a supply shock raises real output by one unit, shifting the *AS* curve right from AS_1 to AS_2. If households perceive this increase to be permanent then consumption rises by one unit as well (since we continue to assume that $mpc(y_p) = 1$). *Ceteris paribus*, this shifts the *AD* curve to the right by one unit. In the money market, the increase in y_1^* raises the demand for money and shifts the money demand curve to $m^d(y_1^* + 1)$. This causes a (temporary) rise in the interest rate to r_2 at point B. The rise in r then causes investment to fall which dampens the rightward shift in the AD curve caused by the rise in consumption. Thus, the net effect is that the AD curve shifts right, to $AD_2(y_1^* + 1)$ in Figure 8.5A, but by less than the rightward shift in the AS curve. This creates an excess supply of goods that causes the price level to fall from P_1 to P_0 where goods market equilibrium is restored at point C.

Returning to the money market, the decline in the price level to P_0 increases the real money supply, shifts the money supply curve right to (M_1/P_0), and returns the interest rate to its initial level of r_1 at point C. How can we be sure of this result? We know that in the new general equilibrium the total demand for goods must equal the higher aggregate output $(y_1^* + 1)$. And since this rise in output is permanent and $mpc(y_p) = 1$, consumption must rise by exactly one unit. But if consumption spending absorbs all of the additional output, investment spending must remain unchanged. This can happen only if the equilibrium interest rate is unchanged.

What if the supply shock is temporary? In all essential respects, the macroeconomic consequences of a temporary supply shock are identical to the earlier example (captured in Figures 8.4A and 8.4B) in which it was assumed that consumption depends on current income with the $mpc(y) < 1$. A one-unit, temporary rise in y_t^* raises permanent income by less, possibly much less, than one unit. This means that consumption rises by less than one unit as well. Therefore, in final equilibrium, investment spending has to rise to make up the difference. But this will happen only if the interest rate falls.

Needless to say, incorporating the PIH into the model opens the door to a host of other important issues. The Ricardian Equivalence Theorem and temporary vs. permanent changes in government tax and expenditure policies, for example, follow logically from the PIH and are easily addressed using the respecified $ADAS$ model.

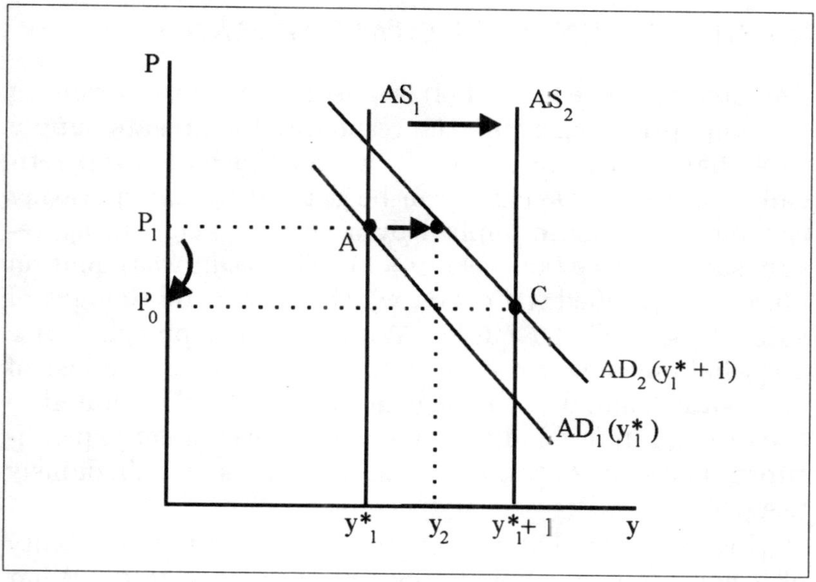

Figure 8.5A

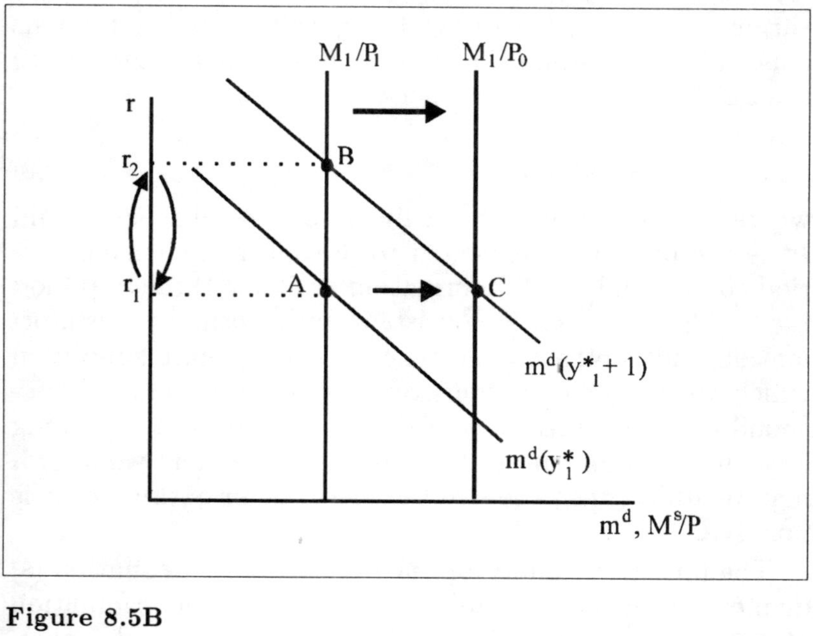

Figure 8.5B

8.5 SHORT RUN AGGREGATE DEMAND

As noted above, equation (4) is a generic *AD* curve awaiting an assumption regarding the response of aggregate supply to a change in P. In section 3, we showed how a theoretically consistent *AD* curve can be derived by incorporating the supply response implied by a vertical long run aggregate supply curve (i.e., $dy^s/dP = 0$). The result was equation (6), our respecified *AD* curve, which can also be thought of as a "long run" *AD* curve. With output supplied, hence household income, constant in the long run, the response of aggregate demand to a change in the price level is limited to the direct, interest-induced, impact on investment expenditures. The slope of this long run *AD* curve is unambiguously negative.

Now, suppose that we were to incorporate the possibility of a nonzero short run supply response for dy^s/dP. What form might this short run response take? Since the primary focus here is on aggregate demand, not on the merits of the various competing theories of aggregate supply, it seems reasonable to assume that output is supplied according to the following Lucas-type function:

$$y^s = y^* + \alpha(P - P^e) \qquad \alpha > 0 \tag{8}$$

where y* continues to be defined as natural output, and P^e is the price level expected to prevail in the current period conditional on all information available through period $t-1$. This equation is consistent with both the misinformation and contract-wage theories of aggregate supply, in which short run deviations of P from P^e generate corresponding departures of y^s from y^* with output returning to y^* in the long run as P^e converges to P. The value of α may be different in the two theories, but in both cases it is positive.

The important point for our purpose is that equation (8) defines the income variable relevant for the determination of desired consumption expenditures and, therefore, aggregate demand in the short run. Suppose, then, that P falls

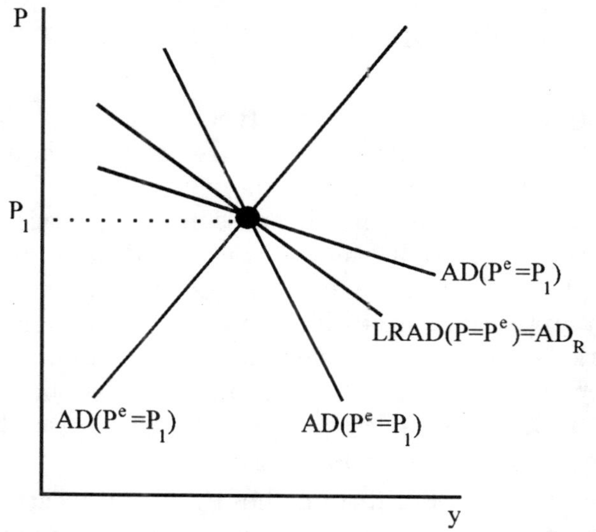

Figure 8.6

holding P^e constant, say at P_1. In addition to the supply response incorporated in the long run AD curve, there are two short run effects working in opposite directions. On the one hand, the decline in P lowers aggregate demand because the resulting decline in income lowers consumption expenditures. On the other hand, the decline in income lowers the demand for money (over and above the decline resulting from the fall in P) which, in turn, lowers the interest rate and increases investment expenditures. Not only might this short run AD curve be steeper or flatter than the long run AD curve, but if the output-induced decline in consumption expenditures is sufficiently large the short run AD curve will be *positively sloped.* These three possible outcomes for the short run AD curve (in relation to the long run AD curve) are illustrated in Figure 8.6. The adjustment dynamics for this short run AD curve as P^e changes can be complicated and would take us too far afield to pursue here.[14]

[14] For a more detailed discussion see Fields and Hart (1990).

8.6 PRICE LEVEL AND INTEREST RATE DETERMINATION IN ADAS MODEL

The textbook *ADAS* model teaches students that the price level is determined in the goods market while the interest rate is determined in the money market. This, however, is most certainly not the case in the classical version of the textbook *ADAS* model considered here. It would seem that this misimpression is the result of excessive concentration on partial equilibrium analysis of the money and goods markets. The former gives the mistaken impression that the interest rate adjusts to equilibrate the money market, the latter the mistaken impression that the price level adjusts to equilibrate the goods market.

In general equilibrium, however, the interest rate is independent of monetary disturbances, leaving only the price level to equilibrate the money market. This, in turn, leaves the interest rate to clear the goods market. To illustrate this important point, consider the general equilibrium effects of a monetary disturbance in the textbook *ADAS* model. Figure 8.7A, illustrates the aggregate demand and aggregate supply curves. Equilibrium initially occurs at point A where the price level is P_1 and output is at its natural level y_1^*. Figure 8.7B illustrates the money demand and supply curves (given an exogenously determined money supply of M_1 and equilibrium output from the goods market of y_1^*). Money market equilibrium occurs at point A where the interest rate is r_1.

Now suppose that the central bank doubles the nominal money supply from M_1 to $M_2 = 2M_1$. The interest rate falls from r_1 to r_0 as the money supply curve shifts right to M_2/P_1. Equilibrium in the money market is restored at point B. In the goods market, the decline in r raises investment demand, shifts the AD curve right from AD_1 to AD_2 and creates an excess demand for goods at the initial price level of P_1. The excess demand for goods causes the price level to rise to P_2 where goods market equilibrium is restored at point C. In the money market, the rise in price

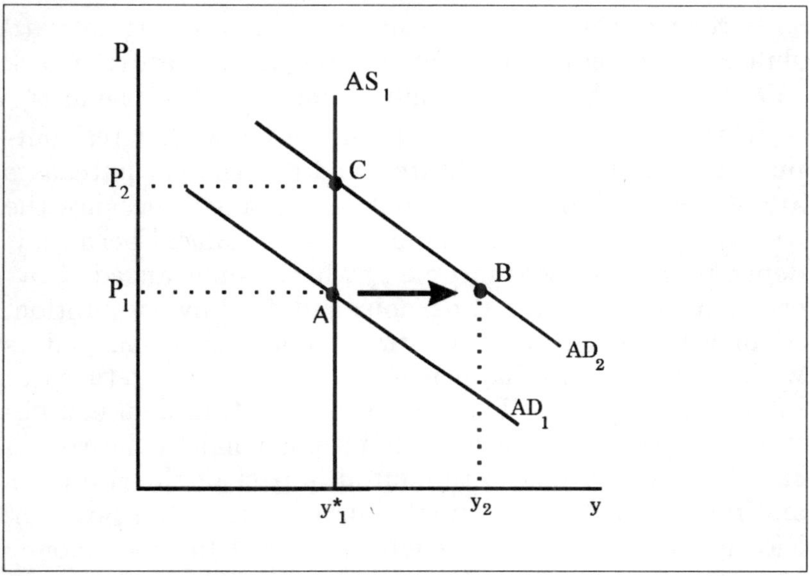

Figure 8.7A

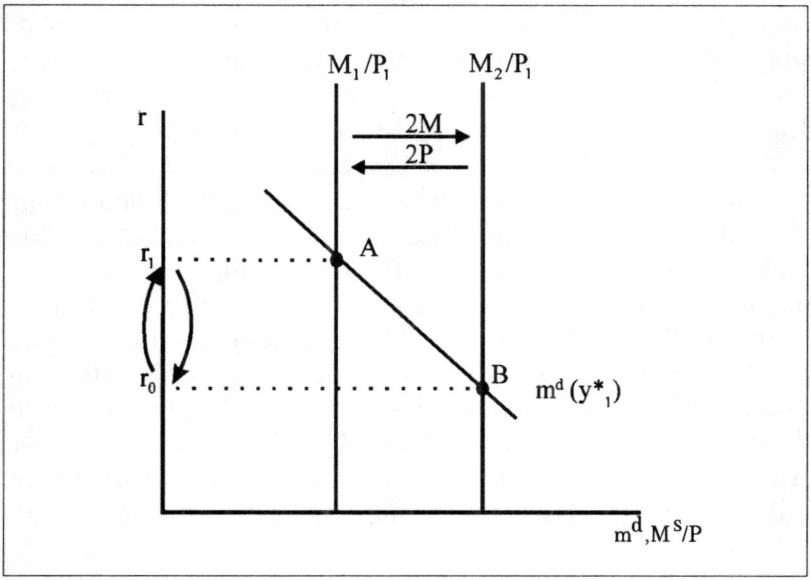

Figure 8.7B

to P_2 reduces the real money supply. The resulting leftward shift in the money supply curve raises the interest rate back to r_1 thereby offsetting the initial impact of the rise in M.

In the new general equilibrium, we know that real output, consumption expenditures, and government purchases are all unchanged. Real output is unchanged because the AS curve is vertical. Consumption is unchanged because it depends on household income y_1^* which is unchanged. Government purchases are exogenous and fixed by assumption. It follows directly that investment must be unchanged as well. But this only happen if the interest rate returns to its initial level of r_1. This also means that, in final equilibrium, the rise in price to P_2 is proportional to the rise in M. This exactly offsets the initial impact of the rise in M and returns the money supply curve to its initial position, leaving no net change in the interest rate.[15] In short, money is neutral, and the quantity theory holds. The critical issue for our purposes is that while we teach this *as if* the price level is adjusting to clear the goods market, it really doesn't happen this way. The rise in the price level from P_1 to P_2 plays no role whatsoever in equilibrating the goods market. Instead, as is evident in Figure 8.7B, the price level, not the interest rate, is adjusting to clear the money market (by offsetting the impact of the rise in M). And if price equilibrates the money market, it necessarily follows that the interest rate is equilibrating the goods market. This fact is evident in the textbook $ADAS$ model, its emphasis on partial equilibrium analysis notwithstanding. Notice in Figure 8.7A that the number of goods demanded starts out at y_1^*, rises to y_2, and then falls back to y_1^*. Why did the number of goods demanded rise? Because the interest rate declined (temporarily) and caused investment to increase. And why did the number of goods demanded return to its initial level y_1^*? Because the interest rate returned to its

---

[15] In all essential respects, the general equilibrium effects of an exogenous change in money demand would be the same. That is, after the economy has fully adjusted, y^*, c, i and r are all unchanged.

initial level, causing investment to return to its initial level as well. In short, the interest rate adjusts to clear the goods market.[16]

What difference does this make for the analytical development of the *ADAS* model? The most obvious difference is that the *AD* and *AS* curves should really be plotted against the interest rate, not the price level, and that money supply and money demand curves should be plotted against the price level.[17] In this alternative specification, the aggregate demand curve is a downward-sloping function of the interest rate. Its slope is derived by differentiating equation (2) with respect to r, holding constant all variables other than output that influence aggregate demand, and solving for dy^d/dr. This gives:[18]

---

16 To make the same point more formally, consider equations (2) and (3) which represent the equilibrium conditions in the goods and money market, respectively. In the goods market, P is absent from both sides of equation (2), implying that y^*, c, i and g are all independent of the price level. Aggregate supply is constant at y^* and, given y^*, consumption is completely determined. In addition, government purchases are fixed exogenously. This leaves the interest rate as the only variable free to equilibrate the goods market. Therefore, in the textbook model the equilibrium interest rate, r^* say, is completely determined in the goods market. Now consider equation (3). The nominal money supply (M) is exogenous and fixed, and the interest rate is determined in the goods market and equal to r^*. This leaves P as the only variable to equilibrate the money market.

17 This is precisely the approach taken by Barro (1993).

18 Since the textbook model assumes that aggregate supply is perfectly elastic with respect to changes in aggregate demand, output supplied varies along this version of the *AD* curve too. Intuitively, this curve is downward sloping because a decrease in r raises the investment component of aggregate demand. This direct impact is captured by the numerator of equation (9). The direct effect is then augmented by the multiplier, captured by the denominator of equation (9), as consumption expenditures respond positively to the assumed increase in aggregate supply. Stated somewhat differently, *(continued)*

$$\frac{dy^d}{dr} = \frac{\partial i/\partial r}{1 - \partial c/\partial y^s} < 0. \tag{9}$$

The AS curve is vertical because we have assumed throughout that the supply-side of the economy is independent of the interest rate.[19] When these AD and AS curves are superimposed, they determine the equilibrium interest rate (say r_1). In the money market, the money demand curve is vertical because the real demand for money is independent of the price level. The location of the money demand curve is determined by y_1^* and the equilibrium interest rate. By contrast, given the nominal money supply (M_1), the real money supply curve is a downward-sloping function of the price level since a decrease in P raises the real money supply, *ceteris paribus*. When the money demand and supply curves are superimposed, they determine the equilibrium price level (say P_1).

Let's consider the effect of an increase in the money supply using this alternative version of the model. In Figures 8.8A and 8.8B, the initial general equilibrium corresponds to the set of points marked A. Now suppose that, starting from the initial equilibrium, the central bank doubles the money supply from M_1 to $M_2 = 2M_1$. This raises the real money supply, shifts the money supply curve right from M_1/P to M_2/P, creating an excess supply of money at the initial price. This causes the price level to rise to P_2 which restores equilibrium in the money market at point B. It is evident that $P_2 = 2P_1$ since the real demand for money is the same in both the initial and final equilibrium. Therefore,

---

the IS curve becomes the textbook AD curve. In our theoretically consistent $ADAS$ model, by contrast, the slope of this alternative specification of the AD curve would be limited to the numerator of equation (9). This is because there is no multiplier when output supplied is constant at its natural level of y^*.

19 This is equivalent to assuming that there are no intertemporal substitution effects on labour supply arising from variations in the interest rate.

the real money supply must be unchanged as well. But this can only happen if the rise in P is proportional to the rise in M. In the goods market, the *AD* and *AS* curves remain stationary at their initial positions since neither is affected by a change in M or P. Consequently, the interest rate remains unchanged at r_1.

Comparing the results in Figures 8.8A and 8.8B with those in Figures 8.7A and 8.7B, we see that the textbook approach and the alternative approach imply the same general equilibrium response. Furthermore, it would certainly appear that the alternative approach is an easier framework for students to understand and manipulate. After all, it eliminates the need for complicated discussions of the interplay between the goods and money markets inherent in the textbook *ADAS* model.

If, then, the interest rate equilibrates the goods market while the price level equilibrates the money market, why does the textbook *ADAS* model continue to teach just the opposite? We believe that authors present it this way, whether consciously or unconsciously, because the textbook *ADAS* model has an important pedagogical advantage over the alternative approach. Specifically, the textbook model contains a more convincing explanation (i.e., tells a better "story") of what is going on "behind the scenes" as the economy adjusts from one equilibrium position to another following an economic disturbance.

Consider, for example, the story told by the alternate model regarding the effects of an increase in the nominal money supply. In the money market, the increase in M creates an excess supply of money balances which causes a proportional rise in the price level. In the goods market, the interest rate is unaffected because neither the *AD* or *AS* curve are affected by a change in M or P. End of story.

How does one respond when students ask: "What is the process by which the rise in M causes the price level to rise?" The alternative model is silent on this point. This is in direct contrast to the textbook *ADAS* model which provides a story of the dynamic adjustment process that students

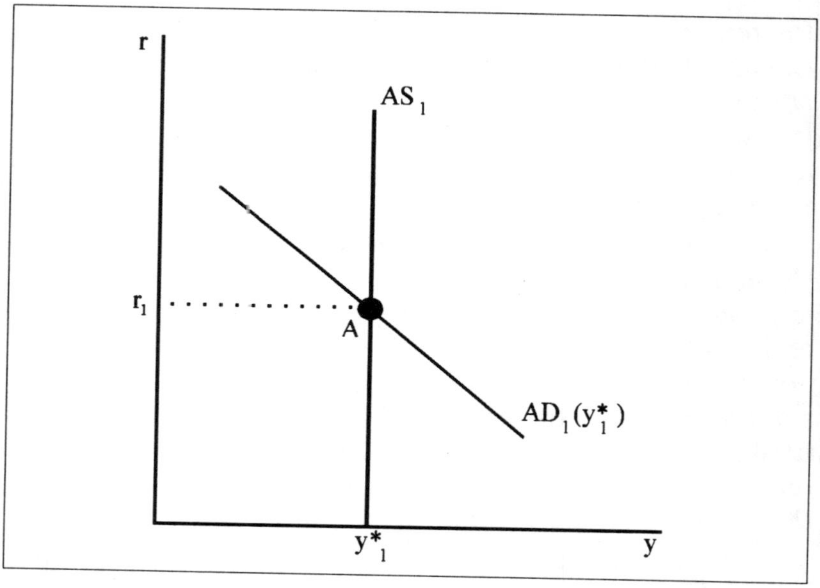

Figure 8.8A

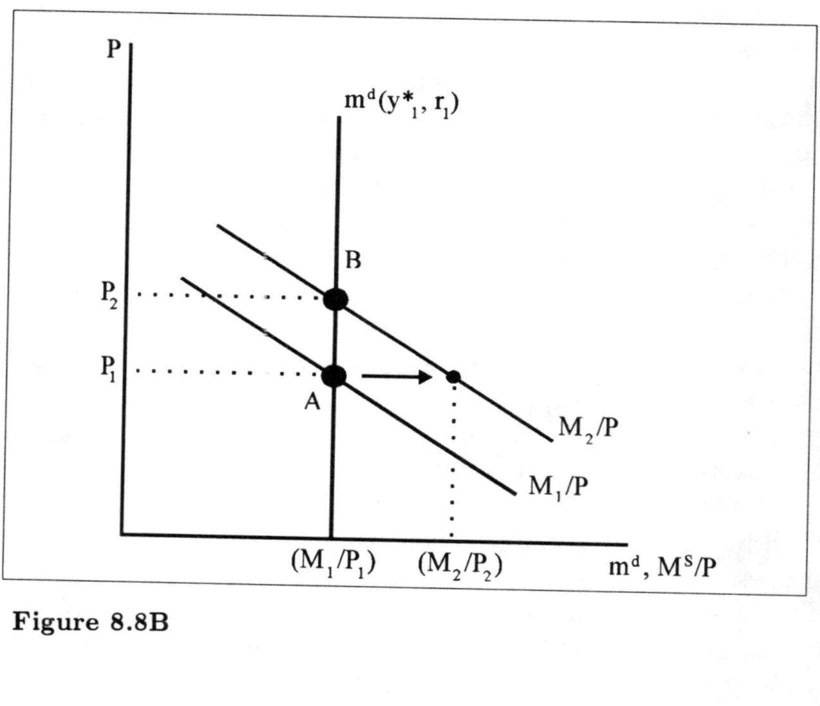

Figure 8.8B

find to be intuitively appealing and reasonably convincing.

So in this regard at least, we find the textbook *ADAS* model to be defensible. Surely, it is reasonable to argue that an increase in the money supply at least temporarily lowers the interest rate (otherwise how could private sector agents be induced to expand their money holdings absent a rise in either real output or the price level?). This should be interpreted, however, as an "intermediate equilibrium" interest rate – which is an important point not made explicit in most textbooks. The lower intermediate equilibrium interest rate then stimulates investment spending, which raises aggregate demand and the price level. This shifts the (real) money supply curve leftward and ultimately eliminates the excess supply of money. But this more compelling story should not be allowed to obscure the critical feature of the model, which is that the price level is being determined in the money market and that the interest rate is being determined in the goods market.[20]

Our defense of the textbook *ADAS* model on pedagogical grounds, however, does not dampen our criticism of the conventional *AD* curve. To the contrary, we believe it strengthens the argument for deriving the *AD* curve in a manner that is internally consistent with its companion *AS* curve. If the textbook *ADAS* model is defensible because it tells a "better" story (and we believe it does), it is our contention that the stories we tell students should be theoretically correct as well. As previously demonstrated, however, such is not the case with the textbook *ADAS* model.

8.7 CONCLUSION

We have argued in this chapter that the textbook *ADAS* model is internally inconsistent in two respects. First, the

[20] Our criticism of the alternative model notwithstanding, this alternative, Barro-type, approach is useful if one wants to emphasise the intertemporal substitution effect on labour supply (an effect that is critical in real business cycle models if one wishes to explain how fiscal policy can affect real output).

conventional *AD* curve is inconsistent with the *AS* curve with which it is paired to determine equilibrium price and output. Second, the textbook *ADAS* model teaches students that the price level is determined in the goods market and the interest rate is determined in the money market when the opposite is true, at least in the long run. While we believe that the latter inconsistency may be defensible on pedagogical grounds, the former inconsistency is another matter entirely. We have shown that the textbook model incorporating the conventional *AD* curve is fundamentally flawed. Moreover, the theoretically consistent *ADAS* model that results when the *AD* curve is properly specified does not appear to be inherently more difficult for students to understand. Indeed, in light of the model's flexibility, we believe it is a viable and useful pedagogical device for teaching macroeconomics.

9 Acceptable and Unacceptable Dirty Pedagogy: The Case of ADAS

David Colander and Peter Sephton

9.1 INTRODUCTION

Teachers of economics must simplify enormously to reduce the complex ideas that make up economics into models that are sufficiently simple to be conveyed to undergraduate students. This simplification is done in the knowledge that it violates some of the more complicated ideas of how the economy works, but it is justified in the name of simplicity.

Despite the importance of the simplifications, little direct analysis has gone into optimal simplification, and a wide variety of simplifications are all justified in the name of "dirty pedagogy". The argument of this chapter is that not all simplifications are justifiable; specifically, a simplification is unjustified if an alternative simplification exists that conveys the ideas that a teacher wants to convey, but does so in a way that is less misleading, and more consistent with high-level thinking, than the alternative.

This chapter will discuss one simplification that is prevalent throughout macro texts: the *ADAS* model.[1]

The central thesis of the chapter is that the *ADAS* model, as generally presented, is unacceptable dirty pedagogy. Specifically, this chapter will argue that there exists

[1] There are many variations of this *ADAS* model. The one we are referring to has the *AD* curve derived from the fixed-price *ISLM* model and the *AS* curve derived from the labour market, with the long-run *AS* curve, assuming wage-level flexibility, perfectly inelastic.

an alternative model that accomplishes all that teachers of economics wish, or should wish, to convey with the *ADAS* model, but that avoids many of the pitfalls of *ADAS* analysis.

9.2 WHAT THE ADAS MODEL IS SUPPOSED TO ACCOMPLISH

Professors need a relatively simple model to demonstrate to students the effect of macro policy on the economy. They need to be able to show graphically the effects of shifts in government spending, taxes, and the money supply on important macroeconomic variables such as real output, interest rates, and the price level. The 45 degree *AEAP* model on the introductory level, and the *ISLM* model at the intermediate level, fit the bill until the price level and inflation had to be incorporated into the core macro models. The evolution of the core macro model to the *ADAS* model occurred because the *ADAS* model incorporated the *ISLM* model as well as the price level. It fit the bill – it was easy to teach, easy to understand, easy to draw, and it conveyed the effects of monetary and fiscal policy that most economists saw as reasonable.

9.3 PROBLEMS WITH ADAS ANALYSIS

The movement to *ADAS* did not occur without objection. *ADAS* analysis has been attacked by many economists, including many in this volume. Among the complaints about *ADAS* analysis are:

1. The *ADAS* terminology misleads students into thinking the curves are essentially partial equilibrium curves, which they definitely are not.

2. The *AD* curve is not an *AD* curve. It is a conjectural aggregate equilibrium curve at all points on which $AS = AD$.

3. The terminologically justifiable *AD* curve is not a curve derived from the *ISLM* model; it is a curve that incor-

porates only the effects of changes in the price level on quantity of aggregate demand, and it is likely interconnected, in some fashion, with the aggregate quantity supplied.

4. The foundations of the *AS* curve presented in principles books blends those for a formal *AS* curve (an aggregate equilibrium curve conveying the condition that labour supply equals labour demand) with those for a curve reflecting price level institutional rigidities.

5. The dynamics that are implicit in the *ADAS* analysis presented in textbooks assume that wage-and price level flexibility will bring about full employment through effects operating through the hypothesised effects of price level changes on the quantity of aggregate demand. These dynamics are not those that most economists believe characterise the dynamics in our economy. Specifically, price level decreases have generally not brought about full employment and real wages have not moved in the predicted manner.

6. *ADAS*'s equilibrium specification makes the model impossible to use for comparative statics since there is no presumption that the curves will remain constant as one moves along the other curve. Yet it is continually used in that fashion, with books implying that if the new equilibrium exists, the dynamics of the economy will get it there.

7. The typical textbook derivation of the model is from two disparate models. The goods market equilibrium curve is derived from a model assuming quantity adjustment, given a fixed price level. The labour market equilibrium curve is derived from a model assuming flexible prices. This can lead to, and in introductory textbooks generally does lead to, logical inconsistencies in the discussion of disequilibrium dynamics.

Despite these problems, which are well known, and which are accepted generally, *ADAS* analysis continues to be used, and justified under the assumption of "dirty pedagogy". In this volume Peter Kennedy takes this position. His disagreements with those of us who are critics of the model concern items 5, 6 and 7 on the above list. Kennedy argues that if the standard *ADAS* model is treated as a pure equilibrium model, and discussions of dynamics allow the economy to be off the curves, these problems can be avoided. (He agrees, however, that in practice, they generally are not avoided in the textbooks.) Specifically, he argues that "when people append dynamics to *ISLM* to produce stories of how the economy moves to a new equilibrium, they supplement *ISLM* and implicitly supplement the corresponding *AD* with a supply story (and not a very good one). But when one moves to the *ADAS* model, one scraps that supply story, replacing it with one told around the *ADAS* curves. The old supply story is thrown away because it is not genuinely a part of *AD* – there is no inconsistency."[2]

Rao (1991), Nevile and Rao (1996) and Colander (1995) claim that if the derivation of the *AD* curve comes from a Keynesian fixed price *ISLM* model, as it generally does, from a pedagogical standpoint there are implicit dynamics built into the explanation of the curves, and the inconsistency in alternative supply specifications cannot be avoided. They claim that once a story has been told to students, the instructor cannot throw away that story and substitute another story. In the pedagogical use of the model, the stories told in deriving the curves become part of student's understanding of the curve. Students have heard and learned the first story; it cannot be scrapped.

As is evident from the above discussion, Kennedy's dirty pedagogy justification does not work for us. If we had our druthers we would deep six the entire *ADAS* model as it is currently taught, and replace it with a carefully specified alternative model. In this alternative model the *AD* curve would not be derived from a Keynesian model at all, and one would not assume an underlying perfectly competitive economy. In this model there would be no supply curve but, instead, a price-output curve reflecting the aggregate of the strategic pricing decisions of firms. This alternative

---

[2] From private correspondence between Kennedy and Colander.

model would focus on dynamics.

That model might make sense, but it is not what we are arguing for as the core principles macro model in this chapter. We are textbook authors, and as textbook authors we are well aware of the pressures for a simple macro model, and of the enormous inertia that will keep some version of the *ADAS* model central to the pedagogical exposition of macro for the foreseeable future. As our publishers, and our reviewers, have told us: An introductory book will not be successful without it.

Initially, Colander (1994, 1996) tried to define alternative *AS* and *AD* curves and to discuss the interrelationship between them and did reasonably well in the market. In his revised *ADAS* model, the *AS* curve was a hybrid curve – representing the quantity response of suppliers in seller-price setting markets to falls in the price level, holding expectations of real demand constant. That curve could shift due to expectations of demand. Colander's *AD* curve was a deductively derived curve that included only the initial effects of a fall in the price level on aggregate demand (for example, the Keynes and Pigou effects); it did not include the multiplier effects, since the curve was not derived from the Keynesian model. The difference is that the standard *AD* curve, derived from the *ISLM* equilibrium, includes multiplier effects in it since those multiplier effects are embodied in the IS curve. A fall in the price level causes the quantity of aggregate demand to increase. In that standard *ISLM* model, that increase causes supply, and hence income, to increase by an equal amount. That initial increase in income is multiplied by some amount dependent on the size of the multiplier and the shape of the *LM* curve. In Colander's revised *ADAS* model the *AD* curve included only the initial effects of a change in the price level. Thus Colander's *AD* curve was always less elastic than the standard *AD* curve.

The advantages of this aggregate demand curve and hybrid aggregate supply curve were that they allowed dynamics to be discussed separately from equilibrium, with the possible interdependency between the aggregate supply decisions and aggregate demand decisions directly incorporated into the presentation.

Colander's alternative *ADAS* model was logical and, we believe, insightful. But the formal foundations are complicated, and most economists were unwilling to accept a model that had a curve that looked like an *AS* curve shifting with expectations.[3] Because of this many reviewers kept telling him that his alternative macro model, while not wrong, was more complicated, or, at least, too different from the standard model, than the standard professor was willing to accept. If he wanted to move to be a market leader (which he did) he had to create an easier macro model that was more consistent with the standard model. Hence, the evolution of the model; in the third edition of Colander, and in the first Canadian edition, co-authored with Peter Sephton, the co-author of this chapter, we have developed the *macro policy model* – a model that looks and feels like the *ADAS* model of the standard texts, but that avoids many of the problems inherent in that model. It is this macro model that we believe makes the *ADAS* model a model with unacceptably dirty pedagogy.

9.4 MACRO POLICY MODEL

The basic macro policy model is shown in Figure 9.1. It consists of two curves: (1) the Aggregate Supply path – a curve that looks like the "aggregate supply curve" in the *ADAS* model; and (2) the Aggregate Equilibrium Demand Curve (*AED*) – a curve that is essentially a relabeled *AD* curve. Thus, the geometry of the macro policy model is identical to the geometry of the *ADAS* model found in the principles books but there are three differences: (1) the

---

[3] Those foundations require the introduction of a shift factor, co-ordination, in the production function which allows output supplied to change independent of any change in the real wage, but simply in response to a change in aggregate demand. The chapter by Allen and Stone in this volume discusses that model.

names of both curves; (2) the implicit microfoundations of the curves and (3) a more limited claimed applicability for the model. Let's consider those differences.

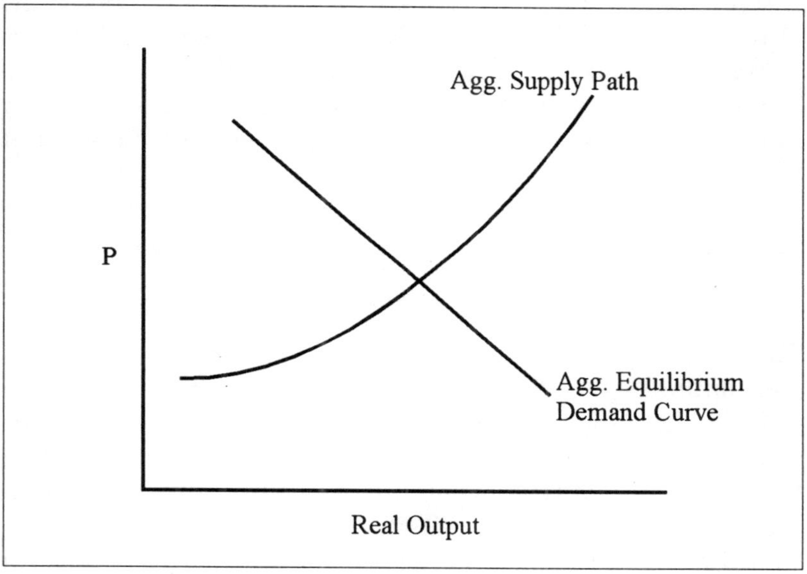

Figure 9.1

9.4.1 The Renaming of the AED Curve

The first change that the macro policy model makes is that it relabels the AD curve the AED curve. The purpose of this change is to remove the current misleading terminology. Renaming the AD curve makes clear to students that it is a curve reflecting goods market equilibrium, and is not an aggregate demand curve. Such a change, as argued by Colander (1996), is absolutely required by truth in labeling. Given that supporters of $ADAS$ analysis all agree that what is currently called an AD curve is really a price/output space equilibrium curve, and that the AED curve is a curve at which the goods market is in equilibrium ($AS = AD$), we can see no legitimate complaint with changing the name, unless the purpose is to deceive students.

The only complaint can be that we did not go far enough in relabeling the curve: Why call it an *AED* curve at all? Why not just call it a goods/money market equilibrium curve? Our answer is that it is derived from a Keynesian model in which demand plays a central role. This renaming of the *AED* curve resolves complaints (1) and (2) above, but it does nothing to complaints (3) to (7).

9.4.2 Using an Aggregate Supply Path Rather than a Supply Curve

To help meet complaints (3) to (7) we replace the aggregate supply curve with what we call an Aggregate Supply path. The Aggregate Supply path has roughly the same shape as the typical aggregate supply curve presented in the introductory textbooks, but has quite different microfoundations. Specifically, it is an empirically based curve that reflects the observed price-setting strategy of real world firms; it makes no pretense of being an *AS* curve reflecting marginal costs since it is based on an assumption that the goods market is not perfectly competitive. Whether the shift in output and prices reflect static or dynamic considerations is not an issue with this empirically based curve, and one can easily relate it to stories involving inventories, customer markets, and strategic pricing issues that characterise our real world economy. It is a curve that students can relate to, even if they cannot "derive it". It is a curve that can be influenced by the policy regime chosen, since firms' pricing strategy will reflect that regime.

The aggregate supply path allows for, but does not require, the Colander *AD* curve and the aggregate quantity supplied to be interconnected (solving complaint 4); its ambiguity allows easier integration of a variety of dynamics into the stories one tells about adjustment (solving complaint 5); and its definition lets it be used in discussions of dynamic shifts of the *AED* curve. Finally, it allows one to incorporate different assumptions about price level flexibility, resolving complaints 6 and 7).

Stating how the supply path differs from the aggregate supply curve in principles texts is difficult because of the ambiguity that surrounds the principles presentation of the aggregate supply curve. In intermediate books, the supply curve is clear – it is a labour market equilibrium curve. In most principles books there is implicit in the discussion a sense that the *AS* curve is the same curve as is formally developed in intermediate books – a labour market equilibrium curve, with the upward slope existing because of a fixed nominal wage assumption. But few principles texts ever explicitly come out and say that, nor do they explain why that labour market equilibrium curve would be perfectly elastic at low levels of output, as the *AS* curve is generally drawn in principles books.

The perfectly elastic portion of the curve could be explained by assuming the production function has constant marginal returns at low levels of output, but that assumption is hard to justify intuitively, and is not used in most principles books. Instead, to explain the perfectly elastic portion of the *AS* curve, the standard principles book generally switches explanations, and discusses issues involving institutionally sticky prices. Our problem with this approach is one of incompatibility of the two explanations; they come from different models that analytically are far apart. Sticky prices, based on seller price setting behavior is inconsistent with a model in which a supply curve provides a meaningful reference point. A model in which an unchanging supply curve is a meaningful reference point is a model which assumes sellers are price takers.

One way to resolve the problem would be for principles books to use the standard *AS* curve, and to tell "off the curve" stories of dynamic adjustment. There are two problems with that "solution". One of these is pedagogical, and the other involves the intuitive reasonableness of the story being told.

Let us consider the pedagogical problem first. Principles

books cannot tell "off the curve" stories because principles students don't yet have a real understanding of what it means to be on the supply and demand curves. It is to avoid telling "off the curve" stories that principles books use inconsistent explanations of what underlies the aggregate supply curve. Such inconsistencies are necessary to keep steps along the adjustment process on the supply curve when telling the Keynesian dynamic story of aggregate adjustment-stories that remain central to most principles book's underlying analytic presentation.

The second problem involves the intuitive logic of the dynamic adjustment process. That problem is best seen by considering a specific downward adjustment such as that in Figure 9.2A.

Say there is a shift back in aggregate demand of 10. Given that shift of 10, the aggregate equilibrium demand curve shifts by a multiple of 10 – the multiple determined by *ISLM* analysis that has not been presented to students. In that standard dynamic story, shown in Figure 9.2A if one wants to incorporate sticky prices, the initial leftward shift of the *AED* curve must move the economy to a point such as *A*, off the *AS* curve. To complete the analysis one needs some reasonable explanation of how the economy moves from point *A* to point *B* – the point consistent with the *ADAS* fixed nominal wage equilibrium implicit in the intermediate interpretation of macro equilibrium. It is here where the problem arises. Economists do not have a good dynamic story of how the economy moves from point *A* to point *B* which would entail firms increasing output as the price level falls, wages remaining constant. Most economists accept the institutional reality of a downward rigidity of prices, and that a significant fall in the price level would undermine financial markets, thereby making downward price level flexibility an undesirable alternative. Thus, given institutions, point *A* can be a quasi-equilibrium. Once the economy arrives at *A* there are no realistic dynamic forces

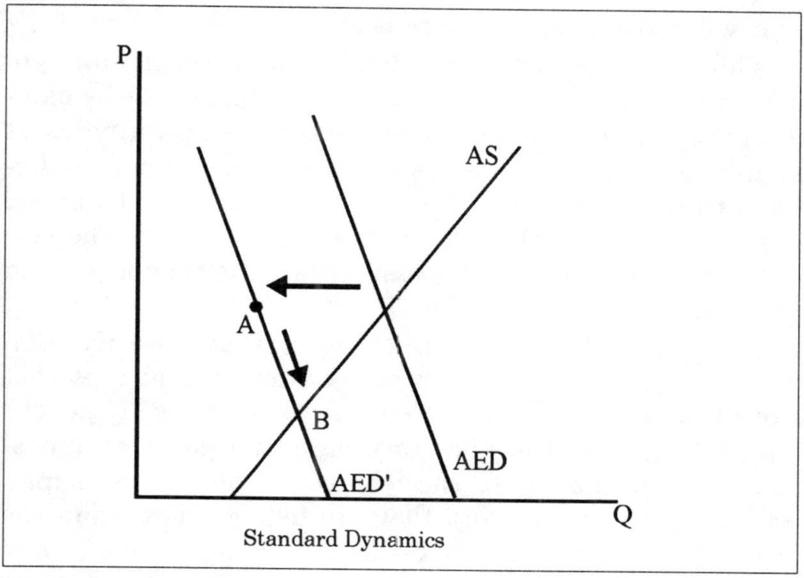

Figure 9.2A

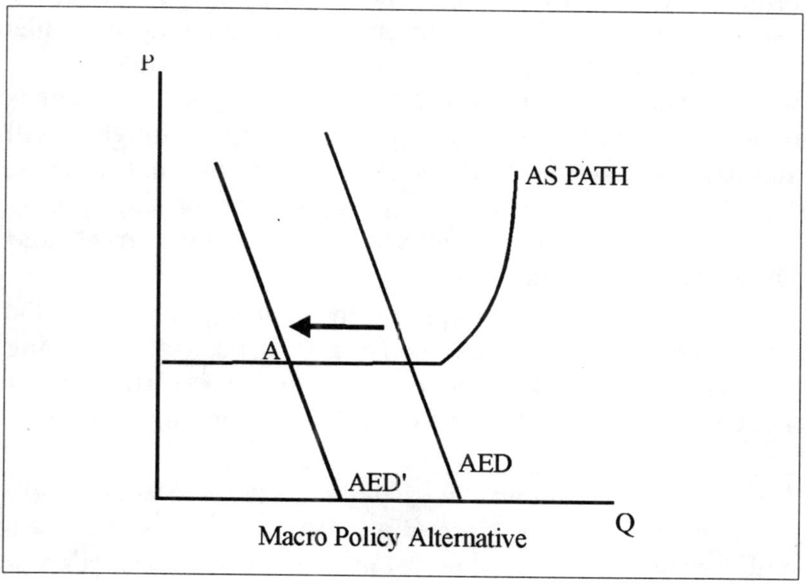

Figure 9.2B

that will move it unless there is another shock.[4]

This lack of an acceptable dynamic adjustment story going through point A is solved in intermediate books by eliminating point A. The intermediate story simply eliminates all dynamics from the analysis and focuses on final equilibria with its assumption of perfect competition. The model implicitly assumes that the economy can move to the new equilibrium at point B. By assumption the economy could be at no other point.

In a full mathematical presentation, that perfectly competitive goods market story becomes clear, and it is that story that economists like Kennedy say is logically consistent. We agree. But the story lacks the intuitive appeal and the applicability to the real world that the principles books require of the story they are telling. Herein lies the problem: the introductory books are trying to tell *a more complicated story* that involves a movement to point B via point A. *It is in mixing these two stories where the intuitive dynamic logic of the story is questionable.* If the economy has actually moved to point A, and output supplied has fallen, one must explain what underlies the firm's supply decision that led it to point A, and how, once the firm is at point A, what the nature of the incentives are that will lead it to change output to point B. That explanation must incorporate a discussion of any implication of that supply decision, such as feedback effects on the labour market, and on aggregate demand.

Essentially one must explain how, as the price level falls, nominal wages remaining constant, firms are increasing their output, and why, when the adjustment to point A occurred, the demand for labour curve remains constant.

[4] We do experience disinflation; interpreting the vertical axis as the price level relative to the expected price level allows us to get downward flexibility relative to expected price levels, and provides a reasonable set of dynamics if the economy has an ongoing inflation. But for that to work, there must be underlying inflation in the economy above the level of the disinflation needed.

If, in the quantity adjustment to point A, and firms actually reduce output which is what one is saying happens when one states that the economy is at point A, *the disequilibrium interdependencies between the goods and labour market must be included in the analysis.* The level of aggregate demand will become a determinant of the marginal product of labour, and hence a determinant of the amount firms choose to supply. Specifically, when firms reduce output, they will reduce their demand for labour. As they do so the effective marginal product of labour will fall, and as it falls, what might be called the effective supply curve of firms – the labour market equilibrium curve given a level of aggregate demand – will fall.

Notice what the assumption of non-perfectly competitive markets does to the analysis of downward shifts of the AED Curve. It removes perfectly competitive equilibrium as a meaningful reference point, and requires one to explicitly state how the economy will return to an initial equilibrium, if shocks push it away. The new supply path AED equilibrium is a real world equilibrium. Aggregate supply equals aggregate demand, by definition of the AED curve. It is true that long run equilibrium can only exist if there is no labour market disequilibrium. So, at this equilibrium there will be some downward pressure on the wage, and, through the wage, on the price level. But the existence of that pressure in no way tells us that the perfectly competitive equilibrium is a meaningful one. One could, for example, argue that the required fall in the price level would disrupt the institutional structure and cause a significant fall in aggregate supply as that deflation transfers money from debtors to creditors, and forces many debtors, firms and entrepreneurs, into bankruptcy.

If this is true that price level changes can affect supply, aggregate equilibrium is path dependent, and cannot be considered independently of disequilibrium dynamics that accompanies it. The reasonableness of the dynamic argument is asymmetrical. For expansions, with a technologically determined output maximum, there is a fixed point beyond which the economy can only expand temporarily, but, for contractions, if major short run falls in the price level are not institutionally feasible, the fixed point is lost.

The problem of creating an acceptable textbook macro model is not one of pedagogy; it is a problem of macroeconomic theory. The currently held macro theory – which is essentially an expansion of the intermediate macro story is logically consistent given perfect competition, but has not yet provided an acceptable foundation onto which one can incorporate dynamics and possible path dependencies. The currently in-vogue model with its assumption of perfect competition in the goods market eliminates, by assumption, my interpretation of Keynesian economics as a simple example of possible disequilibria expectational effects affecting the final equilibrium. All such effects are eliminated by the assumption of perfect competition in the goods market. If there were perfect competition in the goods market, aggregate demand would play no role in the economy, and there would be no role for Keynesian economics.

The above is not an argument to return to Keynesian economics; its dynamics are too simplistic to be generally acceptable. It is, however, an argument that the macro model we use take into account the interdependencies between supply and demand decisions that characterise many of our real world markets.

The standard principles presentation of the issues does not solve the problem; it simply presents aspects of both the Keynesian model and the perfectly competitive *ADAS*, mixes the two, and creates an analysis that involves inconsistencies that naturally flow from combining two models – one the intermediate perfectly competitive model, and the other the institutionally fixed price model. In doing so, in our view, the standard principles presentation crosses the line between acceptable and non-acceptable dirty pedagogy.

9.5 THE AGGREGATE SUPPLY PATH ALTERNATIVE

Our proposed solution is to explicitly *choose a non-perfectly competitive market as the underlying framework for the principles presentation of macro issues,* and to explicitly incorporate the institutional rigidities into the explanation of what happens to the price level. Our aggregate supply path is essentially a more precise name for the curve the principles books are trying to describe with their institutional story. It is an empirically determined curve, not a deduced curve. Calling it a supply path alerts students to the fact that the curve is not a supply curve, and that the dynamic story it is telling is not based on a perfectly competitive institutional structure. Because it isn't a perfectly competitive model, the supply path reflects real world firm's strategic pricing behavior within semi-oligopolistic markets.

We expect that a likely complaint about our macro policy model is that the *AS* path has ambiguous microfoundations. We fully admit this. We can do so because the problem with the standard *ADAS* model for us is not ambiguity, it is "hidden ambiguity". We believe that it is unacceptable pedagogy to hide the ambiguity behind the AS curve and to imply to students that an institutionally based curve has definite micro underpinnings in a perfectly competitive market. But this is precisely what one is doing when one calls the institutionally-determined price output path an aggregate supply curve.

The relabeled aggregate supply path allows the model to deal more easily with what we consider the standard case relevant to short run output fluctuations in the real world: the case in which both the price level and the wage level are semi-flexible. In this case a fall in aggregate demand can affect the demand for labour independently of any change in the real wage, *making labour market equilibrium conditional on the state of the goods market.* Expectational coordination problems can lead to a fall in the marginal product of labour, causing unemployment, even if wages are as inflexible as prices (meaning the real wage, W/P, hasn't changed). Thus, the standard Keynesian interpretation of the model as a model of demand-constrained markets (what Hicks and Rao call Q-markets) can be presented as consistent with the supply path, as can the New Keynesian coordination view (that Colander was arguing for in his alternative $ADAS$ model) without moving off the curves. In the current $ADAS$ model, these interpretations of the workings of the economy are difficult, if not impossible, to incorporate into the model.

9.6 THE MORE LIMITED APPLICABILITY OF THE MACROPOLICY MODEL

The third difference between the macro policy model and the standard $ADAS$ presentation is that the macro policy model is not presented as a complete model of the economy. The reason is that the analytic micro foundations of the AS path are to be found in game theoretic strategic pricing models that are not yet fully developed. At best, our ability to predict what will happen in such models is limited to considering first order differences – what will happen to an existing historically-determined equilibrium, given a shock. These models might be called first order difference models – they tell how the economy will adjust from a historically given equilibrium; they do not tell how the economy arrived at the equilibrium to begin with.

Similarly, in the macro policy model there is no formal graphical analysis of the movement to long run equilibrium, or what long run equilibrium is. Such a formal analysis is, in our view, beyond what we can hope to acceptably present in a principles course. That doesn't mean that we can't talk about the different views, and give students a flavour of the arguments, but to pretend that any formal model of that process we could present to them at the principles level is any more than a suggestive story would, in our view, be inconsistent with the state of modern macro understanding.

While the macro policy model takes slowly adjusting

short run prices as an institutionally given, it need not be given a Keynesian interpretation. It can be used to illustrate both Keynesian and New Classical views. For example, in the third edition of the U.S. edition of the Colander text, the Keynesian multiplier story is questioned specifically by considering the strategic decisions that would likely undermine it, and the New Classical argument that any expected policy would be incorporated into expectations is presented as part of the discussion of the strategic decision model of the economy.

In the macro policy model there is no implicit assumption that an economy with such price setting institutions, left on its own, will achieve the desired equilibrium, nor is there a presumption that it will not. In that it is consistent with what we consider is the highest level macro theory. Instead of being a positive model, the macro policy model is primarily a descriptive model of what is observed in the economy. It is an institutionally-based, not analytically based, model. At the principles level of macro such a descriptive model is the most one can realistically hope to convey to students. Given the state of current macroeconomic theory, pretending to be doing more is misleading unacceptable dirty pedagogy.

9.7 SUMMARY

Albert Einstein once said that a theory should be as simple as possible, but not more so; the same holds true for models. We think the problem with the standard *ADAS* analysis is that it is "more so". Specifically, it has been trying to be both a two dimensional summary of what happens in the real world, and a model of what happens in a perfectly competitive model. In combining the two, it has been neither; it has, instead been a mishmash of terminological inconsistencies and unexplained assumptions.

There are a number of pedagogically acceptable solutions to the problem – one possibility is to forget the real world, and develop a model that applies only to a perfectly competitive world – that is the intermediate macro book solution. On the principles level that solution does not work because the appropriate model is too complicated, and too far from the real world to present to the introductory students. The alternative we propose here is to limit the applicability of the model we present to students to one relevant to the institutional structure of the economy they live in. One can do so using the same curves as are currently used in principles texts, but slightly relabeling them, and providing a honest description of the institutional assumptions that underlies them. The macro policy model described here does that; in doing so it achieves all the goals that a good teacher should want from the *ADAS* model, and thus we urge its much broader use as a pedagogical device. It's still dirty pedagogy, but it is a lot less dirty than the current *ADAS* alternative.

10 Aggregate Demand and Supply Analysis: A Story in the Wrong Language*

John W. Nevile

10.1 INTRODUCTION

As Colander (1995) has reminded us, undergraduate teaching in economics is largely a matter of telling stories. We present highly simplified models to students and use them as a peg on which to hang our stories. The models are not just to show students that economics is an analytical subject. Their main purpose is to help students remember the major features of the stories we tell. Thus, in microeconomics it is usual to present a typical Marshallian picture of the market for a particular good, with the demand curve sloping downwards and the supply curve sloping upwards, and then use this to talk about what happens if there is a demand shock or a supply shock. For example, if the price of raw materials rises, the supply curve will shift upwards, prices will rise and the quantity sold will fall. The relative importance of each of these changes will depend on the slope of the demand curve. We know that the model is grossly oversimplified: that the competitive market it assumes may not exist in the industry in question and that part of the reaction may be a shift in advertising to try to change the

* This chapter benefited from discussions with Bill Rao and Trevor Stegman, but as I did not always follow their advice, the normal caveat is more than usually important.

slope of the demand curve. We know that strictly speaking it is a purely static model and if a shock moves the amount bought and sold away from equilibrium, the market may never reach a new equilibrium, (for example, when the cobweb theorem holds) and so on. But the story and the model are consistent and capture what we think is usually important in the real world. There is widespread consensus that the model and related story is a useful teaching tool which is rarely misleading.

In macroeconomics the situation is not so happy. This is only partly because there is less consensus about the essential features of the story we want to tell. It is more because economists simple models are essentially comparative statics. Comparative statics theory is useful for analysing many micro problems. It is far less useful in analysing macro problems, which are generally dynamic in nature. As the better macro textbooks make clear, the models that they present are equilibrium models. In microeconomics, comparing two equilibrium positions is usually helpful by itself. In macroeconomics the interest is often in how to get from A, say a current situation with unemployment at 10 per cent, to B a desired situation where unemployment is much lower. Comparing the equilibrium conditions necessary to remain at either A or B may be interesting, but it gives no reliable information about an economy that is not in equilibrium. This point is widely recognised in the literature. If challenged, textbook authors would no doubt argue that they tell intuitutively appealing stories about economies that are not in equilibrium and since the conditions for the new equilibrium position are based on their theoretical model the story of how the economy gets there need not be all that rigorous.

This chapter argues that fudging the difference between comparative statics and dynamic analysis can lead to error and that the intuitive stories told in macroeconomic textbooks are not only formally incorrect but may well be seriously misleading. The shock that moves an economy from equilibrium or what happens when the economy is not in equilibrium may change the conditions for equilibrium. These issues are discussed in section 2 of the chapter. The use of misleading stories about the paths of an economy after a policy change or other shock is encouraged by the general equilibrium nature of macroeconomic textbook models. Microeconomic textbooks start with Marshallian particular[1] equilibrium models which are not quite so rigorous, but which allow the model, and the story it supports, to fit together better. Perhaps macroeconomic textbook writers could learn from this. This point is discussed in section 3.

This chapter argues that the issues covered in section 2 encompass the most fundamental problems in the use of aggregate demand and aggregate supply analysis, and that these problems are aggravated by use of general equilibrium models rather than a Marshallian approach. Nevertheless a wide variety of criticisms have been made of textbook models of aggregate demand and aggregate supply.[2] One that is not generally acknowledged is set out in section 4. To extend the metaphor in the title of the chapter, not only do the textbooks choose the wrong language, but in addition they speak in dialect unfamiliar to students.

In section 5 an alternative to the approach criticised in previous sections is sketched. Then a brief conclusion draws the threads together.

10.2 LANGUAGE OF GENERAL EQUILIBRIUM COMPARATIVE STATICS

The demand curve for fresh fish tells us how much fish will be demanded in a market at each possible price, assuming other things are equal. It is a behavioural relationship. It

[1] The rather oldfashioned term "particular" (see Boulding, 1948, p.638) is used deliberately, as it can also mean the equilibrium that holds for particular values of the variables assumed to be constant.

[2] See Nevile and Rao (1996) for both criticisms and a list of references.

tells us how people would behave in various hypothetical situations. The aggregate demand curve is completely different. It tells us nothing about how people will behave. It tells us how they must behave if equilibrium is to be achieved. In the words of one, particularly careful, textbook, the aggregate demand curve

> shows all the possible crossing points of a single *IS* commodity market equilibrium curve with all the various *LM* money market equilibrium curves drawn for each possible price level. Everywhere along the curve *both* the commodity and money markets are in equilibrium (Gordon 1990, p.159, italics in the original).

This definition is for the common case in which the aggregate demand curve is derived from *ISLM* analysis. But even when it is based on the simpler Keynesian cross, or 45 degree diagram, the aggregate demand curve is still a locus of points in which both the goods market and money market are in equilibrium. The difference is that *ISLM* assumes that the money supply is fixed exogenously and the interest rate is endogenous, whereas the Keynesian cross assumes that the interest rate is exogenous and that the money supply is endogenous and of no great importance for the analysis in question.[3] However, either way the aggregate demand curve traces out those combinations of the general price level and the aggregate amount demanded that are consistent with equilibrium in both the goods market and the money market.

Similarly, the aggregate supply curve is the locus of points that are consistent with equilibrium in the labour market. Keynes (1936) spent a lot of time discussing his aggregate demand function but very little discussing his aggregate supply function, perhaps because he thought it was only a reconcoction of our friend the [Marshallian] supply function (1973, p.513). Modern textbooks typically

[3] There is more that can be said on this and the matter is discussed at greater length in section 4.

spend much more time deriving the aggregate demand curve than the aggregate supply curve, but their aggregate supply curve is just as different from the traditional supply curve as their aggregate demand curve is from the traditional demand curve. On occasion some textbooks gloss over this and speak of the aggregate supply curve as analogous to a Marshallian supply curve for a single industry.[4] Nevertheless, the derivation of the aggregate supply curve makes clear that is a curve giving the conditions for equilibrium in the labour market. Thus, the point where the aggregate curves intersect is the one point that is consistent with equilibrium in all three markets; goods, money and labour.

The equilibrium nature of aggregate demand and supply analysis leads naturally to comparative static analysis, and indeed is only suited to answer comparative static questions. Comparative statics compares the states of two different economies (or parts of economies). Because the two different economies are in equilibrium, expectations are fulfilled. Since expectations are fulfilled, either both the economies are relatively stable with little change occurring or a fairly long period must be under consideration to allow for uncertainties to be overcome and mistakes to be corrected. Or perhaps expectations are never completely fulfilled, but the focus is on the average performance of the economy over a long period and what, in this context, are relatively minor divergences from equilibrium do not matter. As Hicks puts it in his discussion of comparative statics:

> By the *state* of a given economy one would appear to mean its average performance over a fairly long period, short run fluctuations being cancelled out (1985, p.8, emphasis in the original).

This sort of comparative equilibrium analysis can be applied to dynamic states of an economy as well as to stationary states. It does have a role to play in macroeconomics e.g.,

---

[4] See, for example, Parkin and Bade, 1988, p.149.

in answering questions such as why did the German economy grow faster than the American economy in the 1950s and 1960s, or why did the Australian economy grow faster in the 20 years before 1973 compared to the twenty years after that date. However, by its nature, it is not suitable for answering questions about short term fluctuations. It is about conditions which must be fulfilled if an economy is to be in equilibrium and can tell us nothing about what happens when an economy is not in equilibrium. Hence, it cannot be used to describe what happens in an economy when a shock displaces it from an equilibrium position. It may be able to give valuable clues about the effects of different monetary or fiscal policies that are kept in place over decades but is not helpful as a tool to analyse stabilisation policy or to describe how to get from point A to point B in a relatively short period of time.

Of course macroeconomic textbooks are interested in the effects of external shocks on the economy and in stabilisation policy. They tell stories about what happens when there is a change in the money supply, in government expenditure, in various other exogenous variables or in parameters such as the marginal propensity to consume. They describe how such a change puts the economy out of equilibrium and how it will return to a new equilibrium position.

Neverthless, this is illegitimate. As we have seen, general equilibrium comparative statics gives no information about what will happen when an economy is out of equilibrium. It only tells us the conditions for equilibrium before and after a change in an exogenous variable. Thirtyfive years ago there was unease among textbook writers about the stories they told describing what happened when an economy was not in equilibrium. To quote Ackley, in this sort of pedagogy

> We tread perilously close to misleading statements ... as well as being forced to bring dynamic considerations into what is supposed to be static analysis (1961, p.372).

This unease has not stopped the continuing use of this sort

of pedagogy, and the unease seems to have diminished as the years have passed. To give just one example from a recent book, Hall and Taylor (1993) go to the other extreme. Their aggregate demand curve is derived in the usual way from *ISLM* analysis as a curve of the locus of points of equilibrium in both the goods and money markets. Despite this, they assert that this aggregate demand curve tells how much people will demand at a given level of prices (p.200). Hence, they argue that, when a demand shock occurs, e.g., a fall in aggregate export receipts, not only does the aggregate demand curve shift, but also the economy is initially at the point on the new aggregate demand curve corresponding to the equilibrium price before the shock, and that it moves down the new aggregate demand curve until equilibrium is reached at the point where the new aggregate demand curve cuts the aggregate supply curve (p.233).[5]

Hall and Taylor are no doubt aware that their description of the aggregate demand curve is incorrect and that their story about what happens after a demand shock cannot be deduced from static equilibrium analysis. Presumably they feel that the invalid use of equilibrium theory is justified in order to get across the way they believe a demand shock will affect output and prices.

Teaching students things that they will later have to unlearn, if they proceed with the study of economics, can be challenged. In my view the use of simplifying assumptions, even gross oversimplification, is justified if the simplifying assumptions are made explicit. But the use of invalid analysis is not. Even if students do not notice the logical flaws, teaching invalid analysis may sweep important problems under the carpet without their being acknowledged and lead to ways of thinking which give misleading conclusions in many contexts.

---

[5] This is not an isolated example of aggregate supply and demand analysis being used to analyse what happens out of equilibrium. Hall and Treadgold (1982, p.40) list many other examples in various textbooks.

Underlying the example from Hall and Taylor is an important problem. Comparative static general equilibrium analysis assures that expectations are fulfilled, since this is one of the conditions of equilibrium. Hence expectations largely drop out of the picture and in many text books are not even mentioned in aggregate demand and supply analysis. However, a revival of Keynes (1936) emphasis on expectations is a mark of macroeconomics over the last twenty years. The Hall and Taylor analysis outlined above ignores the fact that a fall in export income may affect expected returns from investment. A fall in the terms of trade may well lead to the postponement, or even cancellation of investment projects. General equilibrium comparative statics does not consider the effect of a shock to one exogenous variable on other exogenous variables or that the equilibrium position may in part be path determined. Thus, it is not a suitable basis for describing the effects of shocks to an economy or how monetary and fiscal actions can reduce short run fluctuations. But these are at the heart of the problems teachers and students want to discuss in introductory and intermediate macro classes.

10.3 MARSHALLIAN ANALYSIS VERSUS GENERAL EQUILIBRIUM

The previous section uses the lengthy phase general equilibrium comparative statics to classify aggregate demand aggregate supply analysis. The significance of the words equilibrium and comparative statics has been discussed but the fact that it is general equilibrium rather than Marshallian particular equilibrium analysis is also significant. The use of general, rather than particular, equilibrium analysis aggrevates the problems that occur when a comparative static model is used in a relatively short run disequilibrium situation. Microeconomic textbooks start with Marshallian particular equilibrium analysis and Keynes used this method in the General Theory.[6] Perhaps we should learn

[6] Nevile (1997, forthcoming) discusses this point in more detail.

from those examples.

Clearly macroeconomic analysis cannot use Marshallian particular equilibrium models unchanged. A macro model cannot be for a particular industry. It can be for a particular country, as opposed to the whole world, but that is not the point. The distinction that I want to make is not between the coverage of the models, but the methods of analysis. On the one hand general equilibrium analysis treats all variables not determined by the model as exogenous. They are either policy determined variables (Tinbergen's instruments) or variables assumed to have constant values irrespective of what happens to the instruments or the variables determined by the model (Tinbergen's data). On the other hand Marshallian particular analysis proceeds on the basis that the values of a number of variables can be assumed to be constant, or approximately constant, for the purpose in hand.

Tinbergen's use of the term "data" is revealing. Calling variables exogenous leads to a different mode of thought than does the assumption that for the purpose in hand the variables are at least approximately constant. Exogenous variables can be changed at will and an examination made of the effects of a change of a single exogenous variable on the conditions for equilibrium. Textbooks universally engage in this practice. As we have seen, the disequilibrium story of what follows a change in an exogenous variable does not follow from aggregate demand and supply analysis and may be misleading. Moreover, the implication, or often explicit statement, that the change in the exogenous variable will cause a change in the economy, rather than a change in the equilibrium conditions is incorrect.[7] These errors are

[7] Strictly speaking there are no causal relationships in general equilibrium comparative statics. One should not say that a change in g causes a change in h. All that the theory states is that if an economy is thrown out of equilibrium by a change of so much in g then h will have to change by a specified amount, other things being equal, if the economy is to again be in equilibrium.

encouraged because there is nothing inherently illogical in assuming that an exogenous variable can be changed at will.

It is far less easy to vary at will the values of variables that are assumed to remain approximately constant, locked for the time in a pound called ceteris paribus as Marshall put it (1920, p.366). The assumption that a number of variables remain approximately constant does not imply that one variable can change significantly while all the others remain the same. When discussing the demand for an individual commodity, say soap, microeconomic textbooks commonly assume that money income and the prices of all other commodities are held constant. They certainly do not imply that it is useful to consider the effects of a large increase in money income on the demand for soap, while keeping the assumption that the prices of all other commodities remain the same.

The difference between the general and particular equilibrium approaches can be highlighted by comparing modern textbook analysis of an increase in the nominal money supply with that of Keynes. The textbook analysis is well known. As a result of the larger money supply, the interest rate is lower, and investment and hence output are greater, if the aggregate supply curve is horizontal. If the aggregate supply curve is vertical output remains the same, but the general level of prices rises to such an extent that the real money supply is unchanged and equilibrium is restored at the same level of output. If the aggregate supply curve is neither flat nor vertical but upward sloping both output and prices rise to some extent.[8]

[8] Telling this as a causal story is appealing but not correct. Many textbooks talk about the increase in the money supply shifting the *LM* curve, and hence the aggregate demand curve to the right. If the aggregate supply curve is flat, the equilibrium level of output increases, if it is vertical that of the general level of prices rise and if it is upward sloping a bit of both occurs. For the moment the point is not the nature of the path from one equilibrium point to another but the effect on the economy of a change in an exogenous variable.

Contrast this with Keynes' discussion about whether an increase in the money supply will increases output and employment. Keynes thought that

> A moderate increase in the quantity of money may exert an inadequate influence over the long-term rate of interest, whilst an immoderate increase may offset its other advantages by its disturbing effect on confidence (1936, pp.26-7).

Keynes was alert to the possibility that changing one of the variables in the ceteris paribus pound could bring about a change in another variable in that pound. The textbook analysis ignores the possibility of an increase in the money supply affecting expectations and the marginal efficiency of capital.

It is ironic that expectations are treated as exogenous in aggregate demand and supply analysis and are often completely ignored. Almost all the shades of thought in modern macroeconomics consider expectations very important. The implications of rational expectations on the effectiveness of policy on the one hand, and the post Keynesian complaints that the neo-classical synthesis neglects the important role of time in a capitalist economy on the other,[9] are alike not considered in the textbook analysis set out above.

A second advantage of Marshallian particular equilibrium theory is that while it is still static analysis it leads more naturally to dynamic analysis than does general equilibrium comparative statics. As Hicks puts it it gets very

---

[9] In a formal sense time has a large role to play in aggregate demand and aggregate supply analysis. The past is important as the determinant of the capital stock, the state of technology and other factors which affect the shape and position of the aggregate demand and aggregate supply curves. The future is important since expectations determine both the marginal efficiency of capital and liquidity preference. However, time and exceptions of future real demand are rarely mentioned, though expectations about price level changes do play a part in the analysis in some textbooks.

close to dynamics (1985, p.51). Keynes used a Marshallian particular equilibrium framework in the General Theory. This led naturally to a dynamic theory based on Keynes work quickly being produced by Harrod.[10]

Marshall stressed that the assumptions that other things are equal was only provisional (1920, p.380). This often prompts a dynamic story. If profits are very high (or quasi-rents are large in Marhsalls terminology), it is natural to suppose that this will lead to net investment and an increase in the capital stock. This is not a rigorous argument. A well formulated dynamic model would have to bring expectations into the analysis since high profits will not necessarily lead to investment if they are thought to be temporary. But the lack of complete rigour enables the story to flow naturally from the model. Similarly, in the General Theory the assumption of a constant capital stock cannot be combined with positive net investment without some lack of rigour. The capital stock can only be approximately constant. This leads to a consideration of what happens when the change in the capital stock is too large to be considered even approximately constant. The teaching model set out in section 5 is designed to be interpreted as a particular equilibrium model with a number of things assumed to be locked in Marshall's ceteris paribus pound. As an example, one important dynamic story is told which involves things in the pound changing in a systematic way when a shock moves the economy from an equilibrium position.

10.4 NOT ONLY THE WRONG LANGUAGE BUT AN UNFAMILIAR DIALECT

The most common derivation of the aggregate demand curve is from *ISLM* analysis. A fixed nominal supply of

[10] Harrod's 1937 exposition of the essence of the General Theory finished with suggestions about dynamic extensions of the theory and a year later Harrod published a full blown dynamic Keynesian model.

money is assumed so that when the general level of prices is lower the real money supply is greater. Hence the equilibrium interest rate is lower and output greater giving a downward sloping aggregate demand curve. But students do not read in their newspapers articles speculating on whether or not the central bank will increase the nominal money supply. They do not, any more, even read articles about how the nominal money supply is growing too rapidly and that the central bank should take actions to lower its rate of growth. If they read the financial sections of their newspapers, what they will see are articles discussing whether the central bank is likely to raise interest rates, or lower them as the case may be. They will see articles arguing that the central bank should take action on interest rates, or should have taken action on interest rates some time ago, but nothing on the money supply as an instrument of monetary policy.

In this case the journalists are more correct than the textbook writers. In today's world of deregulated financial markets, not only is the money supply endogenous but changes in it have little correspondence with changes in interest rates. Substantial rises in interest rates may be accompanied by a large rise in the money supply. For example, it is generally agreed that the prolonged recession in Australia in the early 1990s was precipitated and made more severe by very tight monetary policy.[11] Short term interest rates rose from June 1988 to December 1989 and then remained constant for the first few months of 1990. Yet over the year to December 1989 $M3$ increased by 22 per cent and broad money by 14 per cent. Over the same period nominal gross domestic product increased by 9 per cent.[12]

[11] The 1990 annual report of the Reserve Bank of Australia stated "Financial conditions were tight throughout 1989/90" (p.21) and the previous years annual report had described monetary policy as tight since the June quarter of 1988.

[12] I owe this example to Reimers (1996).

Some textbooks derive the aggregate demand curve from the Keynesian cross. This can be drawn assuming a constant volume of money in nominal terms, a constant marginal efficiency of capital schedule and a given general level of prices, but the assumption that, along with the marginal efficiency of capital, the interest rate is exogenous and the money supply endogenous is a more straightforward justification of the assumption that the level of investment in fixed capital is constant. In this latter case the weakness discussed in this section obviously does not hold. Instead there is the problem of explaining why the aggregate demand curve slopes downwards to the right.

While various justifications are presented in textbooks, which do not base their analysis on ISLM, none are likely to have a large effect on the slope of the aggregate demand curve. It is perhaps not a matter of great moment whether the aggregate demand curve is vertical or just fairly close to vertical. However, it is helpful not to use models that depend on a constant exogenous money supply.

10.5 A POSSIBLE ALTERNATIVE

Critics of teaching models have more credibility if they can suggest an alternative approach. If one rejects the conventional aggregate supply aggregate demand analysis is there a simple alternative? The Keynesian cross, as taught in the 1950s and 1960s, worked well then, but returning to it alone would mean once again ignoring the supply side as well as, in practice, expectations. At the intermediate level I would recommend a recursive historical model.[13] The algebra of elementary difference equations is not all that difficult and in any case students can be given a feel for more difficult cases (e.g., those which involve complex numbers)

[13] The term historical model is used in the sense of Joan Robinson (1962, pp.24-25) to describe a model which begins with a set of data (actual or hypothetical) about where an economy was yesterday and predicts where it is today and will be tomorrow.

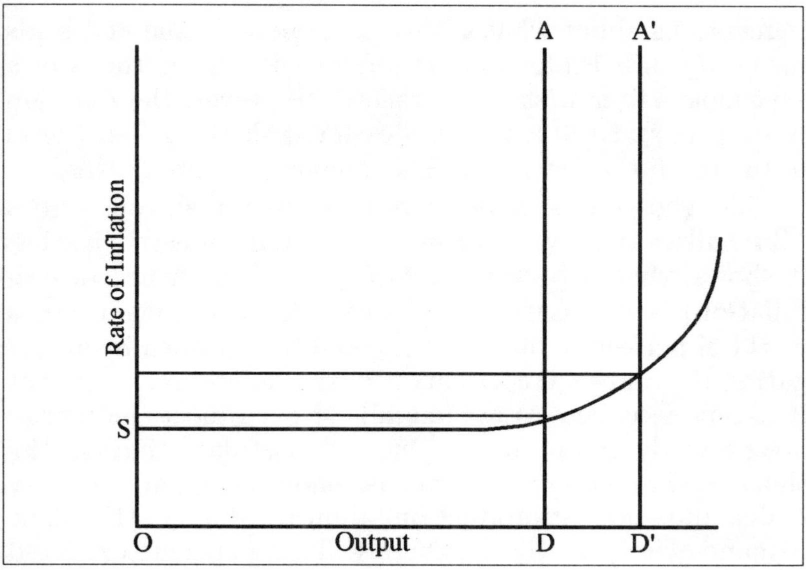

Figure 10.1

by numerical examples. However, at the principles level it is desirable to have a simple diagram on which to hang the exposition. The following is not meant to be prescriptive, but just an outline of one possible approach.

The basic diagram is set out in Figure 10.1. On the vertical axis can be measured either P, the general level of prices, or ΔP or the rate of inflation. This may seem like a fairly formal choice. Certainly, the difference between P and ΔP is merely where one puts the origin and changing from ΔP to the rate of inflation is only a matter of the scale used on the vertical axis. Each choice has some advantages, but I prefer the rate of inflation.

Despite large falls in typical inflation rates in many OECD countries, the rate of inflation is still usually positive and significantly different from zero.[14] Putting the rate of inflation on the vertical axis accords with student's

[14] In the last 25 years the annual rate of growth of the consumer price index in Australia has never been zero or negative. Over *(continued)*

perceptions about what is the actual policy issue and leads naturally into Phillips curve analysis if that is the way a textbook writer wishes to proceed. However, the diagram is simpler and the exposition easier with the general level of prices on the vertical axis and some may prefer this.

The aggregate supply curve is defined analogously to a Marshallian supply curve in a particular industry, in that it shows what expected level of prices (and hence rate of inflation) is necessary to elicit each level of output. In a world of perfect competition it could be obtained by aggregating the marginal cost curves of the individual firms, but it is not necessary to assume all, or even most, industries are perfectly competitive. One can postulate that, in the short run, monopolistic firms assume a constant elasticity of demand for their product but allow for shifts in the whole demand schedule. Hence, there will be a specific expected price associated with each level of output of their product. This price is a constant multiple of marginal cost.[15]

---

the same period there have only been four occasions when it was zero or negative in any of the 26 countries for which statistics are given in the OECD Economic Outlook. These four rare exceptions were Germany in 1986, The Netherlands and Luxembourg in 1987 and Japan in 1996.

[15] Economists are used to summing marginal cost curves to obtain aggregate supply curves when perfect competition prevails. However, the necessary condition is not perfect competition, but that each firm assumes a (firm specific) constant elasticity of demand, which does not change with short run shifts in the demand curve. If this is the case, since

$$MR = P(1 + \frac{1}{\eta}) \text{ or } P = \frac{\eta}{(\eta + 1)} MR$$

when profits are maximised

$$P = \frac{\eta}{(\eta + 1)} MC \text{ or } P = a_i\ MC$$

where a_i is a firm specific constant and the other variables have the usual meanings.

As marginal cost is a function of output, for each firm *(continued)*

The left hand portion of the aggregate supply curve can be drawn horizontal, or rising slightly and it must finish with a vertical section at the extreme right of the diagram. In between there should be a section with an upward slope which increases noticeably as one moves to the right. It would be possible to use a right angled supply curve, but that throws away realism without any great gain in a simpler analysis. It also limits the use of the diagram in the analysis of inflation.

The aggregate supply curve is a Marshallian short run curve based on the assumption that the capital stock is more or less constant. Once one takes into account the effect on the capital stock of investment in fixed capital, the analysis moves into growth theory. This is a different ballpark altogether.The upward slope of the supply curve occurs because of rising marginal costs that are not the result of rises in factor prices. In addition to conventional diminishing returns, costs may rise as output increases because less efficient labour is used, even if it is only less efficient because it does not have valuable firm-specific experience and skills. The aggregate supply curve is drawn assuming that short-run expected wage rates (or wage rate rises) do not change as output increases.

The aggregate demand curve DD' is based on a Keynesian cross that is set out in real terms. Hence it is a vertical line in Figure 10.1. Because of this it is necessary to explain that analysis based on the diagram only holds when the aggregate demand curve is to the left of the vertical section of the aggregate supply curve. This is not a problem since it is easy to give a verbal description of what happens if the aggregate demand curve is so far to the right that it does not intersect the aggregate supply curve.

Where the aggregate demand curve and the aggregate supply curve intersect is at least a temporary equilibrium

---

there is a specific price associated with each level of output, and these individual supply relationships can be summed across firms to obtain an aggregate supply curve.

position. It may only be a temporary equilibrium because, in the exposition of the aggregate demand and supply curves, the point is made that they assume a large number of other things are equal, and that this may only be the case for a relatively short period of time. Also the exposition should point out that, if something in the ceteris paribus pound changes, one must be alert to the possibility that this may cause changes to other things in this pound.

The analysis of shocks to the economy is straightforward. If there is a change in autonomous expenditure the aggregate demand curve shifts by the size of the autonomous expenditure change times the multiplier, e.g., from AD to AD' in Figure 10.1. The story to explain how the economy shifts from an output level of OD to one of OD' can be that as aggregate demand increases stocks are run down, firms realize that demand has increased and raise both production and prices until equilibrium is reached at the new intersection point. This could be the end of the story but it would be possible to continue with the $NAIRU$ type story sketched later in this section. Supply shocks are treated in a similar manner, e.g., an increase in input prices (say an oil price shock) will raise the whole supply curve including the horizontal section, so that output level OD now is associated with a higher level of prices or rate of inflation.

If one wishes to tell a story about inflation that is focussed on the $NAIRU$, this can be done using the diagram in Figure 10.1. While the $NAIRU$ does not appear in the figure it is easy to introduce the concept by designating some level of output as the one corresponding to the $NAIRU$ for a given suply curve. If output is above this level wage inflation increases, and if output is below the designated level wage inflation falls. The inflation story starts by making explicit that, when the aggregate supply curve is drawn, one class of things locked in the ceteris paribus pound is expectations about the rate of growth of factor prices, including wages. Assume that an economy is in equilibrium with output equal to OD and that OD is the level of output corresponding to the $NAIRU$. A shock shifts the aggregate demand curve to$A'D'$. The new equilibrium position is at a higher level of output and a higher rate of inflation (for final output). Before long wage inflation will rise causing a rise in the expected rate of wage inflation. This will shift the supply curve upwards leading to a higher rate of inflation again and the process will continue indefinitely. To halt the acceleration in inflation either the aggregate demand curve must be shifted to the left, say by a cut in government expenditure, so that it is again at a level of output corresponding to the $NAIRU$, or the supply curve must be shifted to the right in a way that increases the level of output corresponding to the $NAIRU$, for example by an increase in the supply of employable labour through labour market programs. In the first case the equilibrium rate of inflation will be higher than that before the demand shock (unless output is held for a time below the level corresponding to the $NAIRU$). In the second case, involving a shift in the supply curve, the new equilibrium rate of inflation depends on the exact nature of the shift in the supply curve. More generally, the diagram is more useful in suggesting the ongoing inflationary consequences of demand shocks rather than of supply shocks, since with a supply shock one has to determine arbitrarily the size of the effect has on the $NAIRU$.

One final point: much of aggregate demand and aggregate supply analysis has been criticised for combining in the one model two inconsistent models of supply. The aggregate demand curve is often based on an analysis which assumes a horizontal aggregate supply curve, but the aggregate supply curve drawn in the diagram is not horizontal (Rao, 1991, Colander 1995, Nevile and Rao 1996). Can this criticism be applied to the approach set out in this section. Certainly the Keynesian cross normally implies a horizontal supply curve and the aggregate supply curve in Figure 10.1 is not horizontal for much of its length including the section around the point of intersection with the aggregate demand curve. The question is not really about the slope of the aggregate supply curve, but about the assumption regarding price determination which underlies that slope. The analysis underlying the derivation of the aggregate demand curve in most textbooks, and in the model pictured on Figure 10.1, assumes that the labour market is, a fixprice market, to use Hicks convenient terminology. A fixprice market is not one where prices never change but one in which in the presence of a difference between the amount demanded and the amount supplied price does not change rapidly to equate demand and supply, so that the assumption demand equals supply is not a useful one. An aggregate demand curve based on a fixprice labour market cannot be combined with an aggregate supply curve which assumes a flexprice labour market in which price changes adjust supply and demand to maintain full employment.

The aggregate supply curve in Figure 10.1 is compatible with the assumption of a fixprice labour market. Except when the curve becomes vertical rises in the price level necessary to call forth increased output are because of diminishing returns and because inherently less productive labour must be drawn into the productive process as output rises. If a story is told about inflation which implies a Phillips curve situation where lower unemployment increases the bargaining power of workers and raises wage levels in the near future, this does not imply a flexprice labour market. There can still be involuntary unemployment when wages are rising. Like most models in the general Keynesian tradition, that in Figure 10.1 escapes the criticism of inconsistent assumptions about supply.

10.6 CONCLUSION

Aggregate demand and supply analysis as presented in textbooks is general equilibrium comparative statics analysis which gives the conditions for an equilibrium position but provides no reliable information about an economy out of equilibrium. It ignores the possibility that a shock to one exogenous variable may cause changes to other exogenous variables and that the equilibrium position may be, in part, be path determined. However, textbooks base on it stories about what happens after a shock to the economy and how an economy moves from point A to point B. These stories can be very misleading.

Moreover most expositions of aggregate demand and supply analysis assume constant nominal supply of money determined by the central bank. This conflicts with the actual situation and with what students read in the financial sections of their newspapers which discuss the central banks using interest rates as the instrument of monetary policy and assume that the money supply is endogenous.

An alternative exposition is suggested in which the interest rate is a policy instrument and the money supply endogenous. This exposition is Marshallian in character and emphasises that, if one thing assumed to be constant changes, this may cause changes in some of the other things assumed to be constant. This approach is considered both more faithful to the underlying economic theory and more appealing to students.

11 A Simple Analysis of Price and Output Determination: A Model with Imperfect Competition

Corrado Benassi, Alessandra Chirco and Caterina Colombo

11.1 INTRODUCTION

The core of any basic course in macroeconomics is the development of a set of instruments for the determination of the level of output, the aggregate level of price, the rate of unemployment and the rate of inflation. As far as output and price are concerned, most macroeconomic textbooks end up suggesting that the many economic forces which lie behind their determination can be described within a demand-supply scheme. This choice is probably justified both by the desire to use intuitive and familiar instruments, and by the simplicity of the reference framework. The idea is that domestic output is a composite good, the demand for which depends negatively on its price, due to a real-balance effect as well as, in open economies, a terms-of-trade effect. Supply of domestic output may or may not depend on this price, depending on whether changes in the price level affect the agents behaviour in the labour market. The supply curve is vertical if the nominal wage adjusts istantaneously to any change in price; it is however positively sloped if the nominal wage is fixed; and finally, it is horizontal if the nominal wage is fixed and technology entails constant returns to labour (or price is historically given). In any case, as for peas or oranges, the intersection between demand and supply determines the equilibrium values of output and price.

There is by now a substantial consensus in deriving a downward sloping demand curve for aggregate output as a reduced form of a standard *ISLM* model. However, in building an aggregate demand-aggregate supply scheme, the first relevant obstacle any economics teacher faces, is to convince the audience that the *ISLM*, fix-price equilibrium relation between output and the price level, can be easily transformed into a behavioural relation of one side of the market – which, by its very nature, should be defined independently of the behaviour of the other side.

Moreover, to this ambiguous demand schedule a supply schedule is typically associated, which is derived under very different (in fact, entirely opposite) assumptions: while demand is based on equilibrium output being demand determined, supply is built by assuming that firms behave as if they were unrationed at any given price. Thus a problem of internal consistency of the model necessarily arises, which emerges more neatly when a nominal wage rigidity is invoked to justify a positively sloped aggregate-supply curve. To be sure, demand and supply are mutually consistent only at equilibrium; but while equilibrium is the only observable position within a fully flexible environment, a nominal wage rigidity opens the possibility that trades occur in disequilibrium. If so, demand and supply plans at any price cannot be defined independently of the nature of the disequilibrium (excess demand or excess supply) in the goods and labour markets. Indeed, a possible solution to the *ADAS* consistency problem is a reformulation of both relations on the basis of the fix-price disequilibrium models; see Rao (1986, 1991), Dalziel (1993) and Chirco and Colombo (1996). This approach, however, has two main drawbacks. The first is that it is not handy enough to be used for pedagogical purposes; the second, which is shared by all fix-price-type models, is that it assumes that the price is fixed, at least in the very short run, within a competitive setup – a setup, however, which cannot justify rigid prices, as agents are price-takers and nobody actually sets the price. The natural development of fix-price models has been in the direction of investigating what happens if agents may relax their quantity constraints by changing prices, that is, in the direction of imperfect competition; e.g., Benassy (1990) and Grandmont (1989).

Imperfect competition is indeed the only theoretical framework which in principle should allow microfounding the observed price rigidities on the labour and goods markets. Moreover, it offers an alternative solution to the $ADAS$ inconsistency problem. Under imperfect competition, price and output determination is not based on the interplay of independently derived demand and supply curves. Firms always choose a point along the demand curve, and in this sense output is always demand determined. The aggregate demand curve turns out to be coherently defined by the $ISLM$ output-price equilibrium: at any price no supply plan can be put forth by firms, which differs from the output actually demanded at that price.

There is no doubt that the development of a macroeconomic framework based on imperfect competition is in some sense (analytically and conceptually) more demanding than the standard perfectly competitive setup; however, we believe that the investment is rewarding. Imperfect competition is widely observed in the labour and in the goods markets;[1] it covers a wider set of economic environments, which cannot fit the straight jacket of perfect competition – be it enough to quote the existence of increasing returns. Finally, imperfect competition allows for equilibrium positions being inefficient:[2] in a macroeconomic scheme, this results in

---

[1] A thorough discussion on the empirical evidence that the labour market does not behave competitively is offered by Layard, Nickell and Jackman (1991, ch. 4). The existence of market power in the goods market has been empirically investigated, among others, by Bresnahan (1989), Domowitz, Hubbard and Petersen (1988) and Hall (1986, 1988).

[2] For excellent surveys of imperfectly competitive macroeconomic models see Dixon and Rankin (1994) and Silvestre (1993).

equilibrium outcomes characterised by under-utilization of the available resources. While price and wage full flexibility leads to full employment under perfect competition, this is not the case in an imperfectly competitive environment.

The main purpose of this chapter is to build a very simple macro-model with imperfect competition, both in the labour and in the goods markets, and to show that its behaviour can be represented through a coherent system of two equilibrium relations in the price-output space, which is similar, but indeed a logical alternative, to the standard *ADAS* model. Sections 11.2 and 11.3 are devoted to introducing the basic ingredients of our reformulation of the *ADAS* model: section 11.2 describes the basic framework, section 11.3 dwells upon the different price rigidities which may be supported by the latter. The analytical structure of the model is presented in section 11.4. Its behaviour and graphical representation under full flexibility and nominal rigidity are studied in sections 11.5 and 11.6, respectively. Finally, section 11.7 provides some concluding remarks.

11.2 AGGREGATE DEMAND AND SUPPLY UNDER IMPERFECT COMPETITION

Under imperfect competition the fact that firms always choose a point along the demand curve makes it obviously meaningless to think of a supply function with the status of an independent behavioural relation. This clearly holds both at the individual firm and at the aggregate levels. However, the way in which firms react to changes in any exogenous demand-variable can be synthetically described by the locus of price and quantity equilibrium pairs associated with different values of that variable. This locus fully describes the 'supply behaviour' contingent on alternative demand conditions. To avoid confusion with the standard *AS* curve, we shall denominate these loci as *PQE* curves.

To catch the intuition behind a *PQE* curve, consider the very simple case of an economy in which a single monopolist faces an aggregate demand curve, where a single policy variable Z is the relevant shift variable. In Figure 11.1, DD is the aggregate demand curve for $Z = Z_0$.

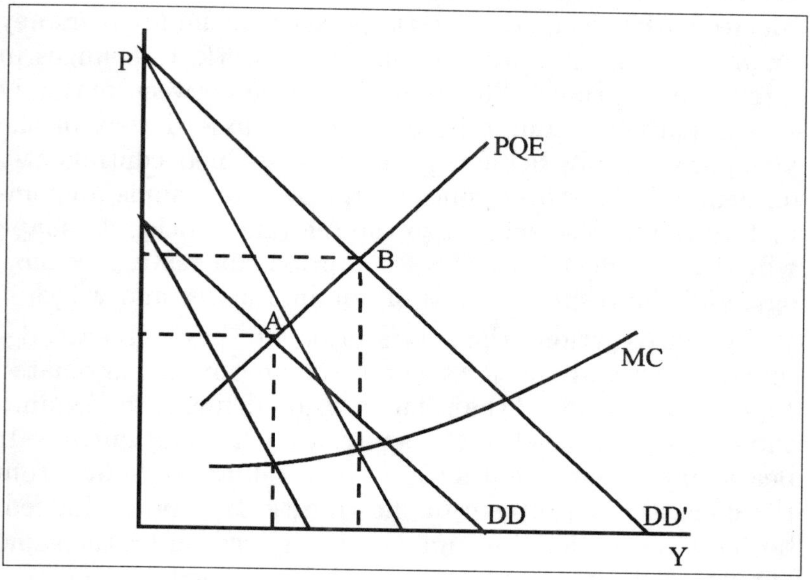

Figure 11.1

Assume that, given this demand constraint and his cost function, the monopolist maximises his profits, by equating marginal revenue and marginal cost, at point A on DD. Then A is a point on PQE curve. Consider now the DD' schedule, which is the aggregate demand curve for $Z = Z_1$. Depending on the behaviour of nominal marginal costs, the monopolist will choose a point on DD'. Assume he chooses point B. Then, B identifies another point on the PQE curve. By repeating this experiment for all values of Z, we obtain the PQE curve. Notice that by construction, given a level of Z, the corresponding aggregate demand curve and the PQE curve intersect at the price-quantity pair chosen by the monopolist for that level of Z.

It must be stressed that when more than one shift demand-variables are present, we may have in principle as many PQE curves as there are shift variables. The locus of price-quantity equilibrium pairs associated with changes, *ceteris paribus,* in the fiscal index may differ from that associated with changes, *ceteris paribus,* in nominal money balances or, in an open economy framework, to changes in foreign absorption.[3] The main difference between perfectly and imperfectly competitive setups, is indeed that in the latter the supply behaviour must be defined contingently on demand. Moreover, since each PQE curve sums up completely the firm's reaction to the relevant shocks, its shape will also be affected by the assumptions on tastes, technology, and the responsiveness of nominal prices and wages.

By construction, the intersection of the aggregate demand curve and the PQE curve (or any of the associated PQE curves, if more than one is to be defined) determines the equilibrium level of the aggregate price and output. It bears emphasising that such a system does not suffer from the consistency problem of the traditional model. Indeed, both curves are equilibrium curves, derived under the same hypothesis that output is demand determined.

11.3 THE ROLE OF WAGE RIGIDITIES

If modelling the economy on the basis of imperfect competition allows to avoid the consistency problem raised by the competitive $ADAS$ model, it also creates the appropriate environment for the analysis of causes and consequences of various types of price rigidities. Traditionally, three hypotheses on price rigidities have been embodied in competitive macromodels. The first is that the nominal wage may be fixed, while the nominal aggregate price is flexible. In this case, it is typically assumed that firms operate

[3] The PQE curves obtained by performing comparative statics exercises on various shift variables may differ if these variables have a different impact on the equilibrium mark-up. In this case, the shape of the PQE curve associated with each variable may also depend on the level at which the other shift variables are held constant. We shall return on this point below.

along their labour demand curve, and workers are rationed on the labour market. The supply curve is therefore upward sloping or flat, according to the shape of the marginal cost curve. The second is that both the nominal price and the nominal wage are fixed, so that both firms and workers cannot realise their desired (notional) plans. The third hypothesis is that the nominal wage and the nominal price are both flexible, but the real wage is rigid – due to some form of wage indexation – at a non-market clearing level. Needless to say, none of these hypotheses can be properly accounted for within a competitive setup. Indeed for price to be rigid there must be price-setting agents, whose choices deliver that very rigidity.[4]

Consider first real rigidities. If prices are set by a Walrasian auctioneer who reacts to excess demand signals, no structure of relative prices can prevail at which one or more markets do not clear. In this sense, non market-clearing calls for some imperfection – as Arrow (1959, p.48) famously observed, "in any situation where supply does not equal demand, it follows the economy will show evidence of monopoly and monopsony". Indeed in an imperfectly competitive world, the agents choices may deliver real prices at which resources are not fully employed, in which case such prices will be insensitive to excess demand or supply. If equilibrium is defined by the mutual consistency of optimal plans, it may occur at terms of trade which may not ensure market-clearing. For example, the existence of a trade union may support an equilibrium real wage at which some workers – though willing to work at the prevailing wage rate – are unemployed; and it may prevent individual underbidding. Clearly, this kind of real price rigidity is perfectly consistent with price-setting agents being able to

[4] Indeed, this is the core of that multifaceted research program which falls under the headings of New Keynesian Economics. The most relevant contributions in this field are collected in Mankiw and Romer (1991) and discussed, *inter alios*, by Benassi, Chirco and Colombo (1994).

adjust freely their nominal prices, in order to achieve their desired (rigid) real price.

The case for imperfect competition as a modeling strategy is perhaps even more compelling when studying the rationale for nominal price rigidities. The latter stem from the agents failure to set their nominal prices at a level consistent with their desired real price. Accordingly, it concerns the procedure through which, by setting a price in nominal terms, agents pursue their objectives defined in real terms. While a real price rigidity may well be individually optimal, nominal rigidities must be justified in terms of frictions which prevent (or make it too costly) attaining the desired real outcome via nominal instruments. These frictions may show up in various guises, such as the presence of adjustment costs, the excessive complexity of the solution algorithm for the optimal nominal price, or the inertial attitude of price setters. Their existence destroys the (zero-degree) homogeneity property of demand and supply plans and, by altering the system of real prices, it distorts the traders perceived incentives. Nominal rigidity makes real decisions dependent on the nominal anchor and the nominal scale of the economy.

In order to keep a clear distinction between real and nominal rigidities, in the following sections we proceed as follows. We first discuss the behaviour of a simple imperfectly competitive economy under the hypothesis that nominal prices and wages are fully flexible, so that the traders optimal real prices are istantaneously attained. We discuss the real rigidity properties of the related equilibrium, while showing that these do not necessarily affect the basic policy ineffectiveness results, which emerge typically in a perfectly competitive setup; indeed, monetary and fiscal policy experiments deliver a vertical PQE curve. Then we introduce nominal rigidities. Following a well established tradition, we first assume that the nominal wage is fixed, while prices are freely adjusted by price setters on the goods market. This allows to derive price and quantity equilibrium loci, which are positively sloped: if the nominal wage is rigid, positive demand shocks are followed by an increase in produced output, with real wages moving countercyclically. Then we add the hypothesis of nominal price rigidity. The model turns out to be observationally equivalent to a standard *ISLM* model of output determination; however, its being derived under imperfect competition implies quite a different evaluation of both the short run effect of policy measures, and the long run adjustment.

11.4 A MACROMODEL OF IMPERFECT COMPETITION

We describe an economy which is characterised by imperfect competition both in the goods and in the labour market. In this economy N goods are produced, which are imperfect substitutes, and each good is supplied by a single firm by means of labour only. Workers are organised in N sectoral unions. Bargaining is decentralised, and each union bargains on the real wage and employment with one of the N firms.

11.4.1 Firm's Behaviour

In the goods market monopolistic competition is assumed. The N firms are identical and face the same demand and technological constraints. The demand for firm i's product depends on its relative price and aggregate demand:

$$Y_i^d = \left(\frac{P_i}{P}\right)^{-\epsilon}\left(\frac{Y^d}{N}\right) \tag{1}$$

where $\epsilon > 1$ is the elasticity of demand, and Y^d is aggregate demand.[5] Whenever $(P_i/P) = 1$ for all i, the latter is evenly distributed among the N firms. We also notice that under imperfect competition output is demand-determined,

[5] For a derivation of a demand function of this kind we suggest referring to Blanchard and Fischer (1989, ch.8).

in the sense that in the aggregate the firm's optimal price-production choice always corresponds to a point on the demand curve. Since the standard *ISLM* based aggregate demand curve is drawn under the same hypothesis (i.e. that for any given price output and income are equal to aggregate demand at that price), we may consistently write aggregate demand as a reduced form of the *ISLM* system:

$$Y^d = Y^d\left(\frac{M}{P}, G\right) \tag{2}$$

where M/P denotes real money balances and G is a measure of fiscal stance. The firms' production function requires only labour and exhibits non-increasing returns:

$$Y_i = \frac{1}{\alpha} L_i^{\alpha} \qquad \alpha \leq 1 \tag{3}$$

The inverse of the production function gives the labour requirement for any given level of output:

$$L_i = \left(\alpha Y_i\right)^{1/\alpha} \tag{4}$$

Firm i chooses P_i in order to maximise the following real profit function, subject to the demand function (1) and the labour requirement (4), and taking the aggregate price level P as given:

$$\Pi_i = \frac{P_i}{P} Y_i - \frac{W_i}{P} L_i \tag{5}$$

where W_i is the nominal wage paid by firm i.

The usual profit maximisation condition that marginal revenue equals marginal cost may thus be written as follows:

$$\frac{P_i}{P}\left[1 - \frac{1}{\epsilon}\right] = \frac{W_i}{P}(\alpha Y_i)^{\frac{1-\alpha}{\alpha}} \tag{6.1}$$

or

$$\frac{P_i}{P}\left[1 - \frac{1}{\epsilon}\right] = \frac{W_i}{P}\frac{1}{L_i^{\alpha-1}} \tag{6.2}$$

We can make different uses of equations (6). By substituting (1) into (6.1), we obtain the optimal relative price of firm i , as a function of the real wage and the exogenous demand variables:

$$\frac{P_i}{P} = \left[\mu \frac{W_i}{P}\right]^{\alpha/\gamma} \left[\frac{\alpha}{N} Y^d\left(\frac{M}{P}, G\right)\right]^{\frac{1-\alpha}{\gamma}} \tag{6.1.1}$$

where $\gamma = \alpha + \epsilon(1-\alpha)$ and $\mu = 1/(1-1/\epsilon) > 1$ is the mark-up. Notice that (6.1.1) is the standard

solution of the firm's partial equilibrium problem within our monopolistic economy, and that the optimal relative price is homogeneous of degree zero in all nominal variables.

Take now equation (6.2). It can be interpreted as the logical equivalent, in this imperfectly competitive model, of the labour demand schedule of firm i:[6]

$$L_i^d = \left[\frac{W_i}{P_i}\mu\right]^{\frac{1}{\alpha-1}} \tag{7}$$

Notice that each firm's desired level of employment is negatively related to its product wage and the mark-up, provided that $\alpha < 1$. If $\alpha = 1$, then the firm is willing to employ any quantity of labour at a product wage equal to $1/\mu$.

11.4.2 Union's Behaviour

We assume that the bargaining between any union and the corresponding firm takes the 'monopoly union' form: by taking the aggregate variables as given, union i sets the nominal wage in sector i, while firm i chooses its optimal level of employment at that wage. Jobs are then allocated randomly among the members of union i.

The union objective function is the expected utility of its representative member:

[6] It is the 'logical equivalent' because firms actually set their own price, while in a competitive framework they determine the optimal labour quantity, given the product wage.

$$U = \nu\Big(\frac{W_i}{P}\Big)\frac{L_i}{\overline{L}_i} + \nu(A)\Big(1 - \frac{L_i}{\overline{L}_i}\Big) \tag{8}$$

where the utilities $\nu(\cdot)$ of the real wage in sector i, and of the outside opportunity in real terms (A), are weighted by the probabilities of being employed or unemployed in sector i, respectively.

A useful specification of the above utility function is obtained by assuming that $\nu(\cdot)$ is linear, so that the union problem collapses to maximising the expected difference between the wage and the outside opportunity:

$$\max_{W_i} Z = \Big(\frac{W_i}{P} - A\Big)\frac{L_i}{\overline{L}_i} \tag{9}$$

subject to the firm's desired employment-product wage relation, $L_i = L_i^d$.

Notice from (7) that the "labour demand" expressed by firm i , the constraint faced by the union, depends on the product wage of that firm (W_i/P_i), while unions and workers are concerned with the purchasing power of the wage rate (W_i/P). However, a sectoral union is aware that the optimal pricing behaviour of firm i depends on the market opportunities of the latter, described by the demand curve (1). In terms of consumption wage, the constraint faced by the union can be obtained by substituting (1) into (7) for P_i and using (3):

$$L_i^d = \Big[\frac{W_i}{P}\mu\Big]^{-\theta}\Big(\frac{\alpha Y^d}{N}\Big)^{\theta/\epsilon}; \quad \theta = \Big\{1/[(1-\alpha)+\alpha/\epsilon]\Big\} > 0 \tag{10}$$

By solving problem (9) subject to (10), the optimal consumption wage for the union is

$$\frac{W_i}{P} = A\frac{\theta}{\theta - 1} = \frac{A\mu}{\alpha} \tag{11}$$

which can be read as a mark-up over the outside opportunity A.[7]

[7] In this formulation, this 'mark-up' depends only on *(continued)*

11.5 AGGREGATE BEHAVIOUR OF FIRMS AND UNIONS

In the behavioural equations of firms and unions some aggregate variables are present, which in a macroeconomic perspective must be made endogenous. Take first equation (11). The outside opportunity A in any sector i depends on the workers earnings when not employed within sector i. We assume that these are given by a geometric average of the unemployment benefit in real terms (B/P) and the average real wage (W/P) prevailing in the rest of the economy:

$$A = \left(\frac{W}{P}\right)^{(1-u)} \left(\frac{B}{P}\right)^{u} \tag{12}$$

where the weighting factor u is the aggregate rate of unemployment, $u = (L - L)/\overline{L}$, and obviously $L = \sum_{i=1}^{N} L_i$ with $\overline{L}$ equal to the total number of workers. By substituting (12) into (11), and recalling that all unions and firms are identical so that $W_i = W$ for all i, we obtain an *aggregate wage setting schedule* for our economy:

$$\frac{W}{P} = \frac{B}{P}\left(\frac{\mu}{\alpha}\right)^{\frac{1}{u}} \tag{13}$$

This upward sloping relation between the real wage and the level of employment is represented in Figure 11.2, as the WS curve. The reason why the WS curve slopes upwards is that a higher level of aggregate employment generates wider outside opportunities for workers in all sectors, and induces unions to choose a higher wage rate in each sector.

Since all firms pay the same nominal wage W, they set an identical nominal price $P_i = P$, so that from (6.2) we may obtain the aggregate relation between the firm's desired level

---

the two elements which influence the elasticity of 'labour demand', namely the degree of the firm's market power on the goods market and the technological parameter α. In a more general formulation of the bargaining process, the difference between the wage and the outside opportunity reflects the relative strength of unions and firms.

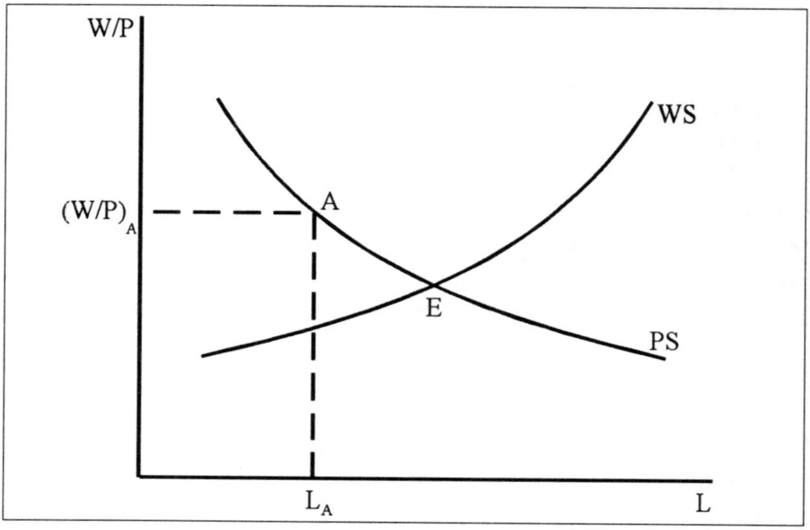

Figure 11.2

of employment and the real wage. This relation is called the *aggregate price setting schedule*

$$L = N\left(\frac{W}{P}\mu\right)^{\frac{1}{\alpha-1}} \tag{14}$$

which is decreasing if $\alpha < 1$. If $\alpha = 1$, the price setting schedule is horizontal and defines univocally the real wage consistent with firms' profit maximisation. This schedule is drawn in Figure 11.2, for $\alpha < 1$, as the PS curve. It summarises the optimal behaviour of the firm under the demand constraint they perceive. Consider a generic point A on the PS curve. Point A laying on PS curve means that the firm will set the price (say, P_A) at which a quantity corresponds on the demand curve which requires employing L_A workers, only in the case the real wage ends up being $(W/P)_A$. A point which must be stressed is that the PS curve is not an aggregate labour demand curve, since P is a choice variable for the firms. Rather it shows the real wage at which any nominal price-quantity pair on the aggregate demand curve can be consistent with firms maximising their profits.

11.6 EQUILIBRIUM UNDER FULL NOMINAL FLEXIBILITY

11.6.1 Determination and Properties of Equilibrium

In order to define the macroeconomic equilibrium under the hypothesis of full nominal wage and price flexibility, we have to determine four unknown variables, $Y, L, W/P$ and P (the nominal wage being implicitly obtained by the latter two). The four independent equations which deliver the required solution are the wage setting schedule (13), the price setting schedule (14), the aggregate demand curve (2), and the employment-output relation holding in aggregate which will be denoted now as (3′):

$$Y = N\frac{1}{\alpha}\left(\frac{L}{N}\right)^{\alpha} \tag{3'}$$

The macroeconomic flexible equilibrium is represented in Figure 11.3, where all the relevant relations are drawn simultaneously. In Figure 11.3a the PS and WS curves are drawn in the $(\frac{P}{W}, L)$ space. In Figure 11.3b the level of employment is translated into output through equation (3′). In Figure 11.3c, along the aggregate demand curve any level of output is associated with the nominal price level at which that output is actually demanded. Figure 11.3d allows to determine the nominal wage as the ratio between P and P/W.

The PS curve and the WS curve intersect at a point E.[8] At E the unions' and firms' choices are mutually compat-

[8] The assumption that technology exhibits non-increasing returns ensures that the equilibrium is unique. The model could be easily extended to the case in which $\alpha > 1$, provided the firm's marginal revenue curve is steeper than the marginal cost curve. Notice that under increasing returns the PS curve is upward sloping in *(continued)*

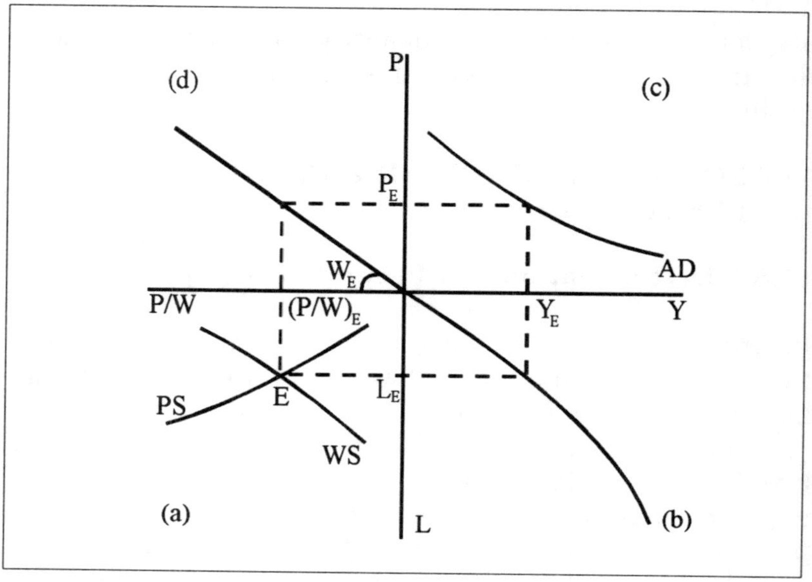

Figure 11.3

ible: on the one hand firms choose to employ L_E workers (i.e. to set a price P_E and produce Y_E in Figures 11. 3b to 11.3c), if the nominal wage is such that a real wage $(W/P)_E$ prevails. On the other hand, if employment is L_E unions require exactly a real wage $(W/P)_E$ and thus, under full flexibility, they maximise their objective function by setting the nominal wage W_E (Figure 11.3d) such that indeed $W_E/P_E = (W/P)_E$ prevails.

It should be clear that under full flexibility our non-competitive economy shares with its standard competitive counterpart two basic properties: neutrality and dichotomy. Neutrality is satisfied since multiplying all nominal vari-

the $(\frac{W}{P}, L)$ space, and that this may cause multiple equilibria to arise. The stability problems which multiplicity may cause in comparative statics led us to exclude this possibility in this simple formulation of the model. Within a very similar framework, the macroeconomic implications of increasing returns are discussed in Kiyotaki (1988) and Manning (1990, 1992).

ables by the same scale variable does not affect the equilibrium value of real variables. Moreover, the model dichotomises in that aggregate output is univocally determined by equations (13), (14) and (3′): the subset of relations represented in Figure 11.3a and Figure 11.3b determines all real variables, independently of the level of aggregate demand.

While neutrality derives immediately from homogeneity of degree zero of all behavioural relations, the dichotomy property requires some comments. As we specified above, in a non-competitive setting, output is in a sense demand-determined: each firm always chooses a point on its demand function, and in the aggregate all firms place themselves along the aggregate demand curve: indeed, the demand curve is the locus of the price-quantity pairs among which firms choose their profit-maximising solution. Output is thus demand-determined, in that firms perceive the demand curve as a constraint on their production decisions: since the price is higher than the marginal cost, they would be willing to produce more at the equilibrium price, should the extra-production be demanded at that price.

However, this *does not* necessarily imply that the equilibrium output is affected by shifts in the exogenous demand variables. Assume that the price-quantity opportunities open to the firms shift in the (Y, P) space, due to a change in these variables. Since in our model this has no effect on the equilibrium mark-up, the behavioural relationships for firms and unions – equations (13) and (14) – are not affected by this change either, and the equilibrium values of L and W/P are unaltered. But this amounts to saying that firms and unions react to the changes in the demand conditions by simply increasing the price and the nominal wage levels: the real equilibrium is accordingly unchanged. In particular, when demand shifts, firms do perceive a change in their price-quantity constraint, but end up choosing a point thereon such that the quantity is unchanged.

While this is a common result in the literature, it must be stressed that it depends *crucially* on the mark-up being assumed invariant to real demand shocks. Were the equilibrium mark-up – and thus the elasticity of demand – affected by demand shocks, the PS and WS curves would not be independent of aggregate demand. The model would no longer exhibit dichotomy.[9]More precisely, output would react positively to expansionary policy measures, whenever the latter end up reducing the equilibrium mark-up. Quite obviously, this possibility can arise only in an imperfectly competitive environment.

Another important feature which distinguishes this flexible equilibrium from the corresponding competitive one is the existence of unemployment at equilibrium. If the labour market was competitive, each worker would be willing to offer his labour services at a reservation wage equal to the outside opportunity, so that $W/P = B/P$: the labour supply curve would be horizontal at B/P. Since (13) lies above B/P for all levels of L, the imperfectly competitive equilibrium exhibits unemployment, in that individual workers who would be willing to work at the prevailing wage are unable to find a job at that wage.[10] If workers organise themselves into

unions and agree with firms on bilateral firm-union bargaining, maximisation of their ex-ante expected utility will make some workers involuntarily unemployed ex-post. This is an example of what in section 11.3 was defined as a real rigidity: due to some market imperfections (like the existence of a union) an optimal, equilibrium real wage prevails, such that the market does not clear at that wage, and which is insensitive to the existence of unemployment.[11] The in-

---

[9] This has been recently stressed by Lindbeck and Snower (1994).

[10] Moreover, in the $(\frac{W}{P}, L)$ space, the PS schedule lies below the corresponding competitive labour demand curve. The existence of market power in the goods market reduces the willingness of firms to employ labour at any level of the real wage.

[11] Other causes of real wage rigidity are analysed in the efficiency wage theory, Weiss (1991), and in the insider-outsider explanation of unemployment; Lindbeck and Snower (1988).

tersection between the PS and WS schedule defines an equilibrium wage, in the sense that the optimal decision makers' choices are mutually consistent at that wage – hence, the market outcome is such that unemployment exerts no pressure towards changing it.

11.6.2 Aggregate Demand and Aggregate Supply Under Full Flexibility

We are now in the position to sum up the properties of the model under full nominal flexibility, in terms of the AD curve and the PQE curve discussed in section 11.2. Here we limit ourselves to a graphical analysis, the algebra being developed in the Appendix.

As we have just seen, neither the price setting, nor the wage setting schedules are directly affected by the exogenous policy variables M and G. The equilibrium value of employment and output, L_E and Y_E, are insensitive to changes in these variables. The

adjustment is realised through the nominal price (and wage) level: an increase in M induces an equiproportional increase in P, while an increase in G fully crowds out private demand – in both cases firms increase P to such an extent that, given $G, M/P$ is restored at the level at which $Y^d = Y_E$.

This ineffectiveness result shows up in the PQE curve associated with changes in M and that associated with changes in G being vertical (and coinciding) in the (Y, P) space (Figure 11.4). However, these vertical supply relations may be shifted horizontally in the same space not only by technological shocks, but also by changes in the degree of monopoly power in the goods market.

11.7 EQUILIBRIUM UNDER NOMINAL RIGIDITIES

So far, the reformulation of the macroeconomic general equilibrium in an imperfectly competitive setup appears to be useful under two main respects: it shows that (a) due to

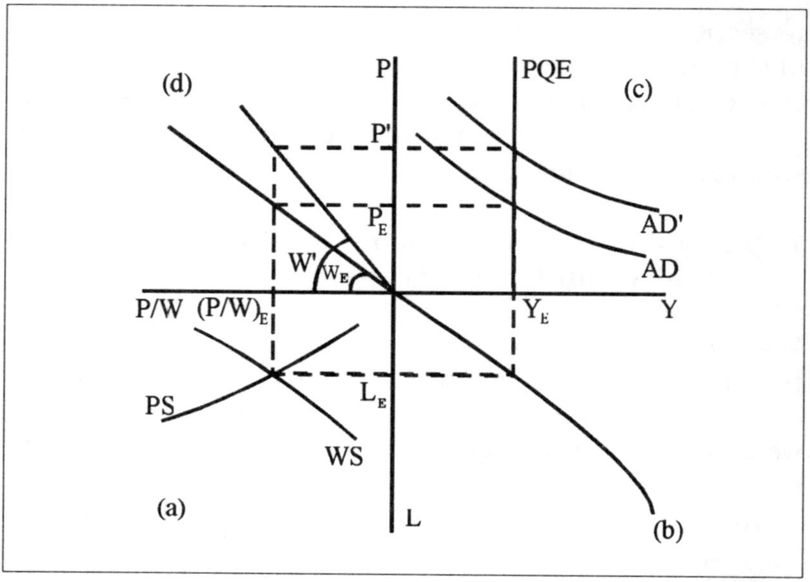

Figure 11.4

monopoly power, rational agents may end up choosing an inefficient level of resource utilisation; (b) a change in the degree of monopoly power may alter the equilibrium level of output and employment. What we want to stress now is that in the above model some agents are identified in each market, who actually set the nominal price in that market – unions set the nominal wage relevant for each firm, firms set the nominal price for their own products. While there is no reason for an auctioneer not to adjust prices (after all, price adjustment is his job!), a union or a firm may have several good reasons to behave inertially: implementing a continuous nominal price adjustment may undermine long run relationships, drain resources, make behaviour less predictable. In a word, it is directly or indirectly costly. Only in a world of price setting agents can nominal prices be kept fixed in the short run if the costs of price adjustment are higher than the gains of a continuous realignment.[12]

[12] See Andersen (1994) for the microfoundations of nominal rigidity.

11.7.1 Equilibrium Under Nominal Wage Rigidity

Assume now unions set symmetrically the nominal wage, and keep it constant in the short run in order to minimise, for example, the informational costs imposed by a continuous revision. Assume also that prices are flexible, i.e. set by the firms at their desired level. We can now see how the model can be worked out in this case. Of course, equation (13) is now replaced by

$$W = \overline{W}. \tag{13'}$$

Accordingly, equations (2), (3′), (13′) and (14) are now the set of independent equations which allows us to solve for the unknown variables $Y, L, P, W/P$. Clearly, the model looses both neutrality and dichotomy: since the nominal wage is fixed, the set of behavioural relations is not homogenous of degree zero in the remaining nominal variables. The model is no more dichotomised, as aggregate demand is necessary to pin down the equilibrium values of the real variables, Y, L and W/P. In order to see this point, consider Figure 11.5. We recall that the PS curve defines implicitly the *price over wage ratio* at which any point on the demand curve can be optimal for the firms. Once W is given, firms may only set that price P^*, at which (a) a quantity Y^* is demanded in aggregate; (b) a real wage $(W/P)^* = \overline{W}/P^*$ prevails at which firms are willing to employ those L^* workers which produce an amount Y^* of output. The position of the aggregate demand curve in the (Y, P) space becomes relevant: if W is fixed, the firms optimal behaviour on the PS curve is determined by the nominal price level which they must set to fulfill the demand constraint.

11.7.2 Aggregate Demand and Supply Under Nominal Wage Rigidity

In terms of our AD–PQE framework, the main consequence of nominal wage rigidity is that the price and quantity equilibrium loci are no more vertical. In Figure 11.5, (Y^*, P^*) is

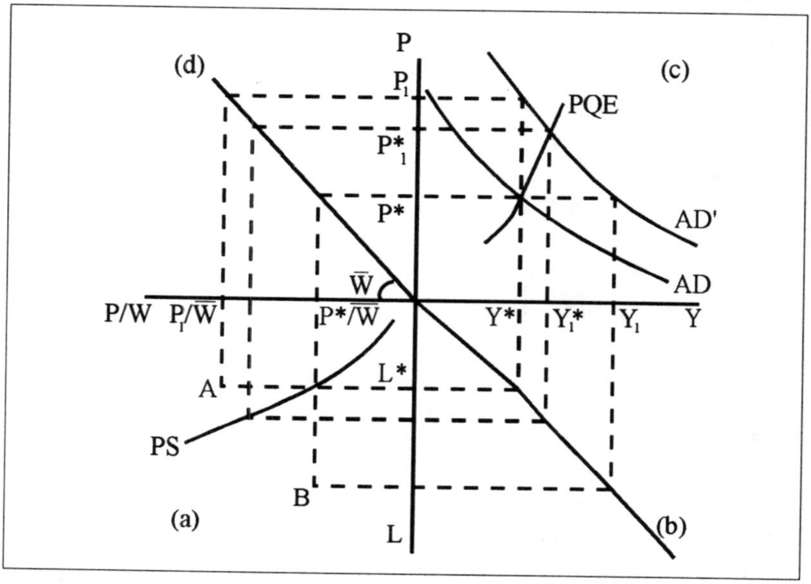

Figure 11.5

the point chosen by the firms along the demand curve AD, when the exogenous policy variables are $M = M_0$ and $G = G_0$. If, for example, M increases to M_1, say, the aggregate demand curve shifts outwards to AD'. In order to derive the PQE curve associated with monetary shocks, let us perform the following experiment. Assume that firms increase the price level to P_1, so that along the AD' curve the quantity still is Y^*. Given $W = \overline{W}$, the real wage would then turns out to be $(\overline{W}/P_1)$, lower than $(\overline{W}/P^*)$. If firms produced Y^* at a real wage $(\overline{W}/P_1)$, at point A the marginal revenue product of labour would be higher than the real wage, and firms would perceive an incentive to produce more. A price P_1 and a quantity Y^* cannot be an equilibrium: the PQE curve cannot be vertical. Assume, on the contrary, that firms keep on setting the price P^* to which there corresponds a quantity Y_1 on the AD'. At the unchanged real wage the firms have no incentive to increase production up to Y_1. If they produced Y_1 at a real wage $(\overline{W}/P^*)$, at point B

the marginal revenue product of labour would be lower than the real wage – accordingly, unless the production function exhibits constant returns ($\alpha = 1$), the PQE curve cannot be horizontal. Thus firms will react to the change in M by increasing the price, less than proportionally, to P_1^*, so that production increases as well, to Y_1^*. The PQE associated with changes in M is therefore upward sloping.

A similar result can be obtained if the aggregate demand curve moves due to a change in G. The price-quantity pairs chosen by the firms for different levels of G lie on a curve which, under the assumption that public expenditure does not affect the elasticity of demand, has the same shape of the PQE associated with changes in M. In the more general case in which the level of G affects the elasticity of demand, changes in this fiscal index not only move the AD curve in the (Y, P) space, but shift the PS curve in the $(\frac{P}{W}, L)$ space, via changes in the desired mark-up. The PQE curve associated with changes in G does not coincide with that associated with changes in M: it tends to be flatter if the mark-up decreases when G increases and steeper in the opposite case. In general, if W is sticky, the crowding out of private expenditure is partial: if G increases, the reduction of real money balances induced by the increase in P is such that aggregate demand increases at equilibrium.

Inspection of Figure 11.5 shows that under nominal wage rigidity the shape of the PQE is also affected by the properties of technology. With a constant mark-up, the PQE is upward sloping in the presence of decreasing returns to labour, while constant returns imply a horizontal PQE curve. This is a restatement of the well known result, that with constant marginal costs, sticky nominal wages and isoelastic demand, the price is insensitive to isoelastic demand shifts. That has frequently been claimed to be a microfoundation of price insensitivity to demand; the above discussion should have made it clear that price being insensitive to demand is neither a consequence of flat marginal costs, nor does it derive from the mark-up being constant. Rather, it depends crucially on the sticky wage assumption. Should the nominal wage be fully flexible, constant returns and constant mark-up would be consistent with a vertical PQE curve.

11.7.3 Equilibrium Under Nominal Price Rigidity

So far we have assumed firms to be on the PS curve: i.e. that they be always able to set a nominal price such that their maximum profit is achieved, for any given levels of the nominal wage and the aggregate demand. But, as for unions, a continuous realignment of nominal prices to an ever changing environment may be costly, and this may cause individual prices and the price level to be rigid. We shall discuss here neither the many reasons why changing prices may be costly, nor the different rules of dynamic price adjustment which have been derived under various assumptions on the nature of adjustment costs.[13] Rather, we shall concentrate on the static and comparative static properties of the fix-price equilibrium, when the latter is explicitly derived within a imperfectly competitive setup. We recall that the hypothesis of sticky nominal wages allowed us to replace the union behavioural equation (13) with equation (13′), which defines the level at which the wage is fixed. This amounts to saying that unions do not typically realise their desired (flexible) plans at the $AD\text{–}PQE$ equilibrium. If both wages and nominal prices are fixed, then firms do not realise their desired (flexible) plans either, and equation (14) must be replaced by

$$P = \overline{P} \tag{14'}$$

which defines the price level at which the price is fixed. Equations (13′), (14′), (2) and (3′) fully define the equilibrium value of W, P, Y and L. Equation (2) defines univocally the level of output given M and G, while (3′) determines the

[13] For a textbook discussion of the dynamic adjustment rules, see Blanchard and Fischer (1989, ch.8). An updated collection of some important chapters with a thourough introduction is presented by Sheshinski and Weiss (1993).

level of employment required in the aggregate to produce that output. Needless to say, the model collapses to a standard *ISLM* formulation. The *PQE* curves turn out to be horizontal in the (Y, P) space, and 'supply' plays no role in output determination.

There is however an important difference between the competitive and the non-competitive formulation of the model with fixed wage and price. Assume that in both cases the nominal wages and prices are initially set at their flexible equilibrium values. In a competitive setting, both a demand expansion and a demand contraction would make firms as well as workers worse off, which is due to the optimality properties of that equilibrium. For a demand expansion to be accomodated by an increase in production, workers should supply labour at a real wage lower than the marginal disutility of labour, and firms should employ workers at a wage higher than their marginal productivity.[14] A demand contraction is followed by a reduction in output and employment, so that the real wage falls below the marginal productivity of labour, while it turns out to be greater than the marginal disutility of labour.[15] In both cases, the two sides of the labour market would gain from full nominal adjustment, and indeed this is the deep justification for the traditional stabilisation macropolicies, whose stated aim is to minimise the economy's deviations from its flexible ("full employment") equilibrium.

In a non-competitive setting, the flexible equilibrium does not exhibit the same efficiency properties. The real wage is greater than the marginal disutility of labour and lower than its marginal productivity: the flexible equilibrium itself shares the typical properties of a Keynesian unemployment equilibrium. Therefore, starting from the flex-

---

[14] Notice that, within the standard Malinvaud-type fix-price model, the increase in demand moves the economy into the repressed-inflation region.

[15] That is, a demand contraction pushes the economy into the Keynesian region (see fn. 14).

ible equilibrium a positive demand shock, *under wage and price rigidity,* would make both the firms and the workers better off, while a negative shock would exacerbate the allocative inefficiency of the flexible equilibrium itself. When price and wage do not properly perform their allocative role – and this is certainly the case under imperfect competition – a widespread nominal rigidity may, in some circumstances, create a favourable environment for welfare improving aggregate demand policies.

The dynamic counterpart of these considerations is that the various mechanisms of wage and price adjustment which have been devised in a price-setting environment do not perform the same welfare improving role they have in a competitive setting. The positive effects of demand expansion envisioned above are confined to the short run. A non-competitive economy tends to long run (flexible) equilibrium positions in which an allocative inefficiency of the Keynesian unemployment type inevitably prevails. In a normative perspective this implies that while there is a case for policy makers to exploit in the short run the welfare improving opportunities created by agents inertial behaviour, the unexploited gains from trade which persist at the flexible equilibrium cannot be recovered in the long run through an aggregate demand expansion. They call for policies aimed at reducing the overall degree of monopoly power in the economy.

11.8 CONCLUDING REMARKS

The model we have sketched in the previous sections is much simpler than those developed in the specialised literature in recent years. In particular, we have drastically simplified the treatment of the demand side. This should be enriched by a detailed specification of consumers' preferences, and the explicit solution of an intertemporal constrained maximisation problem. Moreover, we have followed most of the intermediate macroeconomics textbooks in treating the fiscal index as exogenous. A more satisfactory discussion of the public sector should include a more precise definition of the nature of public expenditure and of its financing. On the supply side, two points must be stressed. On the one hand, the monopoly union model is just one, and the simplest, possible device to describe the bargaining process on the labour market. On the other hand our derivation of the wage setting schedule leaves aside any consideration of the consumers' labour-leisure choice. This latter point becomes especially relevant in the analysis of the supply side impact of a balanced-budget fiscal expansion – which turns out to be magnified in the presence of imperfect competition in the goods market; Mankiw (1988) and Startz (1989).

Finally, notice that we have developed a closed-economy analysis. As Dixon (1994, p.32) has pointed out "There has, as yet, been little literature developing the theme of imperfect competition in open economy models". What is worth recalling here is that a Mundell-Fleming model based on imperfect competition modifies some standard results, such as the beggar-thy-neighbour properties of a monetary expansion under flexible exchange rates (or of an exchange rate depreciation): a unilateral monetary expansion exerts a positive worldwide welfare effect, as both the domestic and the foreign countries take advantage of the subsequent aggregate demand expansion; Obstfeld and Rogoff (1995) and Colombo (1996)

Despite its shortcuts, however, our simple framework offers a more coherent picture of the economic mechanisms at work in non-competitive economies, than that suggested in most macroeconomics textbooks. While it is quite common to find in many of them an explicit reference to non-competitive elements – unions, mark-up pricing, sluggish price adjustment – the latter, and their effects, are not fully integrated into the derivation of the macroeconomic equilibrium.[16]

[16] For example, Dornbusch and Fischer (1994) suggest that prices are set according to a mark-up formula and that nominal wages are sluggish due to long term staggered contracts. But they *(continued)*

Imperfect competition has already become the key reference framework in many other areas of economic analysis. Industrial economics and trade theory have highly benefitted from these extensions. It is somewhat surprising that it has not yet fully embodied in basic macroeconomics. According to many, macroeconomics should aim at explaning why the behaviour of economic aggregates does not merely amplify the individual behaviour. If this is the correct way to pose the basic question of macroeconomics, its basic answer may soundly be grounded on imperfect competition – the latter, even its oldest formulations, creates an environment for individual decision taking, where the invisible hand is no more able to reconcile individual and social optima. This work would like to suggest that moving in this direction is worthy and rewarding, and it may be fruitfully done also at an introductory level.

---

treat the long run (flexible) equilibrium positions as traditional full employment equilibria. Abel and Bernanke (1992) clearly distinguish between the competitive long run vertical aggregate supply curve and a "Keynesian" vertical supply curve, based on real rigidities on the labour market. Their treatment of the goods market is however basically competitive. A textbook entirely based on the imperfect competition hypothesis is Carlin and Soskice (1990), where the appeal to some ad hoc hypotheses leads the authors to consider only a subset of the possible behaviour of the model.

Appendix to Chapter 11

We give here a synthetic account of the basic model in a log-linear version.

(A) The Flexible Equilibrium

The model is made up by four equations: price and wage setting (equations (13) and (14) in the text), employment-output aggregate relation (3′) and aggregate demand (2). The four unknowns are employment (L), the real wage (W/P), output (Y), and the aggregate price level (P). Let ω denote the log of the real wage, and β the log of unemployment benefits in real terms. Then the logarithm version of the model is as follows:

$$\ell = n - \frac{1}{1-\alpha}(\omega + ln\ \mu)$$
$$\omega = \beta + [1/(\bar{\ell} - \ell)]\ (ln\ \mu - ln\ \alpha)$$
$$y = (1-\alpha)n - ln\ \alpha + \alpha\ell$$
$$y^d = \gamma(m-p) + \delta g$$

where lower case letters denote the log of the corresponding upper case variables, aggregate demand is specified in a standard version, and the difference in logs $\bar{\ell} - \ell \approx u$.

Notice that our hypotheses imply that $ln\ \mu - ln\ \alpha > 0$. We can differentiate the system to linearise it around an equilibrium, to get

$$\begin{pmatrix} 1 & \frac{1}{1-\alpha} & 0 & 0 \\ -\frac{ln\ \mu - ln\ \alpha}{(\bar{\ell}-\ell)^2} & 1 & 0 & 0 \\ -\alpha & 0 & 0 & 1 \\ 0 & 0 & \gamma & 1 \end{pmatrix} \begin{pmatrix} d\ell \\ d\omega \\ dp \\ dy \end{pmatrix} =$$

$$\begin{pmatrix} -[1/(1-\alpha)]\ dln\ \mu \\ 1/(\overline{\ell}-\ell)dln\ \mu + d\beta \\ 0 \\ \gamma dm + \delta dg \end{pmatrix}$$

where we have set $d\alpha = 0$. We note by simple inspection that the system is block-recursive: the first two equations (price-setting and wage-setting) pin down the two variables $d\ell$ and $d\omega$ independently of the other variables – as shown by the zeros in the upper right-hand corner of the matrix of coefficients. Accordingly, in order to perform comparative statics exercises on ℓ and ω we can limit ourselves to working with the subsystem

$$\begin{pmatrix} 1 & [1/(1-\alpha)] \\ -[(ln\ \mu - ln\ \alpha)/(\overline{\ell}-\ell)^2] & 1 \end{pmatrix} \begin{pmatrix} d\ell \\ d\omega \end{pmatrix}$$

$$= \begin{pmatrix} -1/(1-\alpha) \\ 1/(\overline{\ell}-\ell) \end{pmatrix} dln\ \mu + \begin{pmatrix} 0 \\ 1 \end{pmatrix} d\beta$$

The equilibrium values of employment and the real wage are unaffected by the policy variables m and g, while they depend on the mark-up and the level of unemployment benefits. By using Cramer's rule, one can easily see that $(d\ell/dln\ \mu) < 0$, while the effect on ω is ambiguous: indeed, an increase in the mark-up shifts both the price setting and the wage setting curves to the left. Clearly, $(d\ell/d\beta) < 0$ and $(d\omega/d\beta) > 0$.

Once employment is determined, the production function sets output, aggregate demand and the price level. Notice in particular that in the last equation dp and dm exhibit the same coefficient γ, which implies neutrality: any increase in the nominal money supply implies that the price level moves in the same proportion, leaving real money balances unaffected. In terms of our PQE curve, we have:

$$\frac{dy}{dm} = 0, \quad \text{and} \quad \frac{dp}{dm} = 1$$

which imply a vertical PQE curve, the elasticity of which is:

$$\frac{dp}{dy}|_{dm} = \frac{dp/dm}{dy/dm} = \infty.$$

The reader may check that the same result applies for changes in g.

(B) Nominal wage rigidity

In the nominal wage rigidity case, the wage setting curve is replaced by condition (13′), which we can render in log terms as $w = \overline{w}$. Accordingly, the complete system is now

$$\ell = n - \frac{1}{1-\alpha}(\overline{w} - p + ln\ \mu)$$

$$y = (1-\alpha)n - ln\ \alpha + \alpha\ell$$

$$y^d = \gamma(m-p) + \delta\ g$$

in the three endogenous variables p, y, and ℓ. In order to perform our comparative statics experiments we again differentiate the system to obtain

$$\begin{pmatrix} 1 & \frac{1}{(1-\alpha)} & 0 \\ -\alpha & 0 & 1 \\ 0 & \gamma & 1 \end{pmatrix} \begin{pmatrix} d\ell \\ dp \\ dy \end{pmatrix} = \begin{pmatrix} -\frac{d\overline{w}}{(1-\alpha)} - \frac{dln\ \mu}{(1-\alpha)} \\ 0 \\ \gamma dm + \delta dg \end{pmatrix}$$

where again we set $d\alpha = 0$. We first notice that fixing nominal wages does away with block-recursiveness. One can easily verify that the determinant of the coefficient matrix is negative. By applying Cramer's rule, we find the natural results that (equilibrium) output and employment increase with g and m, and decrease with $ln\ \mu$ and $\overline{w}$; also, it is easy to check that the equilibrium price level is increasing in all exogenous variables. One noteworthy point is that

$$\frac{dp}{dm} = \frac{\gamma - \alpha\gamma}{\gamma - \gamma\alpha + \alpha} < 1$$

That is, the elasticity of price with respect to money is less than one, so that any given percentage increase in nominal money supply is not translated one-to-one into the same increase in the price level. Indeed, one can easily check that,

$$\frac{dy}{dm} = \frac{\alpha\gamma}{\gamma - \gamma\alpha + \alpha} > 0$$

so that

$$\frac{dp}{dy}|_{dm} = \frac{dp/dm}{dy/dm} = \frac{1-\alpha}{\alpha} > 0$$

and the PQE curve is positively sloped. We leave it to the reader to show that under our hypothesis of constant mark-up the PQE curve associated with changes in g coincides with that associated with changes in m.

Bibliography

Abel, A.B. and Bernanke, B.S., (1992) *Macroeconomics,* Reading, MA: Addison-Wesley.

Abel, A.B. and Bernanke, B.S., (1994) *Macroeconomics,* Reading, MA: Addison-Wesley.

Abel, A.B. and Bernanke, B.S., (1995) *Macroeconomics,* 2nd Ed., Reading, MA: Addison-Wesley.

Ackley, G., (1961) *Macroeconomic Theory,* New York: Macmillan.

Akerlof, G.A. and Yellen, J., (1987) "Rational Models of Irrational Behaviour", *American Economic Review,* Vol.77, May, pp.137-142.

Allen, R.C. and Stone, J.H., (1993) "The New Aggregate Demand Models: A Critical Perspective", *Australian Economic Papers,* Vol.32, December, pp.248-257.

Allen, R.C. and Stone, J.H., (1997) "Walrasian, Non-Walrasian and Post-Walrasian Perspectives on the ADAS Model: Theoretical and Pedagogical Implications", *this volume.*

Amacher, R.C. and Ulbrich, H.H., (1995) *Macroeconomic Principles and Policies,* 6th Ed., Cincinnati: South-Western College Publishing.

Andersen, T.M., (1994) *Price Rigidity: Causes and Macroeconomic Implications,* Oxford: Clarendon Press.

Argy, V., (1992) *Australian Macroeconomic Policy,* Sydney: Allen & Unwin.

Arrow, K.J., (1959) "Toward a Theory of Price Adjustment". In M. Abramowitz, (ed.) *The Allocation of Economic Resources,* Stanford: Stanford University Press, pp.41-51.

Arrow, K.J., (1981) "Real and Nominal Magnitudes in Economics". In D. Bell and I. Kristol, (eds.) *The Crisis in Economic Theory,* New York: Basic Books.

Ball, L. and Romer, D., (1991) "Sticky prices as coordination failure", *American Economic Review,* Vol.81, pp.539-552.

Barens, I., (1997) "What went wrong with IS-LM/AS-AD analysis – and why?" *Eastern Economic Journal,* Vol.23, pp.89-99.

Barro, R.J., (1984) *Macroeconomics,* New York: John Wiley.

Barro, R.J., (1990) *Macroeconomics,* 3rd Ed., New York: John Wiley.

Barro, R.J., (1993) *Macroeconomics,* 4th Ed., New York: John Wiley.

Barro, R.J., (1994) " The Aggregate Supply/Aggregate Demand Model", *Eastern Economic Journal,* Vol.20, pp.1-6.

Barro, R.J. and Grilli, V., (1994) *European Macroeconomics,* Basingstoke: Macmillan Press.

Barro, R.J. and Grossman, H.I., (1971) "A General Disequilibrium Model of Income and Employment", *American Economic Review,* Vol.61, pp.82-93.

Baumol, W.J. and Blinder, A.S., (1997) *Macroeconomics: Principles and Policy,* 7th Ed., Fort Worth: Harcourt Brace.

Benassi, C., Chirco, A. and Colombo, C., (1994) *The New*

Keynesian Economics, Oxford: Basil Blackwell.

Benassy, J.P., (1986) *Macroeconomics: An Introduction to the Non-Walrasian Approach,* New York: Academic Press.

Benassy, J.P., (1990) "Non-Walrasian Equilibria, Money and Macroeconomics". In B.M. Friedman and F.H. Hahn, (eds.) *Handbook of Monetary Economics,* Amsterdam: North Holland, Vol.I, pp.103-169.

Blanchard, O.J. and Fischer, S., (1989) *Lectures on Macroeconomics,* Cambridge MA: The MIT Press.

Blinder, A.S., (1987) "Keynes, Lucas, and Scientific Progress", *American Economic Review,* Vol.77, May, pp.130-136.

Boorman, J.T. and Havrilesky, T.M., (1972) *Money Supply, Money Demand, and Macroeconomic Models,* Boston: Allyn and Bacon.

Boyes, W. and Melvin, M., (1996) *Macroeconomics,* 3rd Ed., Boston: Houghton–Mifflin.

Branson, W.H., (1979) *Macroeconomic Theory and Policy,* 2nd Ed., New York: Harper & Row.

Branson, W.H., (1989) *Macroeconomic Theory and Policy,* 3rd Ed., New York: Harper & Row.

Bresnahan, T.F., (1989) "Empirical Studies of Industries with Market Power". In R. Schmalensee and R.D. Willig, (eds.) *Handbook of Industrial Organisation,* Amsterdam: North Holland, Vol.II, pp.1011-1057.

Brown, W.S., (1995) *Principles of Macroeconomics,* St.Paul: West Publishing Co.

Brownlee, O.H., (1950) "The Theory of Employment and Stablization Policy", *Journal of Political Economy,* Vol.58, pp.412-424.

Burda, M. and Wyplosz, C., (1993) *Macroeconomics: A European Text,* Oxford: Oxford University Press.

Carlin, W. and Soskice, D., (1990) *Macroeconomics and the Wage Bargaining,* New York: Oxford University Press.

Case, K.E. and Fair, R.C., (1996) *Principles of Macroeconomics,* 4th Ed., Upper Saddle River, NJ: Prentice-Hall.

Chirco, A. and Colombo, C., (1996) "The AD-AS Model and Its Solutions: Some New Results in a Disequilibrium Perspective", *Australian Economic Papers,* Vol.35, pp.263-281.

Chow, G.C., (1977) "A Reformulation of Simultaneous Equations Models for Markets in Disequilibrium", *Research Memorandum No.213,* Econometric Research Program, Princeton University.

Clower, R.W., (1965) "The Keynesian Counter Revolution: A Theoretical Appraisal". In F.P.R. Brechling and F.H. Hahn, (eds.) *The Theory of Interest Rates,* London: Macmillan.

Clower, R.W., (1993) "On Truth in Teaching Macroeconomics", *unpublished.*

Clower, R.W., (1994) "The Effective Demand Fraud", *Eastern Economic Journal,* Vol.20, pp.377-385.

Colander, D.C., (1993, 1995) *Macroeconomics,* Burr Ridge, IL.: Irwin Publishers.

Colander, D., (1993) "The Textbook Aggregate Demand Curve", *Unpublished.*

Colander, D.C., (1995) "The Stories We Tell: A Reconsideration of AS/AD Analysis", *Journal of Economic Perspectives,* Vol.9 (3) (Summer) pp.169-188.

Colander, D., (1995) *Economics,* 2nd Ed., Chicago: Irwin.

Colander, D., (1996) "Response", *Journal of Economic Perspectives,* Vol.10, pp.191-193.

Colander, D.C. and Sephton, P.S., (1996) *Macroeconomics,* Canadian Ed., Burr Ridge, IL: Irwin.

Colombo, C., (1996) "Concorrenza Monopolistica, Menu Costs ed Effetti delle Variazioni Monetarie in Economia Aperta" (Monopolistic Competition, Menu Costs and the Effects of Monetary Changes in the Open Economy) *Rivista di Politica Economica,* (forthcoming). English version available upon request.

Cooper, R. and John, A., (1988) "Coordinating Coordination Failures in Keynesian Models", *Quarterly Journal of Economics,* Vol.103, pp.441-463.

Corden, W.M., (1978) "Keynes and the Others: Wage and Price Rigidities in Macro-economic Models", *Oxford Economic Papers,* Vol.30, pp.159-180.

Dalziel, P.C., (1987) "Aggregate Demand Curves in Macroeconomic Theory: Comment", *New Zealand Economic Papers,* Vol.21, pp.105-111.

Dalziel, P.C., (1993) "Classical and Keynesian Unemployment in a Simple Disequilibrium AS-AD Framework", *Australian Economic Papers,* Vol.32, pp.40-52.

Davidson, P. and Smolensky, E., (1964) *Aggregate Supply and Demand Analysis,* New York: Harper & Row.

Dernburg, T.F. and McDougall, D.M., (1976) *Macroeconomics: The Measurement, Analysis and Control of Aggregate Economic Activity,* 5th Ed., New York: McGraw-Hill.

Dixon, H.D., (1994) "Imperfect Competition and Open Economy Macroeconomics". In F.van der Ploeg, (ed.) *The Handbook of International Macroeconomics,* Oxford: Basil Blackwell.

Dixon, H.D. and Rankin, N., (1994) "Imperfect Competition and Macroeconomics: A Survey", *Oxford Economic Papers,* Vol.46, pp.171-195.

Domowitz, I., Hubbard, R.G. and Petersen, B.C., (1988) "Market Structure and Cyclical Fluctuations in U.S. Manufacturing", *Review of Economics and Statistics,* Vol.70, pp.55-66.

Dornbusch, R. and Fischer, S., (1978) *Macroeconomics,* New York: McGraw-Hill.

Dornbusch, R. and Fischer, S., (1984) *Macroeconomics,* International Student Ed., New York: McGraw-Hill.

Dornbusch, R. and Fischer, S., (1994) *Macroeconomics,* 6th Ed., New York: McGraw-Hill.

Dutt, A.K. and Skott, P., (1996) "Keynesian Theory and

the Aggregate-Supply/Aggregate-Demand Framework: A Defense", *Working Paper No.1996-7,* Department of Economics, University of Aarhus, Denmark.

Eklund, R.B. and Tollison, R.D., (1997) *Macroeconomics: Private Markets and Public Choice,* 5th Ed., Reading, MA: Addison-Wesley.

Fields, T.W. and Hart, W.R., (1990) "Some Pitfalls in the Conventional Treatment of Aggregate Demand." *Southern Economic Journal,* Vol.56, January, pp.676-685.

Fisher, I., (1933) "The Debt-Deflation Theory of Great Depressions", *Econometrica,* Vol.1, pp.337-357.

Froyen, R.T., (1993) *Macroeconomics,* 4th Ed., New York: Macmillan.

Gambs, C.M., (1974) "A Note on Macroeconomic Textbooks: the Use of the Aggregate Demand Curve", *Journal of Economic Literature,* Vol.12, pp.896-898.

Gambs, C.M., (1975) "Reply to Havrilesky and Purvis", *Journal of Economic Literature,* Vol.13, p.475.

Glahe, F.R., (1977) *Macroeconomics: Theory and Policy,* 2nd Ed., New York: Harcourt Brace Jovanovich.

Gordon, R.J., (1978) *Macroeconomics,* Boston: Little, Brown & Co.

Gordon, R.J., (1990) *Macroeconomics,* Boston: Little, Brown & Co.

Gordon, R.J., (1993) *Macroeconomics,* 6th Ed., New York: HarperCollins.

Gottheil, F.M., (1996) *Principles of Macroeconomics,* Cincinnati: South-Western College Publishing.

Grandmont, J.M., (1989) "Keynesian Issues and Economic Theory", *Scandinavian Journal of Economics,* Vol.91, pp.265-293.

Greenwald, B. and Stiglitz, J., (1993) "New and Old Keynesians", *Journal of Economic Perspectives,* Vol.7, pp.23-44.

Grieve, R.H., (1996) "Aggregate Demand, Aggregate Supply,

a Trojan Horse and a Cheshire Cat", *Journal of Economic Studies,* Vol.23, pp.64-82.

Gwartney, J.D. and Stroup, R.L., (1995) *Macroeconomics: Private and Public Choice,* 7th Ed., Fort Worth: Harcourt Brace.

Hall, P.H. and Treadgold, M.L., (1982) "Aggregate demand Curves: A Guide to Use and Abuse", *Australian Economic Papers,* Vol.21, pp.37-48.

Hall, R.E. and J.B. Taylor., (1993) *Macroeconomics,* 4th Ed., New York: W.W.Norton.

Hall, R.E., (1986) "Market Structure and Macroeconomic Fluctuations", *Brooking Papers on Economic Activity,* No.2, pp.285-322. Reprinted in Mankiw, N.G. and Romer, D., (eds.) (1991) *The New Keynesian Economics,* Cambridge MA: The MIT Press, Vol.I, pp.387-424.

Hall, R.E., (1988) "The Relation between Price and Marginal Cost in U.S. Industry", *Journal of Political Economy,* Vol.96, pp.921-947.

Hansen, B., (1951) *The Theory of Inflation,* London: Allen and Unwin.

Hansen, R.B., McCormick, K. and Rives, J.M., (1985) "The Aggregate Demand Curve and its Proper Interpretation", *Journal of Economic Education,* Vol.16, pp.287-296.

Hansen, R.B., McCormick, K. and Rives, J.M., (1987) "The Aggregate Demand Curve: A Reply", *Journal of Economic Education,* Vol.18, pp.47-50.

Harrod, R.F., (1937) "Mr Keynes and Traditional Theory", *Economic Journal,* Vol.XLVI, pp.74-86.

Harrod, R.F., (1938) "An Essay in Dynamic Theory", *Economic Journal,* Vol.XLVII, pp.14-33.

Havrilesky, T., (1975) "A Comment on the Use of the Aggregate Demand Curve", *Journal of Economic Literature,* Vol.13, pp.472-473.

Henry, K. and Woodfield, A., (1985) "Aggregate Demand Curves in Macroeconomic Theory: Some Curiously Antipodean Controversies", *New Zealand Economic Papers,* Vol.19, pp.21-34.

Hicks, J.R., (1979) "On Coddington's Interpretation: A Reply", *Journal of Economic Literature,* Vol.17, September, pp.989-995.

Hicks, J.R., (1983) "IS-LM: An Explanation". In J.P. Fitoussi, (ed.) *Modern Macroeconomic Theory,* Oxford: Basil Blackwell, pp.49-63.

Hicks,J.R., (1985) *Methods of Dynamic Economics,* Oxford: Clarendon Press.

Hyman, D.N., (1997) *Macroeconomics.* 4th Ed., Chicago: Irwin.

Kennedy, P., (1984) *Macroeconomics,* 3rd Ed., Ontario: Allyn and Bacon.

Kennedy, P., (1997) "Defending ADAS: A Perspective on the ADAS Controversy", *this volume.*

Kennedy, P., (1996) "The Stories We Tell: The Consistency of AS/AD Analysis", *Journal of Economic Perspectives,* Vol.10, pp.189-191.

Kennedy, P., (1997) *Macroeconomic Essentials for Media Interpretation,* Cambridge, MA: MIT Press.

Keynes, J.M., (1964 [1936]) *The General Theory of Employment, Interest and Money,* New York: Harcourt, Brace & World Inc.

Keynes, J.M., (1936) *The General Theory of Employment, Interest and Money,* London: Macmillan.

Keynes, J.M., (1939) "Relative Movements of Real Wages and Output", *Economic Journal,* Vol.XLIX, pp.34-51.

Keynes, J.M., (1973) *The Collected Writing of John Maynard Keynes,* Vol.XIII, London: Macmillan.

King, R.G., (1993) "Will the New Keynesian Macroeconomics Resurrect the IS-LM Model?" *Journal of Economic Perspectives,* Vol.7, pp.67-82.

Kiyotaki, N., (1988) "Multiple Expectational Equilibria under Monopolistic Competition", *Quarterly Journal of Economics,* Vol.103, pp.695-713.

Layard, R., Nickell, S. and Jackman, R., (1991) *Unemployment. Macroeconomic Performance and the Labour Market,* Oxford: Oxford University Press.

Leijonhufvud, A., (1968) *On Keynesian Economics and the Economics of Keynes,* London: Oxford University Press.

Leijonhufvud, A., (1983) "What was the Matter with IS-LM?" In J.P. Fitoussi, (ed.) *Modern Macroeconomic Theory,* Oxford: Basil Blackwell, pp.64-90.

Levacic, R. and Rebmann, A., (1982) *Macroeconomics,* 2nd Ed., London: Macmillan.

Lindbeck, A. and Snower, D.J., (1994) "How Are Product Demand Changes Transmitted to the Labour Market?", *Economic Journal,* Vol.104, pp.386-398.

Lindbeck, A. and Snower, D.J., (1988) *The Insider-Outsider Theory of Employment and Unemployment,* Cambridge MA: The MIT Press.

Lipsey, R.G. and Courant, P.N., (1996) *Macroeconomics,* 11th Ed., New York: HarperCollins.

Lucas, R.E. and Rapping, L.A., (1969) "Real Wages, Employment and Inflation", *Journal of Political Economy,* Vol.77, pp.721-754.

Makin, J.H., (1975) *Macroeconomics,* Hinsdale, IL: The Dryden Press.

Mankiw, N.G., (1985) "Small Menu Costs and Large Business Cycles: a Macroeconomic Model of Monopoly", *Quarterly Journal of Economics,* Vol.100, pp.529-537.

Mankiw, N.G., (1988) "Imperfect Competition and the Keynesian Cross", *Economic Letters,* Vol.26, 7-13.

Mankiw, N.G., (1990) "A Quick Refresher Course in Macroeconomics", *Journal of Economic Literature,* Vol.28, pp.1645-1660.

Mankiw, N.G., (1992) *Macroeconomics,* New York: Worth Publishers.

Mankiw, N.G., (1994) *Macroeconomics,* 2nd Ed., New York: Worth Publishers.

Mankiw, N.G. and Romer, D., (eds.) (1991) *The New Keynesian Economics,* Cambridge, MA: The MIT Press.

Manning, A., (1990) "Imperfect Competition, Multiple Equilibria and Unemployment Policy", *Economic Journal,* Vol.100, pp.151-162.

Manning, A., (1992) "Multiple Equilibria in the British Labour Market: Some Empirical Evidence", *European Economic Review,* Vol.36, pp.1333-1365.

Mansfield, E., (1992) *Principles of Macroeconomics,* 7th Ed., New York: W.W.Norton.

Marshall, A., (1920) *Principles of Economics,* 8th Ed., London: Macmillan.

McCain, R.A., (1996) "Notes Toward a Simple Game-Theoretic Foundation for Post-Walrasian Economics", http://william-king.www.drexel.edu/top/class/Post-up1.html.

McConnell, C.R. and Bruce, S.L., (1996) *Macroeconomics: Principles, Problems, and Policies,* 13th Ed., New York: McGraw-Hill.

McEachern, W.A., (1997) *Macroeconomics: A Contemporary Introduction,* 4th Ed., Cincinnati: South-Western.

McKenna, J.P., (1955) *Aggregate Economic Analysis,* New York: Holt, Rinehart and Winston.

McKenna, J.P., (1977) *Aggregate Economic Analysis,* Hinsdale, IL: The Dryden Press.

Miller, L.R. and Pulsinelli, R., (1986) *Macroeconomics,* New York: Harper & Row.

Miller, R.L., (1997) *Economics Today: The Macro View,* 9th Ed., Reading, MA: Addison-Wesley.

Mosely, F. and Wolf, R.D., (1992) "Alternative Theories in the Teaching of Economics". In D.C. Colander, and R. Brenner, (eds.) *Educating Economists,* Ann Arbor, MI: The University of Michigan Press, pp.243-248.

Nevile, J.W., (1997) "What Would Keynes Have Thought of the Development of ISLM". In I W. Young and B.Z. Zilberfarb, (eds.) *IS-LM and Modern Macroeconomics,* (forthcoming) New York: Kluwer Press.

Nevile, J.W. and Rao, B.B., (1996) "The Use and Abuse of Aggregate Demand and Supply Functions", *The Manchester School,* Vol.64, June, pp.189-207.

Obstfeld, M. and Rogoff, K., (1995) "Exchange Rate Dynamics Redux", *Journal of Political Economy,* Vol.103, pp.624-660.

Parkin, M., (1982) *Modern Macroeconomics,* Ontario: Prentice-Hall.

Parkin, M., (1997) *Macroeconomics,* 3rd Ed., Reading, MA: Addison-Wesley.

Parkin, M. and Bade, R., (1982) *Modern Macroeconomics,* Oxford: Philip Allan.

Parkin, M., (1988) *Modern Macroeconomics,* Oxford, 3rd Ed., Philip Allan.

Pasinetti, L.L., (1974) *Growth and Income Distribution: Essays in Economic Theory,* Cambridge: Cambridge University Press.

Patinkin, D., (1965) *Money, Interest and Prices: An Integration of Monetary and Value Theory,* 2nd Ed., New York: Harper & Row.

Pesek, B.P. and Saving, T.R., (1967) *Money, Wealth and Economic Theory,* New York: Macmillan.

Pigou, A.C., (1933) *The Theory of Unemployment,* London: Frank Cass.

Purvis, D.D., (1975) "A Comment on the Use of the Aggregate Demand Curve", *Journal of Economic Literature,* Vol.13, p.474.

Rabin, A. and Birch, D., (1982) "A Clarification of the IS Curve and the Aggregate Curve", *Journal of Macroeconomics,* Vol.4, pp.233-238.

Rao, B.B., (1986) "Alternative Aggregate Demand Functions

in Macroeconomics", *Australian Economics Papers,* Vol.25, December, pp.261-264.

Rao, B.B., (1991) "What is the Matter with Aggregate Demand and Aggregate Supply?", *Australian Economics Papers,* Vol.30, December, pp.264-277. Reprinted in *this volume.*

Rao, B.B., (1992) "A Model of Income, Unemployment and Inflation for the U.S.A.", *Applied Economics,* Vol.24, May, pp.597-605.

Rao, B.B., (1993a) "Unit Root Hypothesis, New Classical and Keynesian Models", *Economics Letters,* Vol.31, pp.47-52.

Rao, B.B., (1993b) "The Nature of Transactions in the U.S. Aggregate Goods Market, *Economics Letters,* Vol.31, pp.385-390.

Rao, B.B., (1994) "Disequilibrium Goods Market Model for the U.S.A.: A Disaggregated Approach", *Southern Economic Journal,* Vol.60, November, pp.415-425.

Rao, B.B., (1996) "An Examination of the US Goods Market: Keynes 87% and New Classicals 12.5%", *Discussion Paper No.96/30,* School of Economics, University of New South Wales.

Rao, B.B. and Srivastava, V.K., (1991) "A model of Rational Expectations for the U.K.", *Economic Journal,* Vol.101, July, pp.877-886.

Reimers, D., (1996) "Endogenous Money and the Macroeconomic Curriculum", *Paper presented at the Conference of Economists,* Canberra, September.

Robinson, J., (1962) *Essays in the Theory of Economic Growth,* London: Macmillan.

Romer, D., (1993) "The New Keynesian Synthesis", *Journal of Economic Perspectives,* Vol.7, pp.5-22.

Rowan, D.C., (1975) *Output, Inflation and Growth: An Introduction to Macro-Economics,* Australian Ed., South Melbourne: Macmillan.

Ruffin, R.J. and Gregory, P.R., (1997) *Principles of Macroeconomics,* 6th Ed., Reading, MA: Addison-Wesley.

Sachs, J.D. and Larrain B.F., (1993) *Macroeconomics in the Global Economy,* Hemel Hempstead: Harvester-Wheatsheaf.

Samuelson, P.A. and Nordhaus, W.D., (1995) *Macroeconomics,* 15th Ed., New York: McGraw-Hill.

Schiller, B.R., (1997) *The Macro Economy Today,* 7th Ed., New York: McGraw-Hill.

Schumpeter, J.A., (1954) *History of Economic Analysis,* New York: Oxford University Press.

Shapiro, E., (1978) *Macroeconomic Analysis,* 4th Ed., New York: Harcourt Brace Jovanovich.

Sheshinski, E. and Weiss, Y., (eds.) (1993) *Optimal Pricing, Inflation, and the Cost of Price Adjustment,* Cambridge MA: The MIT Press.

Silvestre, J., (1993) "The Market-Power Foundations of Macroeconomic Policy", *Journal of Economic Literature,* Vol.31, pp.105-141.

Sinclair, P.J.N., (1983) *The Foundations of Macroeconomic and Monetary Theory,* Oxford: Oxford University Press.

Smyth, D., (1989) "Aggregate Demand Curves: Static and Dynamic", *Journal of Macroeconomics,* Vol.11, (Winter) pp.133-140.

Solow, R.M., (1980) "Theories of Unemployment", *American Economic Review,* Vol.70, March, pp.1-11.

Solow, R.M., (1984) "Mr Hicks and the Classics", *Oxford Economic Papers,* November, pp.13-25.

Srivastava, V.K. and Rao, B.B., (1990) *The Econometrics of Disequilibrium Models,* New York: Greenwood Press.

Startz, J., (1989) "Monopolistic Competition as a Foundation for Keynesian Macroeconomic Models", *Quarterly Journal of Economics,* Vol.104, pp.737-752.

Stiglitz, J.E., (1993) *Economics* New York: W.W.Norton.

Taylor, J.B., (1995) *Principles of Macroeconomics,* Boston: Houghton Mifflin.

Tobin, J., (1993) "Price Flexibility and Output Stability: An Old Keynesian View", *Journal of Economic Perspectives,* Vol.7, pp.45-65.

Tregarthen, T., (1996) *Macroeconomics,* New York: Worth Publishers.

Tucker, I.B., (1997) *Macroeconomics for Today,* St. Paul: West Publishing Co.

Weintraub, S., (1957) "The Micro-Foundations of Aggregate Demand and Supply", *Economic Journal,* Vol.67, pp.455-470.

Weiss, A., (1991) *Efficiency Wages Models of Unemployment, Layoffs and Wage Dispersion,* Oxford: Clarendon Press.

Zahn, F., (1975) *Macroeconomic Theory and Policy,* Englewood Cliffs, NJ: Prentice-Hall.

Index

Abel, A.B., 83, 107, 204,
acceptable textbook macro model, 150
Ackley, G., 3, 160
aggregate demand (AD)
  Colander's AD curve, 141
  conventional AD curve, 26
  doubts on the negative slope, 6
  interest rate effects on, 14
  neo classical version, 56
  Nevile's interpretation, 158
  properly specified and conventional AD curves, 114
  without multiplier effect, 73
aggregate demand and aggregate supply model ($ADAS$)
  alternative specification, 140
  birth of, 5
  Colander-Sephton's interpretation, 138
  complaints about, 138
  Dornbusch and Fischer version, 60
  dynamics of, 102
  inconsistency in, 72, 97, 173
  institutional environment, 73
  Marshallian approach, 68
    interpretation of, 75
  mixed sets of coordination environment, 68
  alternatives to $ADAS$, 140
  over determination in, 8, 86
  self contradictory nature, 86
adjustment costs, 184
Aggregate Equilibrium Demand curve, 142
aggregate price setting schedule, 190
aggregate supply (AS)
  as labour market equilibrium curve, 98
  Colander's vertical AS, 78
  in $ISLM$, 158
  Nevile's interpretation, 170
  perfectly elastic part, 145
aggregate supply path, 142
aggregate wage setting schedule, 189
Akerlof, G.A., 63
Allen, R.C., 6, 7, 67, 68, 75, 142
alternative coordination method, 77
Amacher, R.C., 13
Andersen, T.M., 196
Argy, V., 40
Arrow, K.J., 52, 183

Bade, R., 83, 159
Ball, L., 32
Barens, I., 5, 7
Barro, R.J., 11, 21, 47, 62, 63,

64, 83, 108, 109, 117, 131, 135
Baumol, W.J., 13
Benassi, C., 8, 9, 177, 183
Benassy, J.P., 51, 52, 179
Bernanke, B.S., 83, 107, 204
Birch, D., 6, 53, 72, 108, 116
Blanchard, O.J., 185, 200
Blinder, A.S., 13, 64
Boorman, J.T., 29
Boyes, W., 13
Branson, W.H., 31, 83
Bresnahan, T.F., 179
Brown, W.S., 25, 83
Bruce, S.L., 13
Burda, M., 83

Carlin, W., 204
Case, K.E., 13
Chow, G.C., 61
Clower, R.W., 2, 3, 20, 107, 108, 111
Colander, D.C., 6, 7, 8, 9, 17, 19, 20, 21, 23, 67, 68, 72, 77, 78, 79 80, 81, 83, 88, 94, 97, 100, 101, 102, 103, 104, 107, 108, 117, 137, 140, 141, 142, 143, 144, 152, 153, 155, 173
Colombo, C., 203
consequence of nominal wage rigidity, 197
constant returns and PQE curve, 199
Cooper, R., 32
coordination failures, 76
Corden, W.M., 25, 26, 32, 38, 39, 40, 42, 43
Corden's Constant-MV Curve, 39
countercyclical movements in real wages, 185
Courant, P.N., 13
criticisms of
Rowan model, 74
conventional AD, 28
Dornbusch and Fischer model, 61–65
Hall and Treadgold, 53
Rabin and Birch models, 53
Taylor's model, 22

Dalziel, P.C., 67, 73, 75, 79, 178
Davidson, P., 33
demand for labour as derived demand, 89
Dernburg, T.F., 29
difference between
competitive and non-competitive formulations, 201
$ISLM$ and Walrasian general equilibrium, 51
micro and macro demands, 99
difficulty with Rowan's aggregate demand curve, 38
disadvantages of Corden's curve, 40
distinction between real and nominal rigidities, 184
Dixon, H.D., 179, 203
Domowitz, I.,179
Dornbusch, R., 5, 7, 29, 30, 45, 46, 60, 61, 62, 63, 64, 65, 83, 94 107, 203,
Dutt, A.K., 67, 75, 76
dynamic model, expectations and investment, 166

Ecklund, R.B., 13
effects of increases
in money and government expenditure, 195
price change, 17
elasticity of labour demand, 189
employment in the wage-goods

industry, 91
equilibrium through price and quantity adjustments, 3
existence of unemployment in equilibrium, 194

Fair, R.C., 13
Fields, T.W., 8, 37, 38, 67, 74, 108, 112, 117, 127
Fischer, S., 5, 7, 29, 30, 45, 46, 60, 61, 62, 63, 64, 65, 83, 94, 107, 185, 200, 203
Fisher effect, 18
 wealth redistribution effect, 18
fluctuations in employment as a supply side problem, 87
foreign trade effect, 15
Froyen, R.T., 83, 107

Gambs, C.M., 26
general equilibrium comparative statics, 160, 163
general vs particular equilibrium, 164
Glahe, F.R., 30
Gordon, R.J., 5, 83, 86, 107, 158
Gottheil, F.M., 13
Grandmont, J.M., 179
Greenwald, B., 12, 14, 18, 21
Gregory, P.R., 13
Grieve, R.H., 6, 7, 83, 94
Grilli, V., 83, 90
Grossman, H.I., 62
Gwartney, J.D., 13

Hall, R.E., 107, 161, 162, 179
Hall, P.H., 5, 6, 8, 25, 47, 50, 53, 67, 74, 108, 116, 161
Hansen, R.B., 6, 8, 11, 22
Hansen's Law, 20
Harrod, R.F., 166
Hart, W.R., 8, 37, 38, 67, 74, 108, 112, 117, 127
Havrilesky, T., 26, 29
Henry, K., 67, 73, 75, 79
Hicks, J.R., 2, 6, 51, 53, 54, 56, 57, 59, 60, 63, 64, 66, 152, 159, 165, 174
Hicks' $ISLM$, 50–55
Hubbard, R.G., 179
Hyman, D.N., 13

implications of increasing returns, 191
institutional environment of $ISLM$, 68
interdependence of AD and AS, 31

Jackman, R., 179
John, A., 32

Kennedy, P.E., 6, 7, 95, 98, 139, 140, 148
Keynes, J.M., 1, 2, 3, 4, 5, 7, 15, 19, 20, 21, 22, 23, 26, 27, 32, 33, 35, 37, 38, 45, 47, 50, 51, 53, 54, 55, 56, 58, 59, 60, 62, 63, 65, 68, 70, 72, 73, 74, 75, 80, 84, 86, 87, 88, 92, 93, 103, 108, 111, 117, 140, 141, 144, 146, 150, 152, 153, 158, 162, 164, 165, 166, 168, 171, 173, 174, 183, 201, 202, 204
Keynes'
 criticisms of Pigou, 90
 effects of money supply, 164
 use of Marshallian particular equilibrium framework, 166
King, R.G., 19
Kiyotaki, N., 192

Larrain, B.F., 83

Layard, R., 179
Leijonhfvud, A., 2, 3, 4, 45
Levacic, R., 53, 59, 62, 83
limitation of
  the real balance effect to explain *AD*, 14
  general equilibrium comparative statics, 162
Lindbeck, A., 193
Lipsey, R.G., 13
Lucas, R.E., 4, 59
Lucas-type supply function, 126

Makin, J.H., 30
managerial interest in macroeconomic forecasting, 76
Mankiw, N.G., 19, 21, 32, 83, 107, 183, 203
Manning, A., 192
Mansfield, E., 13
marginal product of labour as labour demand, 92
Marshall, A., 164, 166
Marshall–Lerner condition, 49
Marshallian
  approach, 157
  sales-constrained firm behaviour, 75
  particular equilibrium, 157, 162
  particular equilibrium theory, 165
  picture of the market for a particular good, 155
  price and income movements, 75
  short run curve, 171
  supply curve for a single industry, 158, 159, 170
McCain, R.A., 78
McConnell, C.R., 13
McCormic, K., 5, 6, 8, 11, 22
McDougall, D.M., 29
McEashern, W.A., 13
McKenna, J.P., 25, 40
measure of excess demand and supply, 30
  in *ADAS*, 115
Melvin, M., 13
Miller R.L., 13, 83
money supply changes and changes in interest rates, 167
monopolistic firms and constant elasticity of demand, 170
monopoly union form, 187
Mosely, F., 82
multiple equilibria, 192
  in the Colander model, 80

NAIRU, 172
neo classical labour market, 89
neutrality and dichotomy, 192
Nevile, J.W., 6, 8, 68, 83, 95, 97, 103, 108, 140, 155, 157, 162, 173
Nevile's
  simpler approach, 169
  supply based on imperfect competition, 170
Nickell, S., 179
nominal wage rigidity and the shape of the *PQE*, 199
Nordhaus, W.D., 13

Obstfeld, M., 203
optimal relative price of firm, 187

Parkin, M., 5, 13, 45, 47, 83, 107, 159
Pasinetti, L.L., 92
Patinkin, D., 29
permanent income, 122
Pesek, B.P., 98

Petersen, B.C., 179
Phillips curve as AS, 4
Pigou, A.C., 91, 92
Pigou effect, 12, 21, 26, 34, 37, 141
Pigou and Keynes effect, 18, 73, 74, 78, 141
Pigou's
 belief that supply creates its own demand, 92
 critical assumption, 91
 theory of employment, 91
 two-sector model, 91
Pigouvian
 explanations of employment and unemployment, 8
 conception of the labour market, 92, 93
policy ineffectiveness results, 184
price rigidities, 182
price adjustment in partial and general equilibrium models, 20
public good nature of macroeconomic expectation, 77
Pulsinelli, R., 83
Purvis, D.D., 26

Rabin, A., 6, 53, 72, 108, 116
Rankin, N., 179
Rao, B.B., 1, 3, 6, 7, 11, 20, 45, 52, 53, 56, 66, 68, 83, 88, 95, 97, 98, 102, 103, 108, 140, 152, 155, 157, 173, 178
Rapping, L.A., 4, 59
Rebman, A., 53, 59, 62, 83
Reimers, D., 167
Rives, J.M., 5, 6, 8, 11, 22
Robinson, J., 168
Rogoff, K., 203
role of
 Walrasian auctioneer, 68
 Colander's coordination variable, 77
 price level and interest rate in equilibrating money and goods markets, 130
 time in a capitalist economy, 165
Romer, D., 21, 32, 183
Rowan, D.C., 5, 6, 25, 26, 29, 30, 32, 33, 35, 37, 38, 39, 42, 43, 50 53, 55, 67, 74
Rowan's Curve, 33
Ruffin, R.J., 13

Sachs, J.D., 83
Samuelson, P.A., 13
Saving, T.R., 98
Schiller, J.A., 13
Schumpeter, J.A., 11
Scott, P., 67, 75, 76
Sephton, P.S., 8, 9, 137, 142
Sheshinski, E., 200
Silvestre, J., 179
Sinclair. P.J.N., 62
Smolensky, E., 33
Smyth, D., 68
Snower, D.J., 193
Solow, R.M., 50, 58, 65
Solow's interpretation of Phillips curve, 65
Soskice, D., 204
squeezing inflation out of the system, 88
Srivastava, V.K., 3, 52, 53, 56
Startz, J., 203
Stiglitz, J.E., 12, 13, 14, 17, 18, 21
Stone, J.H., 6, 7, 67, 68, 75, 142
Stroup, R.L., 13
structure of $ADAS$, 34
student opinion on $ADAS$, 101

supply-side economics, 96
supply-side shocks, 95

tax-bracket effect, 15
Taylor, J.B., 107, 161, 162
Tobin, J., 12, 14, 18
Tollison, R.D., 13
Treadgold, M.L., 5, 6, 8, 25, 47, 50, 53, 67, 74, 108, 116, 161
Tregarthen, T., 13
Tucker, I.B., 13

Ulbrich, H.H., 13
union objective function, 187

vertical PQE curve, 184

wage increases in
  Keynes's theory
  of employment, 93
Walrasian auctioneer
  and market coordination, 68
  and Keynesian markets, 70
Walrasian model simplified, 69
Weintraub, R., 33
Weintraub's contribution, 33
Weiss, A., 194
Weiss, Y., 200
welfare through nominal rigidity, 202
Wolf, R.D., 82
Woodfield, A., 67, 73, 75, 78
Wyplosz, C., 83

Yellen, J., 64

Zahn, F., 30